FOREVER DOO-WOP

A volume in the series

AMERICAN POPULAR MUSIC

Edited by Jeffrey Melnick and Rachel Rubin

FOREVER DOO/WOP

Race, Nostalgia, and Vocal Harmony

JOHN MICHAEL RUNOWICZ

University of Massachusetts Press

Amherst and Boston

LC 2010027200
ISBN 978-1-55849-824-2 (paper); 823-5 (library cloth)

Designed by Richard Hendel
Set in Scala and Gill Sans by Westchester Book
Printed and bound by Thomson-Shore, Inc.

Library of Congress Cataloging-in-Publication Data

Hersey, John Michael, 1962–
Forever doo-wop : race, nostalgia, and vocal harmony /
John Michael Runowicz.
    p. cm.—(American popular music)
Includes bibliographical references and index.
ISBN 978-1-55849-824-2 (pbk. : alk. paper)—
ISBN 978-1-55849-823-5 (library cloth : alk. paper)
1. Doo-wop (Music)—History and criticism.   I. Title.
ML3527.H47   2010
782.42166—dc22

                    2010027200

British Library Cataloguing in Publication data
are available.

Like a bouquet

of wildflowers

I present this

to my wife, Barbara

CONTENTS

Illustrations follow page 84.

PREFACE

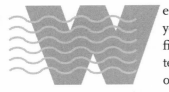e have a special connection to the music of our youth. The words, melodies, and rhythms that fill our relatively uncluttered and still developing teenage brains leave imprints that last throughout our lives. The makers of this music also leave lasting impressions. They are avatars of the optimism and innocence, unbridled energy and impulsive rage, unalloyed joy and intense sadness of our youth, emotions that seem so much more easily contacted through the popular culture of our early years than by other means. The impact of this experience is made all the more poignant by how quickly it seemed to pass. As we, and the music makers, grow older, the music that we shared accumulates ever more layers of meaning and affective power. Music does this for us both individually and collectively.

This book is about a genre of music called doo-wop and the particular meanings and affective power it has come to hold for people today. There have been other books about doo-wop that have focused primarily on its origins and first flowering in the 1950s and early 1960s, but the period of doo-wop's adulthood, from the mid-1960s to today, is when the story gets most interesting for me. What I offer here is a larger and more comprehensive historical and cultural perspective on this music. Doo-wop provides a rich ground to explore American society and culture. Primary is the opportunity to see how black and white Americans interact, to see the truths of the racial complexity of one node of American popular culture. There is, too, the particular phenomenon of doo-wop: a style of music whose heyday lasted only a blink of an eye and whose influence on later music is still vastly underrated, which nevertheless spawned a long-standing, devoted, and now economically influential subculture. To dismiss this simply as nostalgic consumption is to miss the opportunity to examine the intricacies of the role music plays throughout our lives.

Doo-wop's longevity and place in the national "psyche" makes such a study possible. But this particular study is also possible because of my fortuitous proximity to this music. I have spent the last twenty-three years working increasingly closely with one of the legendary doo-wop groups,

Speedo and the Cadillacs, on what is known as the oldies circuit. A social network, what I call the doo-wop community, has supported the performing careers of the members of this group for more than forty years. The doo-wop community coalesced in the late 1960s around American popular music of the 1950s. It comprises the singers, band musicians, promoters, and fans, who all have an often complex stake in its continued existence.

Their story is also my story. It has been and remains at times difficult to know where I end and the community begins. So this is an experimental work in many ways. The up-close and personal nature of my social position has yielded opportunities for insight that would not have otherwise been available. But this same close proximity has also made it more difficult for me to maintain the safe observational distance from which the usual "researcher objectivity" can be claimed. There is always the question, can the storyteller ever be completely removed from the story? Without equivocation, I answer a resounding no. I have become part of what I continue to study—a personal journey that began over two decades ago.

I first met Earl "Speedo" Carroll, the lead singer of the black vocal group the Cadillacs, in the summer of 1987. Peter Millrose, a college friend who was the keyboard player in the Cadillacs' band and who, like me, is white and a generation younger than Carroll, introduced us. I auditioned to be their guitarist not knowing who the Cadillacs were, although Peter had informed me that they were a fairly well-known New York–area "doo-wop" group who had had a handful of hits in the 1950s. (Playing with the Cadillacs was a "good gig," as Paul Schafer, David Letterman's bandleader, once told Peter.) My background as a guitarist was in the white rock music of the sixties, seventies, and early eighties, a musical life with an infancy in the British Invasion (the Beatles and Rolling Stones), an adolescence in album-oriented rock (Led Zeppelin and Yes), and an early adulthood in new wave and punk (Elvis Costello and the Clash). In my time with the Cadillacs, I would learn, among many other things, about the African American origin of much of the white rock of my youth. I did not realize it at the time, but I had just enrolled in the school of rhythm and blues.

I was taught my first lesson during the audition. Following the chord chart, I played along with Peter on keyboard and Carroll singing. During the song "Zoom," an up-tempo, jump-blues number (my first encounter with this term), Carroll stopped the music and good-naturedly instructed me to play the chords not on every beat of the four-bar measure but just on beats two and four. He also asked that I voice or pitch the chords a little higher, and play them more sharply or staccato. It was a subtle but essential aspect of rhythm and blues guitar playing, and it helped me to reconceptualize what it meant to be in a band. In the music of my youth, the guitar dominated the sound. Big, resounding chords and riffs defined the texture of most of the music. In the Cadillacs' band I soon learned that the guitar was just one part of a sonic whole; keyboards, drums, bass, saxophone, and vocals all have an important role to play in the ensemble.

Learning to play the guitar differently was only the beginning of my odyssey with Speedo and the Cadillacs. As time went on and I got to know the singers and my fellow band members, a rich, musically infused social network began to reveal itself. I soon discovered that the Cadillacs are one of many vocal groups with roots in the 1950s and early 1960s that perform on the oldies circuit. Everyone had been in show business for decades, and they had comic, tragic, and inspiring stories to tell.

All the stories I was told or overheard had a quality that made them unique to the oldies circuit—the result of a decades-old social milieu in which race, nostalgia, and vocal harmony were common interrelated themes. At a show somewhere in Staten Island, after about four or five years of steady gigging with the Cadillacs, I momentarily stepped out of my role as guitarist and noticed that something special was going on. The concert featured an equal number of white and black acts for a predominantly white middle-aged audience. The show was billed as a "trip down memory lane," and a picture of a vocal group of indeterminate race was displayed on the program. My "aha!" moment came when I realized that what was being said backstage differed from what I overheard in the audience: the performers and the concertgoers were not necessarily taking the same nostalgic journey. My definition of nostalgia then was "an overly sentimental look at the past through rose-colored glasses." But it did not describe what I was witnessing. African American middle-aged singers were sharing the bill with white middle-aged singers, singing in musical harmony, though not necessarily in the same groups. They seemed to be modeling a kind of social harmony that may or may not actually exist, at least not in the straightforward, simple way that the audience may have perceived it.

About this time I began pursuing a graduate degree in music, and during my first semester I realized that the musical culture of doo-wop, the oldies circuit, and the Cadillacs were a perfect subject for ethnomusicological research. By the spring of 1998, I began interviewing the members of the group, which included lead tenor Earl Carroll, bass singer

Bobby Phillips, baritone Gary Lewis, and musical director and second tenor Eddie Jones. I also began to take notes at the oldies shows I continued to play with the group, effectively turning these gigs into fieldwork sites. At the same time I was reading about and experiencing the complexities of interviewing and doing fieldwork. I discovered the ethical conundrum inherent in the ethnography process: I was no longer just the Cadillacs' guitar-player; I was also their researcher. These were dual roles that I had to explain to not only my "informants" but to myself. They were roles that were often hard to separate psychologically. Who was I when I was with the Cadillacs? I was still a working musician with a well-respected act, a job that I had grown into musically and very much enjoyed, but I was also an aspiring scholar. To further complicate matters, after ten years of being on the road together, the Cadillacs had become my friends as well.

They had come to know me as a fellow musician and now here I was with a microphone in my hand asking personal questions. I had been around them long enough to know the history of economic injustice they had endured. Their music making, and their talk about their music making, has always had potential market value. How was I to strike a balance between my own career ambitions, both in and out of academia, and my desire not to set in motion further exploitation? Maintaining an objective stance toward the Cadillacs proved difficult. In my very first interview with Carroll, this dilemma surfaced. He had started telling me about his family and growing up in Harlem when he abruptly stopped.

"John, I'm giving you my life story, so if you do write a book, let's collaborate on it."

"Of course, man . . ."

[He laughs] "If it do come to a book."

"I—"

"And I've given nobody else this information, believe me. I talk, you know, maybe about what I did in the fifties. But my childhood, and how I got into it, what I'm about, what I'm doin' now—nobody. I was planning on writing a book maybe one day myself."

"Were you really?"

"Yeah, a lot of people have called and asked for a life story, but I won't give it to them. I just, you know, a certain fifteen minutes and whatever, whatever, and that's it.'

"Well, you know, we should talk . . ."

"You're first."

"We should talk about it, because it's an important thing to discuss. You know, I guess I should have started out by saying that what I'm doing right now with you is for a particular class for this semester."

"Right."

"And . . ."

"Well, you see what you get out of it. You got a bit of information here."

"Well, what I'm saying is if we can expand on it—"

"Yeah, maybe we will come up with a book . . ."

It certainly—"

"It's not hard to find a publisher these days. Rock and roll is such a big business today. Believe or not, a lot of people say there's no market for it but they're definitely wrong, 'cause I work around the country quite a bit, and the audiences we get are so, you know, this is their life, rock and roll and rhythm and blues, and so it's a big market. It's still a big market. It's a . . . [slight pause] Getting back to the story . . ."

I did my best to reassure him that I was not interested in anything like an unauthorized biography. Most telling for me in this first attempt at ethnography was that my informant was well aware of the possible financial ramifications of the interview process and that I would have to remain sensitive to what could be catalyzed by my inquiries into his life.

This interview also revealed to me that I was not the first to explore the world of doo-wop. Doo-wop singers are a frequently interviewed social formation. Beginning in the early 1970s, vocal group enthusiasts were committing to print, mostly in fanzines and newsletters but also in a few books, the recollections of numerous street-corner singers. It seemed as though any vocal group, no matter how obscure or commercially ephemeral, was worthy of investigation. This was both good and bad news for my research. On the one hand, I had a vast database to peruse, with numerous case studies to compare. On the other hand, what could I offer to the study of a musical genre that had already been thoroughly examined?

My focus gradually evolved to an ethnographically informed history of doo-wop and a historically informed ethnography of its present-day performance. This approach encompassed not only the singers but band members, concert promoters, fanzine writers, record collectors, and audience members. I began to view the world surrounding the oldies circuit as a community, interviewing and observing its various constituents and their interactions with one another. Eventually I amassed an archive of material that included recorded interviews, audio and video concert tapes, fieldwork notes, and posters, programs, concert flyers, and other print material with the goal of understanding the larger social and cultural environment of the doo-wop community.

Because this community was geographically close, I was able to carry out my research in my own back yard so to speak, where I could integrate my home life, my performing life, and my scholarly pursuits. Such an integrated approach led to certain difficulties. I discovered early on that it was impossible to view these various aspects of my life separately, and I realized that the course to take was to explore how the social realities of my personal and professional lives infiltrated and transformed each other. Although I do not discuss my personal life directly here, a more self-reflexive ethnography can be inferred, especially when I discuss life as a working musician.

In addition, as my role in the doo-wop community evolved and expanded during the time of my fieldwork, from guitarist to musician contractor, second tenor, musical director, and record producer, new avenues for research were opened. As a contractor who would hire the musicians for the Cadillacs' shows, I was able to get to know and make music with a wide range of players, giving me a broader perspective on the life of a working musician in the New York City area. Having a chance to sing doo-wop with some of the pioneers of the style gave me the unexpected opportunity to research this music on an experiential level, to feel what it is like to be in a vocal group. My work as the Cadillacs' musical director gave me more of stake in the quality of our performances, as I was now responsible for mediating between the band and the vocalists on stage. In 2004, I had the privilege of coproducing a new Cadillacs CD, which involved writing, arranging, and rehearsing new material, recording the songs in a local studio, and marketing and distributing the album.

As my relationship with the group deepened I realized that I had received a special gift from these men and their community. They had welcomed me into their lives and embraced me as a friend and a peer. I have endeavored to return their generosity. Over the last several years I have tried to provide whatever support I can to the Cadillacs, calling on my skills as a musician and writer in various ways, from working on their new CD, to website design and maintenance; to writing letters to various philanthropic organizations affiliated with the music business on behalf of the group members; to booking and facilitating performances. As I learned from the ethnomusicologist Steven Feld, one should be prepared for the researcher/informant relationship to be a long-term commitment, a kind of ongoing gift exchange that is to be expected from a deep and extended presence in a community. This book is my gift to my adoptive doo-wop community.

ACKNOWLEDGMENTS

This book would not have been possible without the help of a constellation of teachers, advisers, colleagues, musicians, family, and friends, many of whom are listed below. My gratitude begins with heartfelt thanks to the faculty and staff of the New York University Department of Music who gave me the necessary institutional support to commence this endeavor and provided me with a community of empathic fellow academic travelers as I worked.

For insight and support at early stages, I wish to thank Kyra Gaunt. Gage Averill and Mercedes DuJunco were enthusiastic and inspiring guides through my first encounters with ethnomusicology and fieldwork. My appreciation goes as well to Stanley Boorman, Mirjana Lausevic, Fred Moten, Steven Feld, Robert Moore, Adelaida Reyes-Schramm, Ana Maria Ochoa-Gautier, and Jason King for their invaluable insights and advice along the way. The symposium "Italian Americans and Early Rock and Roll" organized by Joseph Sciorra and sponsored by the John D. Calandra Italian American Institute and the Catholic Center at Queens College in Flushing, New York, proved essential to my understanding of the interracial nature of doo-wop music making.

My acknowledgments to the doo-wop community must begin with Earl "Speedo" Carroll, leader of the Cadillacs and the main informant in my research. His revelations about his own life and the life of the community are the heart and soul of this book. Bobby Phillips and Gary Lewis, the other two current members of the group, were also prime ethnographic informants and musical mentors. Beyond this core are past members of the Cadillacs Eddie Jones and Johnny Brown and past and current members of their band, Peter Millrose, Tass Filipos, Al Cohen, Randy Gilmore, Freddie Cash, Reggie Barnes, Jim Wacker, Bob DesJardins, Richard Ruiz, and Roger Byam.

I owe an enormous debt of gratitude to Shirley Alston Reeves, former lead singer of the Shirelles, and the many members of her singing group and band, with whom I gained additional perspective on oldies circuit performance—singers Iris Lammers and Tanya Alexander and musicians

Greg Woods, Cleveland Freeman, Carl Vreeland, Anthony Vigliotti, Paul Page, and John DiGiulio. Other doo-wop community members who were essential to my research include Bobby Jay, Dave Somerville, Al "Diz" Russell, Vito Picone, Nick Santamaria, Richard and Deborah Nader, Rob Albanese, Pete Mastropaolo, and Andrea Seigel. Through interviews with, observation of, and interaction with these people and many others too numerous to mention, I was granted privileged inside access to this fascinating and dynamic music making community. I also offer special thanks to photographer Julius "Juice" Freeman for providing the wonderful concert pictures of the Cadillacs that illustrate this book and David Booth for archival photos of the group.

My gratitude also goes out to my colleagues and friends in the academic community: Dan Neely, Melvin Butler, William Kingswood, Bernd Gottinger, Dana Richardson, Maria Rose, Tom Brett, Joyce Hughes, Talia Jimenez, Sean Mulhall, Scott Currie, Scott Spencer, Eric Usner, and Rena Mueller. Most special thanks go to the folks at UMass Press, especially senior editor Clark Dougan, managing editor and copy editor extraordinaire Carol Betsch, American Popular Music series editor and reader Jeffrey Melnick and reader Robert Pruter.

My good friend Gwendolyn Corbette, who passed away in 2008, provided invaluable clerical support during all stages of this project, and I miss her dearly. My undying thanks I give to Ettore Toppi, Mike Vassaras, Kurt Gundersen, Dore and Elizabeth Abrams, Brendan Mee, David Rieth II, and Barry Smith for their long-standing and steadfast friendship and support. Mother Gale, father Victor and wife Linda, brother Mark and wife Cookie, brother Chris, sisters Victoria and Kyra, uncle Bill, cousin Ben and wife Jill, aunt Francoise, mother-in-law Zilma, brother-in-law David and wife Sandra, and godmother-in-law Beulah: Thank you for providing the loving familial foundation on which I stand.

Finally, and most especially, my deepest gratitude goes to my wife Barbara. Without her steadfast encouragement, long-term vision, and editorial prowess, the writing of this book would have been mere fantasy. Throughout it all, she has just been there for me with her grace, spirit, and beauty, and it is with profound love and affection that I thank her.

FOREVER DOO-WOP

INTRODUCTION

y association with the doo-wop world as a musician has afforded me an unusual vantage point for studying the roots and meaning of this music. I began to get to know the people of this community more than twenty years ago, but the community itself had developed almost two decades earlier, with the advent of the oldies circuit. The circuit provided new performance opportunities for vocal groups who had formed in the 1950s and early 1960s. And these groups themselves were part of an American vocal harmony tradition with roots reaching back into the nineteenth century.

To help understand doo-wop's evolutionary journey, I have developed three framing concepts. The first, the *racial double helix,* is a metaphorical way of looking at the history of a complex American cultural practice, which illuminates an integral narrative thread that runs through the story of doo-wop. The second concept is *collective nostalgia.* Because of my long-term position within a community defined to a large extant by a nostalgic impulse, I have had the chance to study on the group level the nature and effect of a human condition that is usually studied on the level of the individual. Finally, I explore the nature of my complex and evolving position in this community through the notion of *ethnographic intimacy.*

WHAT IS DOO-WOP?

Before tracing the development of doo-wop, we need to first explore its name, which is a source of debate among those who write about it. Some music historians avoid the term entirely, believing that the music and the musicians are better served by more descriptive and dignified, if cumbersome, classifications such as "rhythm and blues vocal group music." These writers also argue that, because the term was coined more than a decade after the music itself emerged, it is historically, if not politically, incorrect. But in my view the period preceding the adoption of the term is only one part of the history of this music. To avoid using the word "doo-wop" would be to ignore the fascinating social and cultural connotations that it and the music have accumulated over the last half century. The lack of consensus about the name of this genre has led to a multiplicity of spellings, including *doo wop, doowop, doo-wopp,* and *du-wop.* I use what I perceive to be the most common spelling, *doo-wop.* However it is spelled, though, I prefer to use the term because it defines the music at all stages of its evolution, from infancy to nostalgic adulthood.

Admittedly the nostalgic connotations of the word can undermine respect for the music. The word "doo-wop" tends to evoke images of an uncomplicated time and culture. For those of us raised in 1970s, scenes from the television show *Happy Days* spring to mind. As the show's title suggests, these were, supposedly, simpler, more carefree times and, by association, so was the music. If one's only exposure to it were through 1970s popular culture, one might even assume that doo-wop was entirely the product of a lighter—as in whiter—side of American culture.

Like the term "girl group," used for American female pop vocal ensembles from the early 1960s, "doo-wop" as a word discourages regard of the music with the full esteem it deserves.[1] Just as the music produced by girl groups expresses a wide range of adult as well youthful emotional experience, so too is doo-wop music more expansive than its two playful-sounding nonsense syllables connote.[2] One must look behind the veil of 1950s nostalgia to understand the complex story behind the music and its name.

To attempt to define a genre of music that has emerged from a long and continually evolving tradition as doo-wop did is like scooping a bucket of water from a flowing stream. We are merely taking a sample, in the context of a particular time and place, from the much larger flow of history. Doo-wop is not a discrete stylistic category but an important link in a vocal harmony tradition. Its roots in barbershop, gospel, and jazz were infused with new energy and fresh stylistic traits and then passed on to the next generation of vocal harmony, the soul and Motown groups of the 1960s.[3] Yet, it is still useful, and perhaps unavoidable, to look at music as a succession of discrete genres. Time and place necessarily become elements of definition, and within the parameters of a particular time and place, we can further delineate different genres using both musical and non-musical criteria. The consensus among music writers, which is as good a place to start as any, is that doo-wop emerged as a distinctive genre in the 1950s and that it was part of the larger musical category that has been named rock and roll.

Anthony J. Gribin and Matthew M. Schiff have dubbed doo-wop the "forgotten third of rock-'n'-roll."[4] By defining it as such, they are attempting to redress an imbalance perpetuated by many popular music historians. The other main musical currents of the period, *rockabilly*, as personified by the white performers Elvis Presley and Buddy Holly, and *blues*, the black tradition from which Chuck Berry and Bo Diddley emerged, have been deemed more important in the evolution of rock and roll and more worthy of study. The current edition of *The New Grove Dictionary of Music and Musicians* gives only a quarter-page mention to doo-wop.[5] This entry contains an erroneous reference to the supposedly exemplary doo-wop song "There's a Moon Out Again," which was in fact recorded by the Capris in 1981, well after doo-wop's heyday. Likely a reference to "There's a Moon Out Tonight," a hit for the same group in 1961—the mistake typifies the lack of knowledge about doo-wop in scholarly circles. Doo-wop has yet to find its proper place in American musical historiography.[6]

One reason for this lack of understanding is that doo-wop is a genre that shares many characteristics with the other musical currents of the time and place of its emergence. The singing style and distinctive melodic and harmonic material of the blues tradition is evident in both doo-wop and rockabilly. The rhythmic accentuation that sets rock and roll apart from the popular music of the preceding swing era is an essential element in each of the three genres. Doo-wop depends on singing more than the other two, and doo-wop songs feature prominent bass parts, high falsetto leads, and "nonsense" syllable background harmonies (such as "doo-wop"). But these characteristics do appear in what are considered blues and rockabilly songs and are not contained in many tunes considered indispensable to the doo-wop canon.

The definition of doo-wop must encompass more than musical criteria, for it is a genre shaped as much by its social context as by its sonic elements. Doo-wop was primarily an urban phenomenon most prevalent in northern and western cities such as New York, Philadelphia, Washington, D.C., Baltimore, Chicago, and Los Angeles. In its earliest incarnation it was music made by African American teenage males who rehearsed in public places, most notably the street corners of their neighborhoods. At first it was an amateur practice. Impressing girls or just passing the time with friends on a hot Saturday night was just as important, if not more so, as making money and developing a career. This music making initially took place, then, in localized, insular, self-referential social circles, which led to a contagious approach to songwriting and group naming: one group named after a bird, or a car, or a precious stone would lead to another.[7] Not every doo-wop group embodied all these aspects, but some combination of them were present in all doo-wop music making.

Difficulties of genre definition have facilitated music historians' overlooking doo-wop or folding it into a larger category such as rhythm and blues, which itself, has caused confusion in the discussion of American popular music history. In the early 1950s, so-called rhythm and blues, or R&B, emanating from black urban neighborhoods was "discovered," primarily, by white working-class urban teenagers. As this music began to be emulated by white performers and consumed by a growing national white audience, it was dubbed "rock and roll." The term "rhythm and blues" did not disappear, however, but continued to be used for the music of black artists; "rock and roll" became the term for white music.

Perceived racial and social class affiliations affect how genres of music are represented in music historiography. The cursory treatment given doo-wop can be attributed partly to the change in the audience demographic for popular music from primarily working class in the 1950s to more middle class in the 1960s. In the 1960s, when "rock and roll" became simply "rock" music, the tastes of white middle-class young people became ascendant in the popular music fan base.[8] This new audience was listening to folk rock musicians, such as Bob Dylan, and "British invasion" groups like the Beatles, whose music evolved in a few short years from the rhythm and blues–influenced repertoire of *Meet the Beatles* to the popular-music-as-art complexity of *Sgt. Pepper's Lonely Hearts Club Band*.

This decade also saw a growing appreciation of the blues and jazz not as popular music categories but as music traditions. These musical genres were now played not, as they initially were, in dance clubs and ballrooms but in concerts enjoyed by a primarily white middle-class audience, often in the festival format such as at Newport, Rhode Island. Blues performers like Buddy Guy and Muddy Waters, who only a few years earlier had shared the bill with doo-wop groups, were featured at these festivals, but doo-wop, although it was part of a long vocal harmony tradition, was not similarly promoted to traditional music status. It remained associated with teenage pop culture of the 1950s.

Some of the music journalists who came of age in the 1960s helped to perpetuate a music history that excluded doo-wop from serious discussion. Even though rock music was born in the 1950s, rock historiography was born in the 1960s, with the magazine *Rolling Stone* its preeminent venue. *Rolling Stone*'s contributors and columnists for newspapers such as the *New York Times*, who were of and writing for the middle and even upper classes, tended to view 1950s rock and roll, and especially vocal group music, as rock prehistory, a less evolved form of music making. Because the blues was music made by adults about adult experiences, and it was the music emulated by 1960s groups like the Rolling Stones and Cream, it was given pride of place over what was perceived as more teen-oriented music like doo-wop.[9]

The blues was reclassified as *folk music* and given greater historical weight. It could be argued that doo-wop deserves to be restored to its rightful place in rock and roll history in part because it is just as much a form of folk music as the blues is. If one identifies folk as music that has evolved primarily from an amateur music making tradition, then the music that was made on urban street corners fits the definition as well as music that came from the plantations and small rural towns of the South. But this simplifies the case for both genres, for doo-wop, like the blues, is part of a musical lineage whose roots are in both professional and amateur music making.

Furthermore, any measure of the historical value of doo-wop must also take into account its prominence in the communities that spawned it, and an understanding of how doo-wop musical practice reflects wider social processes. Vocal harmony was a vital and meaningful daily activity in the lives of urban African American and later Italian American youth in the 1950s. The image of the street-corner vocal group became a vital cultural symbol initially within and eventually beyond their communities. The songs they sang, the regional styles that developed, and even the clothes they wore became powerful assertions of identity within the larger society.[10]

The birth of doo-wop was more than just the creation and performance of a new musical genre. It was the sonic embodiment of the experiences of particular African American communities. These were experiences informed by individual and collective histories that encompassed social repression, cultural ascendance, and aspirations for a future fueled by postwar American optimism. Their music was a way of channeling and usurping this reality.[11] A similar musical embodiment of social experience occurred in the Italian American community of New York City, as white urban vocal groups emulated their black contemporaries. This racial exchange, that is, the historical sharing of vocal harmony in the 1950s, was part of a larger societal transformation, which is articulated in the name and the music of doo-wop.

THE RACIAL DOUBLE HELIX

The story of the United States in the 1950s is a tale of two epochs. It was the era of an ascendant America, fresh from victory in World War II, often portrayed in its mainstream popular culture as optimistic and morally uncomplicated. White, middle class suburban America was idealized in television shows such as *The Adventures of Ozzie and Harriet* (1952–1966) and *Father Knows Best* (1954–1960). Whatever problems or issues were raised during an episode were resolved by the end of the show, most often with one of the children learning a lesson patiently taught by a parent.

The message that "everything will work out in the end" emphasized again and again, week after week, in the television sitcom format, instilled in the viewer a sense of confidence in the American social structure. Contained in these seemingly innocuous forms of entertainment were blueprints for the pursuit of happiness American style. One need only follow the rules of home and hearth modeled in these conveniently hermetically sealed environments undisturbed by the outside world. This "attainable happy ending" message had a powerful attraction and influence then as it does now. For many people, any contradictory or oppositional message triggered a defensive response—often vociferous, sometimes even violent.

The contradictions and opposition were there, however. This was the other epoch, the dark, disruptive, dangerous world beyond the white, and white-owned, picket fence. The prosperity and placidity so often portrayed in popular culture in the 1950s existed side by side with the stirrings of monumental social change. These stirrings would erupt in the following decade and lead to unprecedented societal transformations in the wake of the civil rights movement, the incipient women's and gay rights movements, and the anti-war movement.[12]

The social ferment brewing in the United States in the 1950s accompanied frightening advances in the technology of destruction, the product of an expanding Cold War. The breakdown of the European and American-based colonial network triggered revolutionary upheaval around the world. *Duck and Cover,* a film produced by the Federal Civil Defense Administration and distributed to schools in 1951, offered instruction for protecting oneself against nuclear attack; it also suggested a response to any social discomfort.

The African American vocal groups, as part of the larger emergent teen culture, embodied the optimism of the post–World War II era. Though the songs they sang were far from political, the sound of their young voices intoning romantic desire was the aspirant sound of those yearning for the attainable happy ending. The music these groups made, and their growing presence and influence in national popular culture, also contradicted and opposed the status quo. For blacks to participate in mainstream middle-class life, the national narrative had to be revised. African American history and culture had to be integrated, which meant that the dominant white American narrative had to be reassessed. This revision began in 1954 with the landmark Supreme Court decision in *Brown v. Board of Education*, which ruled that segregated schools were in violation of the Equal Protection Clause of the Fourteenth Amendment to the Constitution, and continued in 1955 with the Montgomery, Alabama, bus boycott led by Martin Luther King Jr. and others, which protested racial segregation in the public transit system. In the realm of popular music, less overtly political but no less powerful revision was also taking place.

W. E. B. Du Bois, in the beginning of his essay "The Religion of the American Negro," asserts that an essential aspect of African American sacred life is the "frenzy" or extreme agitated state evident in the members of the congregation. Though it may take many forms, from quiet but intense meditative rapture to shouting and dancing, being "in the spirit" was considered a necessary aspect of an authentic religious experience.[13] To the eyes and ears of many white Americans, frenzy was clearly exhibited in the rhythm and blues of the 1950s, which was rooted in part in the black American sacred music or gospel tradition of the previous generation. Music-related frenzy is not a racially specific phenomenon in this country; it is deeply a part of much religious music, especially in the highly emotive evangelical or revival tradition.[14] But in the secular music of the 1950s it emanated from the African American community.

Highly emotive musical performance was not a component of white mainstream popular recordings of the early fifties. The number one song on the *Billboard* magazine chart in 1953 was the nursery rhyme-style novelty tune "(How Much Is) That Doggie in the Window?" sung by the white female singer Patti Page. Her playful and decidedly non-sexually-provocative performance contrasted sharply with the excitedly sung up-tempo numbers and plaintive, yearning ballads of rhythm and blues.

Young white people in 1953 certainly helped make Patti Page a star. But this demographic group was also tuning into a different musical frequency. The advent of the transistor radio and the wider distribution of a greater range of music aided, in part, by a strengthened interstate commerce system, increased white accessibility to that era's black working-class culture. This decade also marked the emergence of an affluent teenage population that sought and found popular culture expressing values in opposition to their parents'.[15] Newly accessible rhythm and blues music was adopted as a marker of rebellion by many white young people of the 1950s, a way of differentiating their tastes from the preceding generation's. The live performances of black musicians, and eventually also of the white performers like Elvis Presley who would emulate them, drew teenagers of both races in large numbers to concerts and dances, where African American musical performance practice was on display as it had never before.

The Cadillacs were one of the groups performing for these young interracial audiences. They were a group that brought the whole package of singing, dancing, and eye-catching attire, inherited, in part, from the vocal harmony, frenetic choreography, and sartorial extravagance of the gospel quartets of the previous and contemporaneous generations. By the early 1950s the separation between sacred and secular black culture had become permeable, and the Cadillacs honed their skills at Harlem's Apollo Theatre, where both gospel and pop groups performed and the fluidity between sacred and secular was strong. Their performance style reflected this and, in turn, was quite influential on their fellow vocal groups.[16]

This new and exciting form of entertainment was finding its way out of the Apollo and similar venues and into the wider, white mainstream, where it was met by a burgeoning receptive young audience. White teenagers' embracing of the music, however, was not equivalent to social acceptance of its black performers. They may have been more instrumental in the development of white teenagers' identities than ever before, but the many eruptions of racial violence among mixed but segregated audiences at concerts demonstrate that the long legacy of racism persisted, even among the young people of the time. Such incidents raised fears among white adults and helped fuel a backlash against rhythm and blues, most notably in the South but eventually across the nation.

In the early years of the 1950s disc jockeys such as Alan Freed had the power to pick and choose what they played on their shows. In his case, this included the black music of the smaller independent record companies. Radio playlists dictated by individual taste meant a greater variety of music on the airwaves. It also meant profits could not be concentrated in a few songs, a few artists, and a few record companies. But such a marketplace free for all could not be tolerated by the major companies. By the end of the decade these companies, in league with radio station managers and program directors who began to severely curtail individual DJ freedom, took control of the situation. They instituted smaller radio playlist formats dominated by major record company product. Taking the conservative approach to getting the most for their money, they redirected the currents of popular culture to the mainstream. Rhythm and blues was now "rock and roll," and it had a decidedly different sound. Songs containing overt sexual references and black or white working-class vernacular speech were either "cleaned up" in white cover versions or simply excluded from the corporate airways.[17]

The backlash against the rising popularity of black music at the end of the 1950s reflects a much deeper historical dynamic. It was not an isolated incident but the resurfacing of an ongoing dialectic of race relations in this country. One way of framing this dialectic is to define the black experience and that of the white mainstream as an interaction with the mysteriously attractive but often threatening "other." Attraction and repulsion, a societal and cultural push and pull are at play on both sides. White America is attracted by but also fears what it perceives as something humanly powerful and essential in black culture.[18] Also at play is white guilt and shame for the history and legacy of slavery. African Americans, while embracing the elemental and vitalizing energy of their own popular culture, also recognize the opportunity for access to mainstream affluence and institutional power. Fear and repulsion accompany this attraction as well, not only the fear of white backlash, a fear of fear, but also the fear of the loss of the safety and power that comes with group identity.

The dance, both actual and metaphorical, continued in the mid-twentieth century. In the 1950s the most powerful and essential element in rhythm and blues was what the white establishment perceived as shameless celebration of sexual desire and pleasure. The condemnation of black music on these grounds had the dual function of continuing both the political, social, and cultural oppression of blacks and the sexual self-repression of whites. White mainstream society was, in part, trying to control what it perceived as its own mysteriously attractive "other" nature. The fear and oppression of sexual pleasure is one tactic in the campaign of political and economic oppression.[19]

The relationship of whites to rhythm and blues is a manifestation of the intertwining of the lives of white and black Americans, the historical racial double helix in the "DNA" of American popular music (and larger social and cultural life). White American popular music can be defined only in relation to black American popular music, and vice versa. Americans of European and African descent have been inextricably interdependent and reliant on each other for their cultural productions and identities. The primary role of the DNA molecule is the long-term storage of information, which can be seen as a kind of code for the future replication, or expression, of molecular structures. The information stored in doo-wop DNA is the deep and complex interracial history of our society.

Contested power relations between the strands of the racial double helix have led to the constantly evolving makeup of this DNA's nature. From the European discovery of the "New World" through the nineteenth century, the relationship was that of the enslaved and the free, and so traditionally has not been that of equals but of outsider and insider or, in terms of social change, radical and conservative. Viewed from this perspective, black culture, because of its outsider status, has usually been perceived by the white mainstream as politically radical, even when there was no overt or obvious political content to that culture.[20] The ascension of black popular culture, such as rhythm and blues in 1950s, can be seen as challenging the power structure, as a kind of covert, if unintentional, radicalism, which requires a response and necessary accommodation on the part of white mainstream. To use the DNA metaphor, for the sake of molecular survival, structural evolution, however contested and negotiated, is necessary.

By using this racial double helix metaphor I am not implying that Americans of African and of European descent are not capable of surviving separately. My point is, rather, that what we have created and are creating, especially in the realm of popular music, is most effectively understood not as the production of separate, interactive social formations but of a single social formation. This social formation, and what is produces, exists because of the close, dynamic relationship of component cultural strands.

We can interpret the emergence of rhythm and blues in the 1950s as a glimpse of the dynamic DNA of American culture, when the racial double helix was laid bare, and the predicable backlash to this revelation occurred. The new music made by black youth and embraced by white youth was marked as dangerous and subversive. It was perceived as the threat to the established order, but, in fact, it was only a reflection of the greater societal upheaval under way.[21] The white backlash against rhythm and blues helped stitch back together the revelatory opening in the social fabric through which vocal groups like the Cadillacs had been able to emerge. But society was forever transformed. The renaming of rhythm and blues as rock and roll and of rhythm and blues vocal group music as doo-wop may have facilitated the reclosing, but contained in performances of this music are echoes of the historical moment of its creation and the continuing expression of the racial double helix.

DOO-WOP IS OLDIES

By the end of the 1950s many vocal group singers could no longer make a living in the business. There was a kind of unplanned obsolescence built into doo-wop production that made it difficult for these singers to continue their careers. Vocal groups were often taken right from the street corner to the recording studio. Records were made and released in a matter of weeks or even days, by small record companies eager to capitalize on what they feared might only be a passing fad.[22] This practice left little time for any real long-term artistic development. In the wake of the British Invasion and with the rise of soul music institutions like Motown and Stax, tastes inevitably changed, but most vocal group singers had not acquired the musical skills to adapt to the new entertainment climate.

Neither were they economically prepared for change. In most cases vocal groups received relatively little remuneration from recording and performing in the 1950s. Their future careers were shaped by the degree to which they had depended on others for the management of their business affairs.[23]

Two of the most important aspects of the music business that would have serious long-term consequences were song copyright and group-name ownership. Many musicians of the era did not fully comprehend these rights or did not have access to the means to secure them. If their business affairs were in hands of unscrupulous managers, the artists were deprived of long-term financial benefits. Because of the lack of support for their artistic development and economic well-being, most doo-wop groups became identified primarily with the music product of their youth, a product, in most cases, they did not own.

Their music careers could well have ended in the early 1960s. However, even before vocal group singers stopped charting consistently, their music was finding new life as fodder for nostalgia. Their songs began to be called "oldies but goodies" as early as the end of the 1950s, and this phenomenon eventually led to a career resurgence for many acts whose initial fame had been brief. By the end of 1960s new performance opportunities arose for artists whose hit-making days had long passed. In 1969 the first major rock and roll revival show was presented at Madison Square Garden in New York City. In the forty-plus years since then, many rhythm and blues vocal groups have found steady if not full-time work as performers in oldies shows. (The Cadillacs' hit-making career lasted only five years, from 1954 to 1959, the golden age of doo-wop, which means their second career as oldies performers has been eight times as long as their first.)

On the oldies circuit, the words "doo-wop" and "oldies" became synonymous in the promotion of concerts featuring the artists of the 1950s be they vocal groups or not. A show featuring a solo artist such as Bobby Rydell, for example, a former "teen idol" from Philadelphia who first found fame on *American Bandstand* in the late 1950s, is often billed as a doo-wop concert. In fact, "doo-wop" has become shorthand for all things 1950s, including the architecture, automobiles, and clothing associated with that era. A nonprofit organization called the Doo Wop Preservation League was founded in the New Jersey beach town of Wildwood. Part of their mission is to "promote the preservation of the largest collection of mid-century or 'Doo Wop' resort architecture found in the United States," the era's motels, diners, restaurants, and vintage neon signs.[24] Doo-wop architecture, according to the league, employs the structural and decorative motifs that represented the globally assertive, economically optimistic, and capriciously playful zeitgeist of postwar America. This includes the space-age rocket-ship textures, the borrowed tropical island décor, and the brash color and form. A word initially used to denote a genre of urban vocal group harmony that was created in an aging built environment has come to represent what was modern, exciting, and decidedly suburban in the mid-twentieth century, today's "kitsch."

The oldies iconicity of the word "doo-wop" also circulates beyond 1950s nostalgia. In Lauryn Hill's video for "Doo Wop (That Thing)" (1998) she juxtaposes two images of herself, one in modern clothes and dreadlocks and one in a 1960s girl group–era miniskirt and vintage Diana Ross hairdo. The music of Motown, the Supremes' record label in the 1960s, is generally not considered to be doo-wop. The soul music of the 1960s was the next wave of black musical culture. Many of the Motown vocal groups did have roots in the 1950s, but the vocal arrangements, rhythm, and sound production were recognizably different. In fact, the popularity of Motown helped relegate the doo-wop sound to that of yesteryear. Nonetheless, the visual allusions in the Hill video seem to equate the look of the Motown era with the word "doo-wop." The meaning of the word, while continuing to refer to a past time, place, music, and look, continues to be open to interpretation.

The oldies iconicity of the *word* doo-wop intensifies the oldies iconicity of the *music* called doo-wop. The impulse behind this musical semantic relationship is the desire to connect to the past. The word most often used to describe this relationship is *nostalgia,* which Webster's defines as "a wistful or excessively sentimental sometimes abnormal yearning for return to or return of some real or romanticized period or irrecoverable condition or setting in the past." It can also be defined simply as "homesickness." Certainly the connotations of "sickness" and "abnormal yearning" are negative, even pathological, and an obsession with the past that detrimentally affects a person's present and future condition could be considered such. But I am interested in the non-pathological implications of a wider nostalgic practice, which comprises all the social, cultural, and economic behaviors surrounding a specific group relationship with the past. The manifestation of nostalgia in the unique and complex social experience of the oldies circuit has a meaning other than pathology or excessive sentimentality.

The economic consequences of a nostalgic practice such as this cannot be ignored. Doo-wop fans put their money where their nostalgia is. For over forty years they have bought concert tickets, listened to commercial "oldies" radio where doo-wop, until recently, was consistently played, and bought CDs of reissued and new doo-wop songs. This activity has helped to make doo-wop in some ways more popular in relation to the records made by solo artists and other non-doo-wop groups in the 1950s and early 1960s. Only 15.4 percent of *Billboard*'s number one hits between 1955 and

1963 were doo-wop songs. However, yearly surveys in the 1990s by New York City's long-time oldies station WCBS-FM show that doo-wop songs consistently averaged a 30 percent share of their all-time Top 500 lists.[25] By this measure, doo-wop has not only weathered the changes in musical style but has carved out a larger niche in the marketplace.

Doo-wop's new popularity is due in large measure to its having become a potent vehicle for nostalgic remembrance. Doo-wop is the music of the first generation of rock and rollers, the most economically influential teenage generation up to that time. In the 1950s, the music that many young people embraced set them apart from their parents' generation, arguably as never before. The music belonged to them and it helped define who they were. This generation has now reached middle and, for many, retirement age. Hearing doo-wop and seeing it performed puts them in touch with a crucial part of their identity.

Of course, the same can be said about the relationship between every generation and the popular music of its youth. Any musical genre can be a powerful form of personal and collective time travel, a kind of sonic portal to a past self—often a much younger self.[26] But because of the longevity of the oldies circuit, this very loyal and now relatively affluent audience has bolstered doo-wop's nostalgic potency and, as a consequence, its economic value. Fifties-centric nostalgic consumption set the standard against which the hawking of the goods of subsequent eras would be measured. Thus it is prime territory for exploring how musical nostalgia plays out over time, its effect on social processes, and for understanding why it is important to both the maintenance and the transformation of society and culture.[27]

For the doo-wop singer, working on the oldies circuit can be perceived as a blessing or a curse. The longtime fan loyalty that supports it exists within a performance framework of expectations for how a concert should look and sound. Even though the rise of the oldies circuit has created a relatively stable market niche in which many doo-wop singers receive much-deserved recognition, this stability is secured by narrow creative parameters. Most shows are billed as nostalgic events, variations on a-trip-down-memory-lane theme, and the audiences expect to hear the songs the artists are famous for. Usually they are not receptive to new material, which can be frustrating for the singers who have continued to write and record. In addition, the received notion about performing on the oldies circuit can injure a performer's self-esteem. Music critics often portray an "oldies" artist or group as having descended into a kind of creative oblivion, banished along with other poor souls who are "past their prime" to spend the twilight of their careers perpetually performing their contributions to an earlier generation's hit parade.

In the 1950s, rhythm and blues vocal groups were part of a music scene that had an integral role in a seminal moment in American history. Today they are called doo-wop groups and are most often promoted as emblems of a bygone era. The danger of excessive sentimentality is always lurking at oldies shows, which can bury what once was vital, exciting, and engaging about this music. The social history of this music, the racial double helix of doo-wop's DNA that was exposed in the postwar period, can easily be glossed over by the veneer of nostalgia. This music, once perceived by many as a threat to the social order, is easily rendered socially innocuous if not irrelevant.[28] When rhythm and blues emerged in the 1950s, its frenzy was perceived by many white Americans as unruly and chaotic, quite literally "noise,"[29] and it had to be reined in. The noise of rhythm and blues was quieted and sold in a less dangerous package. Music that was once cutting edge and even revolutionary was marketed to be consumed as rock and roll lite.

One of the salient features of nostalgia is what the sociologist Fred Davis calls "the muting of the negative."[30] When we contemplate the past our tendency is to block out the unpleasant or complicated and accentuate the positive and less complex. Our past is there for us to access as we choose, and most often we choose to apply it as a balm for present anxiety or discomfort.[31] This concept of muting the negative can be expanded from the personal to the collective level, where those engaged in group nostalgia choose to mute those problematic aspects of a cultural experience that remain unresolved or disputed and instead focus on less politically and socially vexed aspects.

On the oldies circuit, however, the negative may be muted, but it is not negated. The unresolved and disputed history of this music continues to roil beneath the surface and often erupts during this nostalgic spectacle, though not necessarily in obvious ways. Doo-wop harmony contains echoes of the past—past racial tension, past sexual anxiety, past economic injustice—which still inform present experience. The messages, whether purposely conveyed or only intimated on the oldies stage, are there for those who wish to hear them.[32] And they infuse oldies shows with another kind of social tension and imbue the word *doo-wop* with a semantic anxiety that keeps meaning and experience for the doo-wop community not in a fixed state but in slow but steady flux.[33]

COLLECTIVE NOSTALGIA

It has become a journalistic trope to portray middle-aged rock musicians and their fans as without sex appeal or, at best, as parodies of their former sexual selves. In the classical and jazz worlds, aging musicians are usually treated with reverence. Even if they do not play at the virtuosic level they once did, the artistic insight born of their experience is valued. Aging rock and popular musicians often do not command the same respect. Rock music, according to one critic, "is youth music . . . [and] should not be played by fifty-five-year-old men . . . playing songs they wrote thirty or thirty-five years ago and have played some thousands of times since."[34]

Why is rock of middle (or old) ages considered a source of cultural embarrassment? Why is it seen as comical or pathetic when adults are interested in dancing or sex or the communal bonding experienced as young people in school or at rock concerts? Perhaps this embarrassment is really a kind of collective grieving for what has been left behind. The separation from birth family units in adulthood entails the loss of being part of a larger, school-related, community, which had its boundaries and prohibitions, but which also offered opportunities for experimentation and expression not found in smaller, adult, working-life, social units.[35] In the doo-wop community, dancing and allusions to sex are important aspects of the concert experience. In addition to being a cultural site where nostalgia for a particular historical moment is performed and consumed, the doo-wop community can be seen as a socioeconomic formation in which the opportunity to reexperience a youthful connection to body and soul is available.

To understand why we have a powerful connection to the music of our youth, it is useful to conceive of life as a series of stages, childhood, youth, adulthood, middle and old age.[36] Each stage has a particular relationship to time. For most people in American society there is more time to appreciate popular culture in our early years. Nostalgia for youth is, in part, the feeling of loss of greater leisure time, of a more expansive sense of time in general. We have more time to go to concerts when we are young and more time to listen and relisten to our favorite records. We develop a more personal connection with music and music makers. As we grow older the exigencies of family and work tend to curtail our music listening and concert going, And when we reach our thirties and forties many of us begin reflecting on the expansive time of our youth. In the decades that follow, as child rearing and career building become lesser priorities, many of us have more time and money with which to reconnect in a deeper way with the past.

The music that framed an earlier stage of our lives, when listened to in the present, can be a powerful vehicle of emotional time travel, a way of reconnecting to a past self. This kind of individual remembering operates within a larger framework as well, what I call *collective nostalgia*. Nostalgia is a remembering by which the past is refashioned for use in the present. Its two temporal components are of equal importance: our experience of what happened at an earlier time is deeply affected by what is happening in the present.[37] When this process occurs on the collective level, the more popular or potent features of the nostalgic object tend to be more intensely promoted and experienced. If a consensus develops in the nostalgic community that, for example, the music of doo-wop groups is worthy of greater cultural respect, that sentiment will circulate with more power than it would if experienced by individuals in relative isolation. When such a belief is held by a critical mass, it becomes more visible outside the community, and historical importance and economic value is reassessed in the marketplace.[38] Collective nostalgia is a dynamic process with transformational potential on the individual, community, and societal levels.

But doo-wop concerts are not simply venues for reviving or preserving a musical practice or tradition. Even though these concerts feature music from the past, this music, experienced in the present, cannot be the same as its original form. The members of the doo-wop community have aged and, while the songs they hear now on the oldies circuit may have the same lyrics and melodies as before, they experience the music freshly. Their individual and collective histories, their present circumstances, and whatever memories the songs conjure up are all part of the equation. They have complex responses to their music, which are, ultimately, evolving perspectives, transformed by the gestalt of their experiences within and out of the community.

These responses come from engagement in the entire social experience of music making—musicians and singers producing the sounds, dancing, listening, talking or writing about music, promoting concerts, producing records, collecting records, and participating in organizations or groups that support various musical genres.[39] Music making is an activity that fosters a particular way of being in the world, an ontological orientation that differs from, and can transcend, non-musical reality. Participating in music making as a member of a group or community intensifies this differing ontological orientation. One experiences the feeling of being a part of something greater than oneself.

A shared affinity with a type of musical experience helps usurp the social, cultural, and political structures that normally separate us. But what brings people into the doo-wop community, and even various participants' ideas of community, may not be the same. As individuals they may have different relationships with and feelings about the music, and different needs for communal culture. A social activity such as music making highlights the commonalities among the participants, what unites them, but it also illuminates differences. Transcending differences transforms lives.[40] In the doo-wop community the seeds for transcendence and transformation are also contained within the music itself, in the continuing expression of the doo-wop DNA. Doo-wop has been a communal form of music making from the beginning. It sprang from, and was identified with, particular neighborhoods, whose emergence in the 1950s is encoded in its recordings and live performances. For more than forty years doo-wop has anchored its own community bound by love of this music. I am a member of this community, and my role is a complicated one.

ETHNOGRAPHIC INTIMACY

Mitchell Duneier, in *Sidewalk*, his 1999 book about New York City street vendors, discusses the issues involved in doing research when the "social position" of the researcher is different from his or her subjects'. Duneier is white and holds a graduate degree. The street vendors he studied were black and primarily indigent with little formal education. He hones in on the racial and class disparity, pondering what effect it might have on the objectivity of his research. He believes that people act and speak differently depending on the race of the people they are with. A white researcher may not get the same information about a black informant's experience that the informant would give to a black researcher. Because of his lack of trust in the veracity of what people of different race, class, and economic background say to each other, Duneier chose to keep his distance, as it were, and rely more heavily on the participant/observer research method than direct questioning.[41]

In my view, although a healthy skepticism of the cross-racial or cross-class interview is essential, the impact of the ethnographer on the outcome of the research should not be overdetermined. To assume that a researcher's presence itself always elicits a significant alteration in informant behavior is to endow the researcher with more power than he or she actually has. An accepted notion in the science of particle physics is that we cannot observe any phenomenon without changing its nature or behavior in some way. This notion has a valid application in the study of culture and society, but I believe that the changes caused by the observation of human behavior are most often minimal and subtle. The power that ethnographers have to alter the subjects of their research cannot match the influence and power of the social structure within which the subject exists.[42]

That said, racial, class, and economic disparities between researcher and informant, and their potential ramifications for the research process, must be taken into account. But the best a researcher can do is remain cognizant of the situation and to address it in the writing. To dispose of the interview as a research tool is to throw the baby out with the bathwater, but not to acknowledge its inherent shortcomings is also methodologically irresponsible. In fact, these disparities are actually the best place to begin an ethnographic investigation. The researcher should start by deconstructing his or her social position in relationship to the informants and expose the subtleties and possible inequities of their interactions.[43]

Defining my social position vis-à-vis the doo-wop community has become a riot of slashes: white/male/middle class/second tenor/guitarist/ musical director/musician contractor/participant/observer/ , , , In addition to the problem of my ever-expanding list of defining features, I have felt the need to redefine, or at least more specifically define, my academic field to more accurately reflect the nature of my research. In one sense I am an urban ethnomusicologist, since much of my ethnography, and the history of my research subject, is situated in New York City and its environs. But "urban ethnomusicology" is just a general name for what I have done, and it does not aptly describe the evolving method I have used to acquire the data on which I have based my findings.

In my early years with the Cadillacs, when I was not involved in a formal research process, I learned a lot about the doo-wop community through osmosis—I came to know this world inadvertently and even subconsciously. So it could be said that I was engaged in the practice of "accidental ethnomusicology": I overheard and I witnessed.[44] This method evolved into a more conscious, less accidental, but still subtle approach when I entered graduate school. I began to think of myself as being involved in kind of embedded, clandestine, or "fly-on-the-wall ethnomusicology." My approach was to be nonintrusive, not to impede the natural flow of events by, for instance, introducing a recording device or video camera. My hope was that my informants would speak their minds in a less inhibited fashion. My goal was the worthwhile but ultimately vain attempt to both be there and not be there.

As I became more deeply involved in the life of the community, I realized that, try as I might, I could not be "not there," "nonintrusive" or "not impede the natural flow of events." I was a part of the proceedings, right there (as white/male/middle class/second tenor/guitarist/musical director/musician contractor/participant/observer) in the thick of things.[45] So I changed my tack to "experiential ethnomusicology," and my objective became to write about what it actually feels like to be onstage, offstage, and in the audience at an oldies show. But a danger lies in such a self-aware approach, the potential for producing distractingly solipsistic work, crossing the line into auto-ethnomusicology, if you will. This would be a great disservice to the people whose story I, the ethnographer, originally intended to tell. Effective ethnography requires a balance between researcher and subject. More specifically, it requires an understanding of how each influences the other, and how ethnography is the product of that relationship.

When we engage in the ethnographic process we are involved in breaking down or blurring the boundaries that normally separate us. We, as members of families, neighborhoods, regions, and nations as well as races and classes, occupy delineated domains of experience. I believe that there is a characteristic human desire to cross the boundaries of these domains.[46] Beyond or between these boundaries are the places where we encounter and get to know people from other domains of experience. The new experiences we have in this encounter are the product of what Homi Bhaba calls "interstitial intimacy."[47] In the interstices of personal, communal, cultural, and societal interaction is where the re-creation of value and meaning takes place. When we venture into uncharted territories we are compelled to negotiate. We emerge from these negotiations transformed. When this is part of the research process, we experience *ethnographic intimacy.*

Another way to characterize what goes on in the interstices of cultural interaction is to name it dialog. Cultures are apprehended and ethnographies performed as part of a dialogic process. Defining ethnographic research as dialogic enables us to recognize the power and influence of all the agents in the ethnographic exchange. Neither the role of the ethnographer nor that of the informant should be overdetermined.[48] Because all agents are empowered, it is a dialectic and creative process. "Intersubjectivity" is always at work, even when observer and subject, or fieldworker and informant, do not occupy the same physical space. The anticipation and memory of the ethnographic encounter also plays a part in this intersubjective process. The ethnographer is situated not in a static but in an emergent cultural practice, and, ultimately, all exchanges between the dialogic agents are co-creations.[49]

These co-creations are produced through the use of our "voices," which I broadly define as utilizing all forms of communication, including visual images, body language, sign language, and music as well as the spoken and printed word. To have dialogically meaningful experiences one needs to use one's voice, and listen to the voices of others. What better place to do this than the doo-wop community? Doo-wop groups are, after all, vocal groups. To participate in a Cadillacs concert is to be awash in a sea of human voices. From the moment I meet the group at the pre-gig gathering place, the joking, ribbing, complaining, and general discussion of current events begins. By the time we arrive for the sound check, which is usually on the afternoon of the night's show, often as many as ten other doo-wop groups are part of scene, and the density of vocalizing increases. There, men and women, many of whom have been in and out of show business for over fifty years, exchange reminiscences, business contacts, and excerpts of songs. In the background are the sounds of groups running through their routines and the technicians tweaking the PA system. During the show, the voices of the audience, singing along or out in the lobby talking about memorabilia and merchandise, are added to the mix as group members find their places backstage. Everywhere, voices.

The doo-wop community is not just about singers and songs. It is a celebration of the human voice as the embodiment and the expressive tool of lived experience. Our voices are our most direct representation of our corporeal, emotional, and intellectual selves and, thus, our most personally creative tool.[50] To regard the voice in this way is to define it first as a sonic phenomenon and second as a metaphor for the assertion of individual or collective identity.[51] Our voices broadly defined, are the means by which we achieve intimacy. In the doo-wop community, opportunities for transcendent, transformative intimacy are abundant. To seize these opportunities, one must begin by putting one's ear to the ground of doo-wop's history, and then listen in on the contemporary lived experiences of those who sing their songs on the oldies circuit.[52] One will hear voices, both past and present, echo and join together in a complex chorus that contains the consonances and the dissonances of American life.

oo-wop is a musical culture that has a long history. As Greg Woods, a member of Shirley Alston Reeves's band, put it, "Nothing ever happens in a vacuum. Doo-wop did not just spring up over night. It has a legacy. Slave owners didn't like us singing. They were afraid we were passing along information, which we did."[1] There are written examples and accounts of colonial-era European American music making, but traces of pre-nineteenth-century African American musical life are scant.[2] Recognizing and exploring the places in the historical narrative where something seems to be missing—listening for the echoes of the otherwise silent legacies—are critical to filling in the blanks in the recounting of this country's complex interracial legacy.[3] Looking at and listening to an existing long-standing musical tradition is an effective way to search for what has gone missing.

The historical trajectory of American vocal harmony, from the barbershop quartets and minstrel shows of the nineteenth century, through the jazz era and the gospel groups of the first half of the twentieth, to the rhythm and blues vocal groups of the post–World War II era, is filled with echoes. This vocal harmony tradition resonates with the racial interaction that forms the spine of social and cultural America. It is also infused with nostalgia for elements of that interaction—mythological "locations" in the American mind. A comprehensive survey of these vocal group genres would itself require, and deserves, a book-length treatment. I focus here on the relationship of vocal harmony, race relations, and nostalgia, the path where, in Woods's words, important information was and still is being "passed along."

BARBERSHOP QUARTETS

Asked to visualize a barbershop quartet, most people would think of four white men in striped suits with large mustaches singing "Sweet Adeline." This image, propagated for a century in Hollywood movies, Broadway shows, and Norman Rockwell paintings, belies the more complex origins of this music.[4] The story of barbershop, and all American vocal harmony genres, is not black and white but filled with the gray areas of racial interaction and nostalgic exchange. It is the story of an intimacy that usurped and redrew the boundaries that separated blacks and whites.[5] In the nineteenth century, this intimacy included the negotiation of the unequal power relations in daily life—and more publicly and complexly on the minstrel stage.

For a preteen Earl Carroll growing up in 1940s Harlem, the neighborhood barbershop was one of the first performance venues. "On Saturday to get my little movie money I used to go to the hairdressers in the neighborhood and barbershops. At that time Coca-Cola bottles was getting a deposit of two-cents. So I used to get all the bottles together. But before they would give the bottles they'd say 'Earl, we wanna see ya do the Camel Walk.' So I would have to dance for them. And the barber would say, 'Give me an Applejack if you want that box full of bottles over there.' So I'd do a little Applejack and what have you, and I'll have my show fare and go to the movies and have me a little pocket change, you know."[6] At least since the early nineteenth century, the barbershop was an important meeting place in the African American community, a social space where music, dancing, and singing were important. They were safe and stable neighborhood centers where business mixed easily with camaraderie and creativity.[7] Here a tradition of vocal harmony took shape.[8]

The groundwork for this a cappella or nearly a cappella singing tradition was laid in colonial Puritan churches in the seventeenth and eighteenth centuries, during services attended by African slaves and where the use of musical instruments was usually prohibited.[9] Sacred singing coexisted with and perhaps inspired informal, recreational, non-sacred group singing. By the early nineteenth century, when the majority of blacks lived in southern rural areas, young men congregated and sang in small town social spaces like barbershops. Post-emancipation, as blacks moved to the cities, young men would do the same in and around workplaces like train stations and loading docks. The term "barbershop quartet" evolved to encompass any group singing regardless of the location.[10] The intimacy and simplicity of its small-town origin and the nostalgic resonance of the term traveled along with the music.

In the early nineteenth century white people listened in on the black group singing in their midst and reinterpreted it through the filter of their own musical traditions, most notably the secular four-part close harmony of Austrian and German immigrants.[11] Blacks also listened in on the music making of European Americans and incorporated the elements they found most pleasing or useful.

This musical exchange, which had been occurring in a local, informal, everyday manner, when transferred to the minstrel stage became a matter of national public display. On the minstrel stage American vocal harmony began to evolve as a distinct tradition, and the influences of African and European sources coalesced to create something new. This musical evolution was inseparable from the evolution of racial politics, a politics of admiration and mockery, of fascination and ridicule, and, in the words of the historian Eric Lott, of "love and theft."[12]

The first full-length minstrel show was most likely organized by the Virginia Minstrels, a white vocal quartet, in New York in 1843.[13] Minstrelsy was a racial theater of the absurd. Whites transformed themselves visually by putting on blackface and mimicking black dances like the cakewalk.[14] They would also transform themselves *sonically* by mimicking black speaking and singing styles.[15] Throughout the rest of the nineteenth century and into the twentieth, white minstrel performers brought these distorted presentations of black culture to a larger white audience, reinforcing and creating market desire for those distortions. In the process, new performance genres were developed, preeminently barbershop quartet singing. A cultural hybrid barbershop was the product of a uniquely American cultural and social interplay, which incorporated the economic and political power play inherent in the absurd simulacra of musical and choreographic expression, of vocal and body language, and of dress, hair, and complexion.

Also inherent in the performance of minstrelsy was a particular kind of nostalgic longing. Minstrelsy arose from a modernizing, industrializing society supported in large measure by the North American slave trade. Different races and social classes jostled together in close, often volatile proximity. Newly arrived working-class European immigrants, recently escaped former southern slaves, and free-born northern blacks seeking work in city factories, found themselves in often deplorable and degrading living conditions.[16] The American pastoral South of the mind, where, as the minstrel song "Dixie" described, "old times were not forgotten," became a place of psychic refuge, a fabrication born of collective nostalgia that, when invoked on the minstrel stage, was emotionally potent.[17] Black barbershop quartets, even absurd representations of them, became emblems of a perceived lost culture of pastoral innocence.

The racial double helix of vocal harmony was fully expressed for the first time on the minstrel stage. In the sound of the nineteenth-century barbershop quartet one heard the combination, and recombination, of the European and African American strands. The legacy of the German close harmony singing tradition is evident in the way vocal pitches generally remained in close proximity to each other and how chord progressions followed the familiar European harmonic logic.[18] The black influence was heard in the use of drone or held notes; the foregrounding of falsetto or head voice; nonverbal vocalizations that were imitations of instrument, most often drum, sounds; and non-pitched vocal effects such as shouts and low gravelly rasps. Nonverbal vocalizations often came in the form of repeated, periodic fragments accompanying or underscoring the main texted melody of the song. These melodies themselves contained repeated refrains or responses to the call or main sung text of the lead singer or singers.[19] All of these traits would be evident in the vocal harmony genres to follow, especially doo-wop.

Examples of close harmony, call-and-response structure, and black vocal commonplaces have been captured in late nineteenth-century recordings.[20] Barbershop quartets were the subjects of some of the first recordings of any kind in the 1890s, and vocal group records would prove to be the first big sellers in the fledgling recording industry of the early twentieth century.[21] Some of the surviving examples of these recordings include music by the Standard Quartette (1894) on the Columbia label and the Dinwiddie Colored Quartet (1902) on Victor. The recording business, along with the established sheet music industry and the sprawling vaudeville circuit, which had supplanted the minstrel stage as the country's predominant entertainment venue network, would help to make vocal harmony music ubiquitous in turn-of-the-century America.

By the mid- to late 1920s, as jazz became the nation's popular music, barbershop quartet singing came to represent the mythologized halcyon time of nineteenth-century Victorian America. Sheet music typically would have a picture of a group of four white men in small-town barbershop attire on the cover. Such images strengthened the link between this demographic group and the written, standardized versions of the music.[22] As a result, a genre of vocal harmony that evolved in a complex interracial exchange in the socially, culturally, and politically volatile nineteenth century became a signifier for Main Street, small-town midwestern America. In the previous century, the pastoral South was the object of the collective nostalgic impulse. This shift did not result in a complete historical erasure, however. In vocal harmony, the sonic traces, the echoes, remain.

This is true even though barbershop quartet singing became almost exclusively a white male practice, as amateur preservation societies who focused on this activity began to proliferate in the mid-twentieth century. These societies were seeking to preserve not only a musical tradition but a perceived way of life. Their collective nostalgia was selective, emphasizing racial and social purity or at best, simplicity. The black strand in this music's DNA was removed from the preservation narrative. Since nineteenth-century America, in either actual or imagined form, was not a welcoming place for blacks, however, there was not a felt need to counter the narrative. The realties of slavery, minstrelsy, and post-Reconstruction were better left behind. This does not mean that the vocal harmony tradition that emerged in this era, or a different nostalgic relationship born of a different racial experience, was completely discarded in favor of new twentieth-century explorations. Black vocal groups with obvious barbershop pedigrees would come into prominence in the new century.

JAZZ-ERA QUARTETS

Between acts at an oldies concert in November 2000, MC, DJ, and bass singer Bobby Jay announced: "I've been singing since 1955, and it was just the continuation of a great line of singers. Everybody, every group here, owes it all to the group that I say, without hesitation or equivocation, was the greatest vocal group ever, the Mills Brothers. The Mills Brothers opened the door for everything that followed [including] the group that came right after the Mills Brothers, the Ink Spots."

The Mills Brothers grew up in Piqua, Ohio, a small city near Dayton. Their father, John Mills Sr., owned a barbershop and was a singer influenced by the close harmony tradition. He and his wife, Ethel, nurtured the vocal talents of their seven children. In 1925, four of their teenage sons started a group whose initial claim to fame was the surprisingly adroit vocal imitation of instruments. John Jr. played the guitar and imitated the tuba. Harry, Herbert, and Donald imitated other brass and wind instruments such as the trumpet, trombone, and saxophone. They began their career performing in vaudeville theaters, tent shows, and church socials. Within a few years they became the first black act to be given sponsorship on a national radio network.[23] Their career ascent coincided with the ubiquitous popularity of radio in the depression. First in Cincinnati and then in New York, the Mills Brothers' radio broadcasts brought them unprecedented fame that led to world tours, movie appearances, and recordings with some of the biggest stars of the day, including Bing Crosby and Louis Armstrong.

By the early 1940s, the brothers had removed the instrument imitations from their act except for the tubalike bass singing, an aspect of their style that would have enormous influence on the vocal groups of the coming decades. They then began recording an impressive string of hits that would cement their legacy. The mature Mills Brothers' sound was a marriage of the close harmony singing they had learned from their father and styles of the popular white and black artists of the time. The rhythmic foundation of their music—their swing—came from Duke Ellington, whom they had heard on the radio in their youth, and from the many other jazz artists they toured with in the 1930s. White contemporaries Bing Crosby and Rudy Vallee inspired their smooth, crooning style.

The Mills Brothers' recording of "Paper Doll" (1942) is a perfect example of how the group blended all these influences into a style that was at once both traditional and modern. The first verse has a solo singer and gentle three-part close harmony "ooh" accompaniment structure. The only instrument heard on the track is a softly strummed guitar. The mood is unrushed and sentimental, conjuring up images of four men on a barbershop porch on a lazy afternoon in a small Ohio town. In the B section the tranquil spell is broken ever so slightly as the tempo picks up and starts to swing. The vocal arrangement remains the same with the three-part "ooh" in the background behind the lead singer. When the A section returns, the melody is harmonized in a spirited, tight three-part arrangement undergirded by a vocal walking bass line, the same as any heard in small jazz combos in the mid-twentieth century.

Their distinctive style made the Mills Brothers one of the most successful recording and performing acts of all time, with seventy-one chart singles from the early 1930s until the mid-1960s—the most by an American male vocal group.[24] This would not have been possible had they not had a huge white audience. The Mills Brothers were the first black vocal group to achieve such crossover appeal, which has led to characterizations of the group as knowingly catering to a white fan base. But this criticism is the result of unenlightened listening: the echoes are being missed. What can be heard in their harmony is the complex working-out of white and black forms of vocalization and the sonic referencing of and riffing on contemporary and historical styles with the social, often nostalgic, resonances that accompany them.

The Ink Spots, formed in 1934 in New York City, also evolved a style with a wide cross-racial appeal. Initially their repertoire consisted of material that was popular primarily in the black community. At that stage, their vocal style reflected the emotionally expressive approach found in the hot jazz of the 1930s rather than the smooth crooning of the popular white singers of the time.[25] Their 1939 hit "If I Didn't Care" ushered in the stylistic change that made them stars. The vocal arrangement featured the mellow, high tenor lead of Bill Kenny, with a verse performed in understated spoken form by the bass, Hoppy Jones. There is a gentle "ooh" accompaniment by the background singers, as would occur in the Mills Brothers' "Paper Doll," but in this recording it is employed as a response to the lead singer's call. Even though the vocal arrangement subtly references this common black musical gesture,[26] the smoother vocal timbre of the lead and background singers signaled a move away from the more expressive style of the Ink Spots' early years.

This formula proved to be enormously popular with both white and black audiences, producing more than forty hits on the pop charts in the 1940s. The Ink Spots' arrangements featured a slighter wider pitch range than the Mills Brothers', but their smooth approach and gentle "ooh" accompaniment still invoked the spirit, if not the practice, of the close harmony tradition. For a nation embroiled in a frighteningly modern world war, the nostalgia stirred by the sound of this vocal harmony style that was audibly linked to a pre-war performance practice in turn associated with a mythologized Victorian era, contributed to the popularity of the Ink Spots in the early 1940s and the continuing appeal of the Mills Brothers as well.

Ironically, the reasons for their cross-race appeal may have contributed to the Ink Spots' eventual fade in popularity by the end of the decade. Because the lead singer, Bill Kenny, sang in an overly sentimental, old-fashioned style, free of what some considered characteristic black vocal mannerisms, he was perceived as singing "white." This audibly contrasted to the perceived "black" singing style that was being heard by more and more black vocal groups in the 1940s. A reviewer in the October 1, 1941, *Downbeat* refers to "Billy Kenny's sickening, phony and pseudo-dramatic tenor soloing"—clearly criticizing his lack of "authenticity" without using overtly racial terms.[27]

This critique, however, overlooks the subtleties of the Ink Spots' ensemble singing. This recording, in fact, contained an illuminating contrast of "white" and "black" vocalizations. Kenny's supposedly exaggerated "perfect" enunciation in the sung portions was offset by the voice of the bass, Hoppy Jones, who spoke instead of sung the lyrics in the B or middle section of the song with the obvious inflection and lilt of vernacular speech. The Ink Spots were part of a tradition in which a variety of vocal timbres and techniques, including falsettos, drones, shouts, spoken words, and sung non-verbal tones, were employed. Representations of perceived "white" and "black" singing styles could also be read as, simply, more colors in their expressive musical palette.[28]

The wide range of vocal expression within black music is reflective of the wide range of social and cultural experiences and backgrounds of blacks. Some in the white mainstream, exemplified by the *Downbeat* critic, resisted the notion that the black experience was as rich and complex as their own. To accept that idea would have meant that the existing economic and social inequities between the races could not be justified in terms of cultural or biological difference.

A nostalgic impulse, one not focused on a mythologized past but on perceived "authentic" contemporary black practice, was at play in the *Downbeat* criticism of Bill Kenny's singing style. By the mid-1930s, as big band jazz or swing became America's popular music, nostalgia for the small group jazz of the 1920s was manifested by certain enthusiasts, some of whom were musicians but many of whom were just avid record collectors and music lovers. One such collector was Milt Gabler, who owned the Commodore Music Shop on East 42nd Street in Manhattan. In 1935, he founded the United Hot Clubs of America, an organization dedicated to reissuing the jazz records of the previous decade.[29] For Gabler and his ilk, the gritty jazz of the 1920s was the real thing, unlike the smoother swing of the 1930s. Similar enthusiasts and organizations, debating and disseminating notions of black cultural authenticity, would be influential in the doo-wop community many years later.

Despite their critics, the Ink Spots would have a substantial impact on the next generation of vocal groups. The high tenor and prominent bass featured in their style would be a model for the more open, dispersed approach of the 1950s. The "ooh" and "ah" middle voice accompaniment would also be a salient aspect in the sound of the coming decade. Most notably, Hoppy Jones's talking bridge brought new prominence to the bass singer's role and many basses would emulate it. Bill Godwin, a leader of a recent incarnation of the group, even claimed the bridge as a precursor to one of today's most popular vocal genres: "See, the Ink Spots was the original rap. Think about it! When he says, 'If I didn't care' . . . these young fellahs out there now think that they discovered it, and the Ink Spots were doing it in 1939."[30]

The Mills Brothers and the Ink Spots were far and away the most popular black vocal groups of the 1930s and 1940s, and they were the only ones to have great commercial appeal across racial lines. However, many other vocal groups had substantial professional careers and were influential on the next generation of black singers. But these groups, such as the Charioteers, the Deep River Boys, the Four Vagabonds, the Delta Rhythm Boys, the Basin Street Boys, and the Five Red Caps, were in general more influenced by blues and gospel music than the Mills Brothers and the Ink Spots were.

The difference between these two sets of groups was also the result of promotional strategies, both by the groups themselves and by the music industry. The Delta Rhythm Boys recorded a version of "Paper Doll" quite similar to the Mills Brothers', but because they were usually marketed as "Masters of Hip Harmony," they connected more with an exclusively black audience. This orientation toward a "hipper" audience than the white mainstream, however, belied a much wider stylistic range. The Delta Rhythm Boys included both sacred and secular songs and even some European light classical or operetta material, in their performances. Their origins as a college group, in an environment where they were exposed to a wide variety of music, surely contributed to their eclectic repertoire.[31]

That the Delta River Boys and several other blues- and gospel-influenced groups were spawned in college reveals that class background is not a reliable predictor of stylistic choice. (Which is true for performing artists of any race in any era.) The word "choice" is key here. The options available to educated middle- and upper-class people are far greater than those open to artists from working-class backgrounds, who do not have the same breadth of cultural exposure—they do not have the same cultural mobility.

The influence of the less commercially successfully groups of this era, college educated or not, can be heard and seen in the mostly working-class doo-wop singers. The Red Caps' biggest hit, "I Went to Your Wedding," was the lyrical model for the Penguins' "Earth Angel," one of the most popular of all doo-wop songs.[32] The groups of the 1940s also began to establish social models that would be duplicated in the next decade. The Mariners, who formed in the Coast Guard in 1942, were one of the first racially integrated groups, with two black and two white singers.

Unfortunately, the careers of most of these singers did not survive technological change, as they were primarily radio performers, and, unlike the Mills Brothers and the Ink Spots, they did not sell records in the millions. The new medium of the new decade—television—also was initially not accessible to marginal black entertainers, those who did not achieve national name recognition. It would take a much greater groundswell of popularity across racial lines and across the country to break down the barriers of institutionalized racism.

GOSPEL QUARTETS

Doo-wop is a decidedly secular genre, but the influence of the church on it was undeniable. As Earl Carroll remembers, "I did used to listen to quite a few of the groups, spiritual groups, like the Dixie Hummingbirds, the Five Blind Boys, the Swan Silvertones, and Sam Cooke and the Soul Stirrers. You know we used to listen to all of those groups. That was the mother music."[33] These groups were continuing a small-group sacred harmony tradition that had roots in the nineteenth century. In the period following the Civil War, at colleges established by and for blacks, such as Fisk University in Nashville, vocal groups were formed that focused on the Negro spiritual tradition. The Fisk Jubilee Singers eventually traveled and performed for both white and black audiences, solidifying the canon of songs and providing a standard and model for future performance of sacred vocal harmony during the late nineteenth century.[34]

With the new century, however, came new black sacred music practices. In the early 1900s, at the Azusa Street Revival in Los Angeles, Black Pentecostalism was born together with a new musical style that reflected its more emotionally intense approach. This was the frenzy W. E. B. Du Bois witnessed.[35] Dancing, hand clapping, foot stomping, and shouting embodied a more participatory and improvisational style of worship. The Black Pentecostals, expanding on a preexisting charismatic American religious strain, took the already expressive music of the Negro spiritual and added new layers of emotional immediacy that reflected the aspirations, suffering, and hope of a new epoch in black history.[36]

By the 1930s, because of the growing national network of radio, records, and touring exploited by itinerant gospel musicians, Pentecostalism and the music that came from it gained a strong foothold in the black community. A golden age of gospel music that would last through the 1950s had begun. Two areas became centers for gospel quartet singing: the Hampton Roads region of Virginia, which included the overlapping urban areas of Norfolk, Newport News, Portsmouth, and Virginia Beach, and Birmingham, Alabama. Other southern cities such as New Orleans, Atlanta, Houston, and Memphis also spawned influential quartets. In Chicago, the songwriter and choir director Thomas Dorsey and the singer Mahalia Jackson developed a gospel sound that reflected the stylistic interchange between sacred and secular. The exchange flowed in the other direction as well: the Four Southern Singers, the Mississippi Mudmashers, the Four Blue Birds, the Five Jones Boys, and the Golden Gate Quartet were some of the first vocal groups whose secular music was based on spiritual models.[37]

The Cadillacs' baritone Gary Lewis's personal history exemplifies both the stylistic influence of gospel music and the rural-to-urban population shift in the twentieth-century black experience. "I was born in Boston but my parents came from Darlington, South Carolina. My father was in a gospel quartet there. Oh, you can definitely hear the gospel in the music [of the 1950s]. Look at 'Shout' [by the Isley Brothers]. Gospel had more richness. There was more roaming [improvising]. Not just by the tenor, but by all the singers.[38] This roaming or improvisatory vocalizing included dramatic changes in tone and pitch register. One of the pioneers of this approach in the gospel vocal group world was R. W. Harris, the lead singer of the Soul Stirrers, a group who formed in 1929 in Houston, Texas. Harris joined the group in 1937, and was strongly influenced by the blues singers of the day. Under his leadership the group shifted from nineteenth-century jubilee style, with its comparatively more staid arrangements of Negro spirituals, to gospel style. Their innovations included incorporating a second lead singer (expanding the quartet into a quintet), ad-libbing lyrics, and repeating words in the accompanying harmony parts.

In 1950, Harris retired and was replaced by nineteen-year-old Sam Cooke, who further enhanced the Soul Stirrers' reputation with his smooth yet emotional vocal delivery.[39] The Soul Stirrers' 1952 recording of "It Won't Be Long" with Cooke on lead exhibits some of the important aspects of modern gospel vocal harmony which would greatly influence the doo-wop groups of 1950s. The call-and-response pattern is at the heart of the vocal arrangement. The melismatic or ornate lead vocal line and the two-note bass interjection at the end of the second measure effectively fill in the empty sonic space and shadow the "whoa" of the lead singer at the beginning of the song. This sort of intricate vocal interplay would pervade doo-wop style. Cooke became one of the first gospel singers to cross over to popular music, and, although he was killed at the age of thirty-three, his short career helped bridge the gap between the simpler, smoother vocal style of the 1950s, heard in his hit "You Send Me" (1957), and the more emotive approach of the 1960s, as in "A Change Is Gonna Come" (1964).

As blacks continued to move north in the mid-twentieth century, cities such as New York, Chicago, Detroit, and others became strongholds for gospel quartet singing. Gospel music continued to serve as both a link to the past agrarian life and a forge for the creation of a new urban identity. It was an expression of cultural continuity in the flux of the post–World War II era. As Earl Carroll says, it was "the mother music," and it was pervasive as a maternal presence. Most young blacks of that time who tried singing careers came into contact with some iteration of gospel in the course of their lives. The gospel quartet was a popular medium, especially among young black men. They saw the quartets in their churches and listened to their recordings. The popularity of the gospel group singers among women also made them attractive role models for young males, many of whom would seek to join existing groups or start new ones.[40]

The touring, recordings, and radio play of one of the more famous southern groups, the Dixie Hummingbirds, had an immense impact on the vocal groups of the 1950s. One of the defining aspects of the music that would come to be known as doo-wop was the preeminence of the background harmony parts, the distinctly black rhythmic motifs and repetitive, chantlike phrases that underscored the lead singer's melodies. The Dixie Hummingbirds were masters of the craft, and their background repertoire was a rich store from which many groups like the Cadillacs would borrow. Not only the sound but also the look of the Dixie Hummingbirds was influential on future singers. The matching, often flashy, suits they wore when they performed were an essential part of the gospel quartet experience. Doo-wop groups emulated this sartorial practice and took it to even higher levels of extravagance with brighter colors and more daring designs.[41]

The fervent performance style of the gospel groups was adopted by many of the secular vocal groups. Ira Tucker, the lead singer of the Dixie Hummingbirds, was famous for jumping off the stage and running up and down the aisles as he exhorted audience participation.[42] Young audience members like Carroll often witnessed such theatrics at Harlem's Apollo Theatre, where many doo-wop groups got their start. The young singers learned the various ways gospel singers would get audiences to their feet, falling to their knees and reaching to the sky as if in the throes of religious ecstasy. Because sacred and secular acts were often booked at the same venues, the melding of these musical spheres was not surprising. Romantic love and the love of God could be expressed by the same means, often with only a slight change of lyrics. In the late 1950s, when the Isley Brothers performed "Shout" and Little Anthony and the Imperials did "I'm Alright," they were simply borrowing the emotive power, evocative presentation, and magnetic presence of the gospel quartets they shared the stage with.[43]

One of the first groups of the early 1950s to transfer these elements from the sacred to the secular was the Dominoes, started by four recent migrants to Harlem from Durham, North Carolina. Their lead singer was fourteen-year-old Clyde McPhatter, who until then had only sung gospel. The Dominoes' sound and stage presentation were very different from anything seen before. McPhatter injected gospel mannerisms into secular songs with a powerful, emotionally urgent voice and he would go on to do the same as the lead singer of the Drifters. His work helped bridge the gap between gospel and what had recently been dubbed rhythm and blues.

RHYTHM AND BLUES

As Earl Carroll remembers, "Growing up, the Apollo Theatre was my second home. I used to catch people like Nat King Cole, Billy Eckstine, and Louis Jordan there. But the groups we wanted to be like were the Dominoes, the Ravens, and the Orioles."[44] The term "rhythm and blues" signified music primarily by and for blacks. It came into wide use in the music business by the end of 1940s partly because it was an alternative to the offensive term "race music" and partly because the music was becoming immensely popular: *Billboard* magazine instituted "Rhythm and Blues" as a chart category in 1949. The economic foundation for this popularity was a network of independent record companies, music publishers, and independent distributors supported by black radio deejays who often received money (later called payola) from these companies.[45]

It was the music that black people danced to in the postwar era. Jazz had moved into the bebop phase, which was highly respected critically. But when people in New York City wanted to party, instead of going to 52nd Street to hear Charlie Parker, they were more likely to head uptown to a juke joint to dance to Louis Jordan.[46] Jordan was a singer, saxophonist, and leader of a band that came out of the swing tradition of the 1930s but was smaller and emphasized the rhythm section, drums, bass, piano, and guitar. His "jump blues" featured up-tempo, dance-oriented tunes with shouted vocals and earthy, urban-based lyrical themes.

Rhythm and blues was not a monolithic category but comprised a range of types defined to some extent by the kind and size of venue where it was performed. Big bands like Lionel Hampton's and Billy Eckstine's played the dancehalls. In the smaller theaters you could catch blues shouters like Joe Turner and jump artists like Louis Jordan. More jazz-oriented crooners like Nat King Cole (early in his career) and Charles Brown most often could be found leading their piano trios in nightclubs. Neighborhood bars of the cities were the haunts of southern-style blues musicians like B. B. King and Muddy Waters.[47]

The Cadillacs and other doo-wop groups were of a generation whose musical sound incorporated, in varying degrees, jazz-era vocal group style, gospel, and rhythm and blues. But for young black people in the late 1940s and early 1950s, rhythm and blues was *the* popular music of the day. Mainstream pop music with its repertoire of Tin Pan Alley tunes was still an audible influence, but younger groups were gearing their sound more to their peers. The sonic result was a negotiation between past and present, between a black identity with roots in the South and a new identity that incorporated the urban sounds of the North. For many blacks, both the venue and the music were "new homes."

This negotiation involved seemingly contradictory attitudes toward past black musical practices. When the Ravens formed in Harlem in 1945, they continued the smooth, accessible tradition of the Mills Brothers and the Ink Spots. But they were also trying to connect with their peers, young blacks who were forging their own identities in their new urban environment. This, in part, involved the rejection of the traditional blues style of singing they associated with the heritage of slavery. They wanted to be as hip as the new music they were hearing. Their communities were modern and changing, but they also provided social cohesion and cultural continuity based in part on a relationship to long-standing musical traditions like the blues. These were expressive realms where young people could look inward for pride and creativity.[48]

Thus though the attraction to the modern, urban, and sophisticated was powerful, so too was the need for group identification and continuity and what spoke to them more essentially as black people. Consequently, the music of the Ravens and similar groups signified an integration of the sophisticated close harmony singing of the 1930s and early 1940s and the more gospel- and blues-influenced music of the late 1940s and early 1950s. This complex mix reflected the complexity of an emerging, consciously black fan base. The Mills Brothers and Ink Spots may have hinted at melodic blues inflections, jazz bass lines, and gospel call-and-response forms, but the Ravens moved these characteristically black elements front and center. The Ravens and the other vocal groups of the emerging rhythm and blues scene could not easily be mistaken for white.[49]

Jimmy Ricks, leader of the Ravens, was a distinctive bass singer whose greatest influence was Lee Gaines of the Delta Rhythm Boys. Like Gaines, Ricks featured a distinctive use of bass riffs that provided the foundation for the entire harmonic vocal structure. The arrangement of the Ravens' biggest hit, "Count Every Star" from 1950, which begins with Ricks's prominent bass line, became a template used by hundreds of groups in the following decade. In Jimmy Ricks's wake, the bass singer became the indispensible and occasionally most popular member of a group.[50] The Ravens also featured the high tenor falsetto of Maithe Marshall, a sonic element that would become a hallmark of the doo-wop sound. In "Count Every Star" the vocal arrangement has three independent yet integrated parts: the bass line, which provides the root of the chord on the downbeat and thus the harmonic and rhythmic foundation; the inner voices, which simulate chimes lyrically ("bong") on the up-beats; and the floating falsetto line.

The Ravens were also the first rhythm and blues vocal group to feature choreographed dance steps in their act. The moves of their second tenor, Leonard Puzey, established a performance model emulated by many subsequent groups, including the Cadillacs. Choreography made the Ravens more than just recording stars in the black community: they were an act that had to be seen to be fully appreciated.

The Ravens presented exciting music to thousands of young people by touring the "chitlin' circuit," a network of black theaters and small clubs primarily in the East and South. In the days of racial segregation these were venues where black performers could find work and their fans could find them. *Chitlin'*, derived from the soul food staple chitterlings (stewed pig intestines), is a word that connotes familiar, everyday black life and its southern rural past. The circuit was a safe haven where tradition as well as innovation could be freely expressed and readily comprehended.

Venues like Harlem's Apollo (which is still in operation) that lasted several generations provided historical continuity between stylistic eras. Some of the other well-known long-lived theaters were the Regal in Chicago, the Fox in Detroit, the Circle Theatre in Cleveland, the Syrian Mosque in Pittsburgh, the Uptown and the Earl in Philadelphia, the Howard Theatre in Washington, D.C., the Royal in Baltimore, and the State in Hartford. In these venues vocal groups, comedians, dancers, and dramatic actors would share the stage and connect with the audiences. Dancing, comedy, and music were learned and shared by all performers. The chitlin' circuit was the performance school system for transplanted southern blacks and, especially, their progeny.[51]

One of the groups to make a profound impression on young chitlin' circuit audience members of the late 1940s was the Orioles. The group, formed in 1947 in Baltimore, had a simple, cool ballad sound. Instead of relying on reworkings of Tin Pan Alley tunes, they performed and recorded their own material as well as other black songwriters' songs. Like the Ravens, the Orioles sang rhythm and blues harmony, influenced by jazz as well as gospel and blues. Also like the Ravens, their standard vocal arrangement was the doo-wop template of floating high tenor, blended, chimelike middle voices, and prominent bass voice. New in the Orioles' sound was the sweet, soft tenor of their lead singer, Sonny Til. He, like the others in the group, was in his late teens when he made his first record. His voice was the sound of teen and even preteen black America in the late 1940s and early 1950s. His timbre and style reflected a new kind of youthful experience born of the hopes and aspirations of the postmigration and postwar era. This sound would ultimately serve as a sonic bridge to a white teen audience with its own hopes and aspirations.[52]

As sweet and reflective of youthful experience as this strain of rhythm and blues was, it was just as reflective of a new, more extroverted brand of sexual yearning. The vocal group music of the swing era had depended on sexual innuendo and implication. Now, like the raw rhythm and blues of the bars and juke joints, the sexual references of the Orioles' style were more overt, even though still tempered with a more wide-eyed, less world-weary approach. Their choreography, too, was more sexually explicit than what had been seen before. Their songs and style were simpler and more emotionally direct. Even when they performed a Tin Pan Alley standard, they would change the melody and lyrics to make the song their own.[53]

This new explicit yet innocent approach to sex was not initially aimed at a white audience. When the Orioles took the stage at the Apollo and sang their hit "It's Too Soon to Know" in the early 1950s, they were appealing directly to a new young black audience, their peers. Sonny Til became a teen idol and adolescent sex symbol. He would excite the female members of the audience by using his entire body to express the lyrics of his songs, and they responded by screaming and throwing articles of clothing onto the stage.[54] Aspiring young male singers of the early 1950s took note and honed their acts accordingly. Rhythm and blues represented a new musical way of being in the world and being with each other, a way to be separate from their parents though still part of black culture and society.[55] What is more, this generation put their money where their culture was like never before, a trend that became more and more apparent to the white business world.[56]

A complex mix of race, nostalgia, and vocal harmony came into play in an unprecedented way in the 1950s. It was an era of great American myth creation, a period of intense social upheaval, and a moment of monumental fluorescence of vocal harmony groups in the cities of the United States. Notably conspicuous in its absence here, however, is any discussion of the role of female groups in the history of American vocal harmony. This omission is primarily due to the fact that vocal harmony before the mid-twentieth century was a male-dominated arena. Another reason is that scant research has been done on the notable female groups that did exist, such as the white trios the Boswell Sisters and the Andrews Sisters and the black gospel trio the Barrett Sisters.[57] The 1950s and especially 1960s, though, would see a huge rise in the number and influence of female vocal groups.

CHAPTER 2 **THE BIRTH OF DOO-WOP**

n the 1950s, no one was yet calling the music doo-wop, but it was in these years that the nostalgic, racial, social, and economic semantic weight behind the word began to accumulate. One of the most famous New York doo-wop groups is the Cadillacs. Their story is doo-wop's story.

"Well, basically, I'm with a group, as you know, Speedo and the Cadillacs, which is a New York group, born and raised in Harlem, Manhattan."[1] Like Earl Carroll, most doo-wop groups identify with a particular urban neighborhood. It has been estimated that over ten thousand different vocal groups made records during the period from the late 1940s to the early 1960s, the "golden age" of American vocal harmony.[2] The majority of them were formed in New York, Chicago, and Los Angeles, but several other cities had scenes as well, including Washington, D.C., Baltimore, and Philadelphia. Eventually a particular style came to be associated with each different area.[3]

THE STREET CORNER

Within the city, smaller, more intimate social spaces, collectively referred to as the "street corner," became the locus for vocal music making. Long before home entertainment centers were the norm in American homes, when few people even had television or anything resembling air conditioning, leisure time in city neighborhoods in the summer was often spent outdoors, on the stoops of apartment buildings and nearby street corners. It was there that young men not only tried to beat the heat but also socialized.[4] In postwar America, vocal harmony filled black neighborhoods. Many singers began at very young ages, in junior high school or even before, initially just for the love of singing and hanging out with their friends. They listened to the music that was circulating, rhythm and blues and jazz on the black radio stations, the jukeboxes, and the records they would buy, and the white mainstream popular and classical music on network radio.[5]

Music was also learned and performed in school.[6] This was where Earl Carroll (born November 2, 1937) did some of his first entertaining, though not as a member of a vocal group: "Well, I've been in it since I was in elementary school, basically. But at that time I wasn't singing. I was in love with a gentleman, [the early twentieth-century black] tap-dancer Bill Robinson—'Bojangles.' I used to tap dance and I would imitate him and I would whistle 'Sweet Georgia Brown.'"[7] Churches were also important training grounds, although the influence of the church was not necessarily greater than other spheres of society.[8] The sacred and the secular were not separate realms in everyday life. Social and cultural life flowed back and forth. It was the total music world in which these singers grew up that would lead to the creation of doo-wop.[9]

When young singers formed groups, they rehearsed on street corners, apartment stoops, playgrounds, subway platforms, rooftops, in candy stores, bowling alleys, school bathrooms, pool halls, under bridges. The proving ground for teenage vocal dexterity was a collection of public spaces, in view of friends, family members, and rival singers. It was *public harmony*, the continuation of the relationship between voice and place that was rooted in the nineteenth-century barbershop, and now was happening on a much larger, more visible scale.

Forced to live in particular areas of the city, urban blacks came to identify with their street blocks, wards, or district, which were defined both by legislated and social segregation and by the built environment.[10] This imposed physical and social structure, intended to keep blacks out of mainstream white society, also provided opportunity for social solidarity which engendered intense, culturally specific creativity. This is an example of an often-noted irony of segregation: a social structure that was meant to contain actually fostered the means to usurp its boundaries.[11]

Earl Carroll remembers the New York City of the early 1950s as a musical map. "Every young kid in Harlem wanted to be a rhythm and blues singer. I mean, you could go up and down Eighth Avenue or Seventh Avenue or Lenox Avenue, which is in Harlem, and find a group. I remember 142nd Street had a group called the Crows. They had a big record called "Gee." And the Solitaires were out on 141st Street. They had a couple of big records."[12] Formed in the summer of 1953, and originally calling themselves the Carnations because of the flowers they put in their lapels when they performed, Earl Carroll, Bobby Phillips, Lavern Drake, and "Cub" Gaining made the area of Seventh and Eighth Avenues between 131st and

133rd Streets their rehearsal territory and first performed at community dances in nearby St. Mark's Church on 132nd Street.

Fertile ground for vocal harmony was found in other nearby neighborhoods. The Teenagers, the Velvets, the Savoys, the Valentines, the Ebonairs, the Crystals, and the Opals rehearsed in the Sugar Hill section of Harlem, an area on the east side from 145th to 170th Street.[13] The greatest number of groups, though, may have gathered on 115th Street, a critical mass of vocal harmony fueled by a high concentration of record stores, rehearsal spaces, and performance venues.[14] The Five Crowns, the Harptones, the Wanderers, the Willows, the Channels, the Bop-Chords, the Ladders, the Laddins, the Charts, the Whirlers, the Legends, the Matadors, and the Keynotes are some of the better-known groups who congregated and sang there. A little farther north near 125th Street and Mount Morris Park was the territory of the Schoolboys, the Jesters, and the Desires. Another ten blocks north around 135th Street, near the Cadillacs' neighborhood, the Velvetones also worked out their vocal arrangements, and about ten blocks from there the Crows, the Solitaires, the Four Bells, and the Mello-Moods could be found.

This delineation of territory was often reinforced by the presence of teenage gangs. Many groups evolved from gangs, and their music making served as a nonviolent alternative to fighting.[15] Groups from different neighborhoods would compete in singing contests, channeling adolescent energy and anxiety into vocal harmony and away from physical aggression.[16] It was understood that young men could go some places and not others, but during turf wars vocal groups were often given free passes into otherwise hostile territory.

Groups chose rehearsal locations not only for territorial control but also for acoustic viability, especially reverb potential. The Harptones, one of the more highly regarded doo-wop groups, rehearsed in the school yard of Wadleigh Junior High on 115th Street between Seventh and Eighth Avenues, a relatively small area half the size of a city block bounded by high brick walls that made their voices reverberate. The groups colonized whatever space they could find—stairwells, subway entrances, school bathrooms—to get that "echo chamber" effect.[17]

The reverb found in these social spaces helped fill the empty acoustic spaces between the notes of a melody, the pauses for breath and the ends of phrases. It also imbued the singing experience with a resonant aura. The total musical effect became greater than the sum of the vocal parts, making the rehearsal process more pleasurable, or at least less hard on the ears as they each fished for the right notes to fill out the chords. Social and acoustic space melded during these moments, and school lavatories became not just places to sneak a cigarette or catch up with the latest gossip between classes but also refuges to meet with your group to bounce your multilayered "woo" off the tiles.[18] Jerry Butler, the original lead singer of Chicago's Impressions, even called his first group the Toileteers, in honor of their favorite practice room.[19]

Vocal harmony practice was predominantly a male domain. Street corners and school yards were not considered safe or respectable places for young girls to be, so there are few recordings or even written mentions of female vocal groups from the early 1950s. Toward the end of the decade a handful of all-female groups or ones that had at least one female member did start to appear. They simply found other, less disreputable locations to harmonize. For instance, the Chantels, one of the first New York all-female vocal groups to have a hit record ("Maybe," their very influential song of 1958), all played on their school basketball team, and so they would rehearse in the locker room before and after practice.

Female vocal harmony, although not a direct product of the street corner, still had a social and musical relationship with particular kinds of city architecture. In New York, low-income housing projects constructed in the postwar era, which were usually densely populated tall buildings, created opportunities for vocal grouping. The Bobbettes, another of New York's first female groups to gain fame, grew up in the Washington Projects in upper Manhattan, which were built in 1956. The three original members had just moved there from different New York neighborhoods and lived on three floors of the same building. Once they got to know each other, they came up with a unique way of communicating, which exploited the architecture of their building: whenever one of them wanted to rehearse she would bang on the heating pipe; the others would go to their windows, and they would make arrangements for their rendezvous.[20] The Bobbettes eventually became the first black female group in the 1950s to have a Top 10 pop hit, "Mr. Lee" (1957).[21]

The female groups may have initially developed their sound in more private, interior spaces, but they were certainly aware of the harmony style their male counterparts were honing on the street corner. In addition to overhearing the guys' rehearsing through their apartment windows or as they passed by stairwells and school yards, they also attended their performances in school talent shows or at local venues. The girls would absorb the background harmony parts and incorporate them into their own arrangements. Eventually the female groups began to perform as well, first at their local churches and community centers and then, as they made their own recordings, on the same shows as the other young popular performers of the time. They may not have had the record sales and radio play of their male counterparts, but the sound and style of groups like the Chantels and the Bobbettes were influential on many of the popular "girl groups" of the 1960s.[22]

One prevalent reality of 1950s public harmony (or public housing harmony) was the lack of musical instruments. In most cases, their voices were all the singers had, and any prolonged silence might have meant either the intrusion of the noisy environment or a loss of the ever-important beat or pulse. They had to find various ways to fill in and control their acoustic space. One way was to try to sound like snare drums or tom-toms, and the percussive background harmony part became one of the defining characteristics of this music. Background harmony was also created by mimicking other instruments as well, including strings, trumpets, and saxophones.[23] The popularization of the term "doo-wop" in the 1960s was indicative of the importance not only of the notes but of the text used in these often highly inventive parts of the song arrangements.[24]

There were also other means for filling up the acoustic space. Many doo-wop groups used "blow harmonies," a way of singing that lengthens or expands the attack of the tones being sung. In the previous generation, the Mills Brothers and the Ink Spots relied on humming as the default background harmony structure, but doo-wop groups preferred something with a little more resonance. With blow harmonies, the sound of the breath used to create the held note, so-called white noise, was greatly emphasized, making it a salient aspect of the auditory experience.[25] One of the first great blow harmony groups, whose sound had a strong influence on the Cadillacs, was the Moonglows from Chicago. In their ballad "Sincerely" (1954), the middle voices use breathy "w" consonants interspersed with the "oo" vowel sounds. By encasing their harmony within the rushing of air, they brought the sound of the street corner and the outside world into the studio. This aural simulation of open space created an illusion of expansiveness and evoked the desire and longing often found in balladry.

The young black men and women of the 1950s were using public space to make a kind of urban folk music.[26] They were amateurs, albeit often with professional aspirations, interacting with and sonically infusing the surrounding built environment. The street corner singers were also imbuing these spaces with their own experiences. Public harmony was part of the social life of the city. Many of the groups never made it beyond the street corner, but a great many did get a chance to record. In the process, a primarily amateur or folk music making practice was captured on tape, and professional careers were begun.

WHAT'S IN A NAME?

The branch of the music business that supported doo-wop in the early 1950s was a youthful enterprise. Most of the artists were either teenagers or in their early twenties. The business people, mostly men with a few notable female exceptions, were also relatively young, primarily in their late twenties and early thirties.[27] Attracted to the new music for aesthetic and economic reasons, they were aggressive in finding talent and exploiting it. Most of the major record companies, RCA, Columbia, Decca, Capitol, Mercury, and MGM, were interested in white pop and classical music, and paid little attention to black music like rhythm and blues or even white working-class music like country and western. The small independent labels, a few, such as Vee-Jay in Chicago and Red Robin in New York, owned by blacks, but most Jewish-owned, such as New York's Jubilee and End labels, were the companies that recorded, marketed, and distributed doo-wop.[28]

These label owners exercised a great deal of power over the vocal harmony singers, for they not only "discovered" the artists in the first place, they often chose the songs they recorded, organized the recording sessions, and facilitated the song arrangements with band leaders and studio musicians.[29] All these companies made use of the wide reaching and dynamic network of black-oriented if not -owned radio stations, record stores, and performance venues. In some neighborhoods, the radio station and record store were one and the same, with a "goldfish bowl" or sound booth behind a window facing the street. In many cases the owners of these establishments were the first to discover and manage groups.

In this system of operation, cash greased the wheels. The record company paid the store to stock the record, the store paid the radio station and the station paid the DJ to play the record. Any of these entities could also be managing groups and cowriting songs (or, as was often the case, claiming authorship of songs).[30] These were all common and accepted practices in the relatively small market economy of the independent record business of the early 1950s. As rhythm and blues became more lucrative by the end of the decade, payola, or paying to have records played on the radio, became a national scandal and was explicitly outlawed. In the nascent doo-wop world, however, it was just the way business was transacted.

In the fall of 1953, after seeing Earl Carroll's group, the Carnations, perform at the annual talent show at Public School 43 in New York City, fellow singer Lover Patterson gave the group's career a helping hand. "He was a little older than most of us, but he had the inside dope on who to see in the record business. He took the Five Crowns, who became the Drifters, to Atlantic [Records], to [their eventual manager] George Treadwell. And he took my group to Esther Navarro, who was affiliated with the Blaine Brothers who owned Jubilee Records."[31]

Esther Navarro, who was Jewish, was a secretary at the Shaw Booking Agency, which had ties to Jubilee and Josie Records.[32] She liked the group's sound but not its name. According to Carroll, the group put their heads together and came up with a name they thought represented the same kind of sophistication and class as the flower they had been using: the Cadillac. The preeminent automotive emblem of style, it was the perfect fit for the image they wanted to project.[33] This origin story differs from another widely circulated version, that Navarro, in the process of renaming another group, heard someone mention the name "Cadillacs" as a possibility. She allegedly wrote to General Motors and got permission to use the trademark, and then decided to bestow the name on the Carnations.[34] The Cadillacs were the first in a long line of car groups including the El Dorados, the Edsels, the Capris, the Ramblers, and the Lincolns.

There was more at stake here then just bragging rights about starting a trend. Trademark ownership would have unexpected financial implications in the years ahead. Some managers had the foresight or business acumen in the 1950s to register the trademark. Joe Davis, the manager of the Crickets, an early 1950s black group from New York, not the Buddy Holly band, was one of the first producers to own a group's name. Buck Ram and George Treadwell, managers of the Platters and the Drifters respectively, also registered their trademarks. This gave them the power to hire and fire group members as they saw fit, a power they did not hesitate to use. To cite one particularly memorable example, in June 1958, right before a show at the Apollo, Treadwell fired the entire Drifters group and replaced them with the Five Crowns, who instantly became a new Drifters with soon-to-be-famous lead singer Ben E. King.[35]

It was later learned that Navarro never officially trademarked "the Cadillacs" as a vocal group name, but while she was their manager she nevertheless asserted ownership authority, helping to destabilize the group in the process. Even before the Cadillacs made their first record they underwent what would be the first of eighteen personnel changes that occurred between 1954 and 1970. James "Poppa" Clark, who had been a member of the Five Crowns, replaced tenor Cub Gaining. Johnny "Gus" Willingham was added to make the group a quintet. The Cadillacs would eventually have twenty-eight different people credited with vocal contributions to their records, many of whom had recorded and performed with other groups, such as the Solitaires, the Opals, the Vocaltones, the Five Crowns, the Crystals (not the 1960s girl group), the Velvetones, the Crickets, the Fi-tones, the Valentines, the Vocaleers, and the Penguins.

At one point in 1957 there were two sets of Cadillacs, one run by Navarro with all new members and one led by Carroll, both recording for the Jubilee/Josie label. Navarro released the album *The Fabulous Cadillacs* (Jubilee No. 1045) in 1957 featuring songs sung by Earl Carroll and Bobby Phillips, yet neither of them appeared on the album cover. For the 1959 album *The Crazy Cadillacs* (Jubilee No. 1099) Carroll and Phillips, now reconciled with Navarro, did appear on the cover, though one of the other young men in the photograph was not a singer in any group but just a friend from their neighborhood.

A growing aggregation of singers would combine and recombine as the Cadillacs, often very briefly, for whatever recording or performance might come along. The casual, amateur nature of street-corner singing culture contributed to the fluid nature of group personnel. With many gospel groups there were family ties that fostered continuity, but affiliations in secular harmony groups were much more tenuous and ephemeral. It was not uncommon for singers to change groups often, and frequently, the histories of several groups from the same neighborhood or city would be intertwined.

The economic instability of working with small record companies that would regularly go into and out of business also contributed to member fluctuation. The desire of the singers and the companies for hit records and to cash in quickly on what was feared to be a short-lived trend could override bonds between group members.[36] The common denominator was the name of the group, and as a name became established in the marketplace it would develop a life of its own. The singers became all the more replaceable, which sowed the seeds for future discord between the owner of the trademark and the singers who were, however briefly, group members.[37] By 1959, it apparently was unimportant to Jubilee that a Cadillacs album cover include any singers at all—or even that the people pictured be the same race. On *The Cadillacs Meet the Orioles* (Jubilee No. 1117) three young white men in leather jackets with greased-back hair are pictured in the cover photo.

The relative anonymity of individual singers compared with the popularity of the songs associated with the group meant that a particular singer's presence was often not considered a necessity to a trademark-owning manager. In the years following the emergence of doo-wop, it was found that even if a group did not include a member who had actually sung on any of the hit records, concert tickets could still be sold and the audience entertained. While many singers did successfully assert their stake in the music, others, because they had only brief stints in a group, had more tenuous claims to authenticity. All of this fueled tensions between singers and group managers.

THE STORY OF "GLORIA"

The authorship and ownership of particular songs have also been also matters of dispute. Unlike the Tin Pan Alley tunes of the previous generation, which were written by professional songwriters, many of the doo-wop songs that would be become hits were the result of the next stage in the continuing history of African American amateur vocalizing. The songs were inseparable from the singing. They were ephemeral, fluid creations, never to be heard exactly the same way twice. Once these songs were recorded, once they became fixed entities, they were reduced to static sonic representations of dynamic music making.[38] Street songs became doo-wop records. An activity became a commodity, and the predominantly black singers and what they sang were brought into contact with the predominately white and Jewish music industry professionals.

The Cadillacs released their first recording, "Gloria" (Josie No. 765), in July 1954. The writer of this song since that time has been listed as Esther Navarro. According to Carroll, however, "You know, like we wrote most of our tunes, but Esther Navarro got the credit for them because she was familiar with copyrighting and publishing. And we used to sing our songs to her and she would take shorthand and she would turn them in to the Library of Congress and claim that she was the writer on these particular tunes. And a lot of managers did that in those days. It was the day of the Rip-off."[39]

The story of "Gloria" actually began with Leon Rene, a New Orleans songwriter and a cofounder of Exclusive Records, who penned the first version in 1945. It was on the Exclusive label that Johnny Moore's Three Blazers, featuring blues legend Charles Brown on lead vocal, made the first notable recording of "Gloria" in 1946.[40] But it was the Mills Brothers version released in 1948 that would be the most influential on the young New York street corner singers of the early 1950s. According to the Cadillacs' bass, Bobby Phillips, this was the version on which "Gloria" the street song was based, and it was Carroll who was responsible for the distinctive solo introduction and memorable falsetto leap in the melody.[41] Street songs were tunes that many groups knew and that had evolved from their original, sometimes unknown, source through the process of being passed from one group to another.[42]

Comparing the Mills Brothers' 1948 version with the Cadillacs' 1954 version is a good way to examine the stylistic transition that occurred in American vocal harmony in the postwar era and also to illuminate the often controversial issue of doo-wop authorship. Listening to the two recordings one hears how the versions contrast rhythmically. The Mills Brothers' "Gloria" has an easy jazz or swing feel, while the Cadillacs' hints at the backbeat accents that would come to define rhythm and blues. The Mills Brothers' version is very much in the close harmony barbershop tradition with three upper voice parts aligned vertically and spaced within the close range of a major sixth interval. Many of the characteristics of the more open or dispersed style of doo-wop harmony are evident in the Cadillacs' recording, which also incorporates the falsetto, blow harmonies, and more pronounced bass interjections.

Even the lyrics were changed. In the 1948 version, the narrator is chastising a man for playing "the game of kiss and runaway" with multiple lovers until he fell in love with Gloria, who, as fate would have it, was not in love with him. The 1954 version is a more straightforward ballad of requited love. The protagonist in the Cadillacs' rendition is not the victim of an ironic turn of fate where his past rakish behavior comes back to haunt him; he is too young to have yet lived such a life. He just knows "it's not Marie" or "Cherie" that he loves. "It's Gloria," but she's not in love with him. The simplification of the text is representative of the shift in focus and content from adult to teen orientation in the pop music of the 1950s.

With these changes, the Cadillacs' version may well differ enough from the original to warrant new songwriting credit and copyright ownership. On the initial pressing of the Cadillacs' record, no writer was listed at all. But on later pressings and on all subsequent recordings of this "Gloria," the credited writer is Esther Navarro. She claimed that the title of the song had come from another of her clients, singer Gloria "Little Miss Muffet" Smith.[43] There is no public record that Navarro, who died in 2003, ever mentioned any relationship between the Cadillacs' "Gloria" and a version by the Mills Brothers.

The Cadillacs' version has been recorded by many vocal groups, including the Passions (1960), Vito and the Salutations (1962), and Manhattan Transfer (1975). In addition to over fifty-five years of radio play, the Cadillacs' recording was used in the soundtrack for the film *Goodfellahs* (1990). All these uses have generated income in the form of performance royalties for the official writer of the song, Esther Navarro. Navarro's name appears as the writer on a large portion of the Cadillacs' sixty-song catalog. According to Earl Carroll, Navarro did not write any of their songs; she merely put her name down as the writer on copyright forms.

The practice of non-writers receiving songwriting credit was all too common with vocal groups in the 1950s. One well-known example involves the legendary DJ Alan Freed and the Moonglows. In exchange for helping to promote the group, Freed took cowriter credit for "Sincerely," their big hit of 1954, which also became a big hit in 1954 for the white pop group the McGuire Sisters. Navarro, Freed, and the publishing companies associated with them reaped the long-term financial benefits of copyright ownership at the expense of the reputed true writers of the songs, who in many cases were the original performers. Because their songs are legally the property of someone else, the only way these artists have been able to make money in the music business since the release of their records is as performers. Very often the singers were black and the copyright claimants were white, so there is a racial element to the lingering resentment about this matter among doo-wop singers today on the oldies circuit.[44]

Copyright ownership is granted to whoever first files the copyright forms with the Library of Congress. Little proof of authorship is required unless and until there is a dispute. The story of "Gloria" raises some interesting questions about this all-important branch of the music business. How is authorship of a song born of a group, or even communal, vocalizing practice to be determined properly? Many street songs, like "Gloria," were based on preexisting tunes. At what point has a song been so altered that authorship can no longer be said to reside with the writer of an arguably identifiable model? Should the copyright for "Gloria" be held by multiple authors, including, at least, original songwriter Leon Rene and all members of the Cadillacs who participated in shaping the words and music that were recorded in July 1954? Answers to such questions are most often decided in court. More than half a century has passed since Esther Navarro claimed copyright ownership of "Gloria," so proving a case to the contrary would be difficult, time consuming, and costly. For this reason, the surviving members of the Cadillacs, Earl Carroll and Bobby Phillips, have not taken legal action.

THE ICE CREAM CHANGES

"Gloria" is based on a chord progression that is ubiquitous in the doo-wop canon. Cleveland Freeman, a long-time oldies circuit bass player, says of it: "They call them the 'Ice Cream Changes' because using them is as easy as eating ice cream."[45] One of the first songs that many a beginning pianist learns is "Heart and Soul." Played in the key of C, the chords are C-major, A-minor, F-major, and G-major. This is the archetypal doo-wop chord set, which is commonly referred to by musicians as the I–vi–IV–V progression.[46] As in blues music, with its standard 12-bar progression, doo-wop harmonic structure is cyclical, meaning it repeats several times within the course of a song. This harmonic ostinato, or repeating pattern of chords, is the musical backdrop for the song's melody, its vocal arrangement, and the unique use of vocal timbre that typified this genre. After an analysis of some one thousand songs compiled by cross-listing two "best of Doo Wop" sources, I found that, of the 365 songs common to both, 254, or 70 percent, were based on the I–vi–IV–V chord progression.[47] It was the default set of chord changes for doo-wop songwriters.

The ice cream changes were a harmonic prototype common in the A section of many Tin Pan Alley song choruses.[48] Jazz musicians called them "the rhythm changes," since the progression was the harmonic backbone of the George Gershwin song "I Got Rhythm."[49] Like jazz instrumentalists, doo-wop singers would riff and improvise against this harmonic backdrop. This was a chord progression congenial to "basing," the practice of creating a distinctive repeating bass pattern that would provide a foundation for the other vocal lines. Composing a riff in the lower vocal register on which an entire song's vocal arrangement is built is a practice with deep roots in black music history dating back at least to the nineteenth century.[50] It was the combination of this vocal harmony practice and exposure to the Tin Pan Alley standards of the previous generation that led to the regular use of the ice cream changes in doo-wop songs.[51] The compositional result was the foregrounding of melodic and timbral invention against a static but familiar harmonic background.

But the use of this chord progression was by no means uniform. Just as with the blues progression there were many subtle variations on the I–vi–IV–V relationship. In this kind of roman-numeral harmonic analysis, "I" represents the chord with the tonic or home note as its root. For instance, the C-major chord is the "I" chord in the key of C. Since there are seven notes in the major scale (for example, C, D, E, F, G, A, and B in the key of C) a roman numeral is assigned to each chord that is based on a note in the scale. Some chords can have a major tonality represented by uppercase numerals or minor tonality represented by lowercase numerals. Because some of these three-note chords differ by only one note, they are often substituted for each other in chord progressions. Such was the case in doo-wop songs. Some of the more common alternate versions (or flavors) of the ice cream changes using chord substitutes are I–vi–ii–V (C-major, A-minor, D-minor, and G-major); I–I–IV–V (C-major, C-major, F-major, and G-major); I–I–ii–ii (C-major, C-major, D-minor, and D-minor); and I–iii–IV–V (C-major, E-minor, F-major, and G-major).

There were also variations in the harmonic rhythm or the amount of measures per chord change within this chord progression, sometimes in the same song. For example, in the introduction to the Teenagers' "Promise to Remember" (1956), the progression's harmonic rhythm is one measure per chord. When the verse begins, the harmonic rhythm (of the same progression) slows down and there are now two measures per chord. The progression was also used in conjunction with other harmonic ostinati such as the blues progression or sometimes briefly but prominently used only in a song's introduction.[52]

Many vocal harmony songs consisted entirely of this progression, but just as many, adhering to the 32-bar AABA Tin Pan Alley model, had a B section that would usually involve a break from the harmonic ostinato. This section was referred as "the channel," "bridge," or "release," where the groups would often change the mood of the song, becoming more emotive or urgent in their vocal delivery. Audiences would often applaud the most during the channel.[53] It was in this section in the song that singers hit very high or low notes, or they changed lead singers, or they used a particularly distinctive vocal arrangement like the Ink Spots' talking bridge a generation before. The most common channel begins on the IV chord (F-major in the key of C), eventually ending on the V (G-major in the key of C) preparing a return to the A section where the ice cream changes return. In the Cadillacs' version of "Gloria," lead singer Carroll switches to falsetto just as the music comes to a dramatic stop on the channel-ending V chord, a common doo-wop compositional gesture.

The ice cream changes facilitated amateur music making. Like the 12-bar blues progression, these changes were so well known that even young people who did not know one another very well and may not have had much formal music education could come together and sing. This is why so many of the songs of the so-called one-hit wonders, who were usually groups with limited professional experience, were based on the I–vi–IV–V progression. Groups who had longer careers, like the Flamingos and the Platters, tended to record songs that had less harmonic predictability, or, like the Drifters, they evolved away from improvisatory-sounding street songs based on the ice cream changes ("There Goes My Baby") to studio songs written by professional songwriters ("Under the Boardwalk").

Even though these groups may have evolved beyond the amateur music making they started from, however, the distinctive characteristics of that music's sound remained a part of their later recordings. Professional songwriters like Jerry Leiber and Mike Stoller, who wrote for the Coasters, the Drifters, and many other groups, freely employed the ice cream changes. Because of the preponderance of this chord progression in doo-wop harmony, it became a harmonic signifier of a particular period in American musical history and an effective compositional tool for referencing that era's music and the feelings it evokes. When you hear this progression—"Those Magic Changes" as they are called in the musical *Grease*—you think doo-wop.

VOCAL CHOREOGRAPHY

In addition to a sound—the timbre and pitch of the individual voices, the arrangement of vocal parts, the harmonic structure—there is also a look to doo-wop, a distinctive presentation. Doo-wop is not just vocal group music, it is also dance music. The marriage of music and dance has a long history in the black community, and doo-wop performance was a new chapter. All the steps and movements refined on the minstrel, vaudeville, Broadway, and chitlin' circuit stages are in evidence when many doo-wop groups perform. The rhythm and blues era brought new sounds and new sights; the new beats inspired new steps. The Cadillacs under the tutelage of Cholly Atkins continued this evolution.

Cholly Atkins was a well-known tap dancer in the 1930s and 1940s who began helping vocal groups incorporate dance into their stage shows in the early 1950s. He called this practice "vocal choreography." One of his basic principles was that the group members should be in constant motion. When they were not singing, they should be dancing. When they finished their dances, they should have enough time to catch their breath and get back to the microphones to sing again.[54] He emphasized precision and uniformity of movement, and incorporated many of the steps and styles that he learned in his years on the stage with his partner, Charles "Honi" Coles. Atkins's great breadth of choreographic knowledge meant that practically every song had its own unique set of movements. He eventually became the house choreographer at Motown Records, where he worked with many of most successful groups of 1960s including the Temptations, the Miracles, the Supremes, and the Four Tops. In 1989, he received a Tony Award for his work on the Broadway show *Black and Blue*.

In the early 1950s Atkins had just started to work at the Apollo Theatre with some of the up-and-coming artists when Esther Navarro arranged for the Cadillacs to work with him to prepare for Alan Freed's 1955 Christmas Shows at the Academy of Music in New York. Carroll remembers his first rehearsals with Atkins. "You know, we was young kids from the 'hood and we'd say, 'No Cholly, we ain't no dancers, we singers, you know? Ain't none of us can really dance.' And he said, 'Yes you can, guys. Here's what I want you to do. Can you count? I want you to count, but step when you count.' And lo and behold, he had us sho nuff steppin'."[55]

One of the first songs to prominently feature the Cadillacs new vocal choreography was "Speedoo" (Josie No. 785; no. 3 on the R&B chart, no. 17 on the Pop chart), which was released in October 1955 and which would eventually be their biggest hit. This was an up-tempo, jump blues number that, according to Carroll, the group had composed on the way home from a gig in Boston. As Carroll remembers it:

> Well, we were playing an armory up in Boston. When we were leaving they had a bombshell outside of the armory. And they used to tease me quite a bit about my head, saying it was a "steeplehead"—kind of pointy. The ham of the group, Bobby Phillips, came out, and we were all getting ready, getting in the car, and he said, "Hey Speedo, there's your torpedo." I turned to him and said, "Listen, man, my name is Mr. Earl to you, and my name ain't no Speedo." So we got in the car, and before we got back to New York City, we had written the tune in the car "They often call me Speedo, but my real name is Mr. Earl." They had a big record out at the time by the Regals called "I Got Your Water Boilin'

Baby." And, in that tune, they had [in the background harmony] "wa, wa shoobie-do." So we borrowed that "wa, wa, shoobie-do" from the Regals and put it to "Speedoo" with the Cadillacs, and the rest is history.[56]

The Regals had been under the tutelage of Cholly Atkins since the spring of 1955. Their lead singer was Al "Diz" Russell, who is quick to point out that his group was actually the first vocal group to work with Atkins, and that it was not just the music from their song that was co-opted for "Speedoo." (Earl Carroll spells his nickname with one "o" while the official copyrighted title of the song is spelled with two.) "Earl and his group used to come to the Apollo and watch us do our little thing, and the choreography [for "Got the Water Boilin' Baby"] spilled into the Cadillacs."[57] The Regals' song, which was not a big hit for them but became a rockabilly hit for Billy Lee Riley in 1959, has the same chord changes (a variation of the blues progression), basically the same melody, and, as Carroll admits, the same background harmony as "Speedoo."[58] Like the street song "Gloria," "Speedoo" was the product of a fluid, communal composition process.[59] In this case, not only was the music borrowed from a pre-existing source but quite possibly the accompanying dance steps were as well.[60] Although the Cadillacs and Cholly Atkins are given credit for the innovative choreography, once again the official songwriter of "Speedoo" is Esther Navarro.[61]

When performing the song "Speedoo," Carroll had a chance to emulate his childhood hero Bill "Bojangles" Robinson. Atkins incorporated Robinson's signature hat and cane into the routine, and he had the group end the song by marching off stage with Carroll leading the way. The Cadillacs also become famous for their eye-catching tuxedos, usually purchased for the group at F & F Clothes in Greenwich Village.[62] By the time of the Academy of Music shows in New York the Cadillacs had the full package: matching white jackets, black trousers, and white shoes. Atkins had them dancing like the professionals they would become in the next few years.

These shows were in the revue format with several acts, some vocal groups and some solo performers, doing a handful of numbers backed by a full jazz orchestra. The MC, Alan Freed, brought each act on, one after another in rapid succession. By many accounts, the Cadillacs soon became the stars, and other, more established acts like blues singer Joe Williams requested not to have to follow the group in the lineup.[63] They became the proverbial tough act to follow.

CROSSOVER REALTIES

In 1955 "Speedoo" crossed over from the R&B to the Pop charts, as the song "Gee" by the Crows (no. 2 on the R&B chart and no. 14 on the Pop chart) and the song "Sh'Boom" by the Chords (no. 3 on the R&B chart and no. 9 on the Pop chart) had done in 1954. Compiled by *Billboard* magazine, the titles of these charts may be stylistic categories, but they are thin disguises for the delineation of music along racial lines. R&B chart position was based on the amount of airplay on radio stations with a black musical format, the number of records sold in black neighborhoods, and, until the end of the 1950s, jukebox play in those neighborhoods.

It is a formula based on geography. Crossing over, especially in the 1950s, not only was a foray into new cultural and economic territory, it symbolized and presaged the social usurping of physical boundaries that was to come. This symbolic crossing over happened in both directions. The rhythm and blues flowed to young white listeners from the powerful radio transmitters and efficient record distribution of the cities. The curious new audience not only sought out and bought rhythm and blues records in unprecedented numbers, they also called their local mainstream-format radio stations and requested music by black artists.

These kids were attracted by and enjoyed the vitality and novelty of the music for its own sake, but also evident in the white teen consumption of rhythm and blues is the music's potential as a marker of rebellion. White teens resisted parental control by identifying with the stars of *Rebel without a Cause* and *Wild Ones* and vicariously playing in the *Concrete Jungle,* even as they were safely ensconced in the new suburbs. Consuming black music along with white working-class music, country and western and rockabilly, was a portal to exciting, dangerous, and often oppositional cultures that white middle-class teens used to undermine what they felt to be the oppressive norms of postwar America.[64] It should not be forgotten, though, that through this same portal they could always safely return to the confines of their suburban homes; rhythm and blues and country music were nice places to visit, but they did not necessarily want to live there.

White teens did bring back the sonic and visual souvenirs of their sojourns, one of which was the latest incarnation of the socially and politically resonant American vocal harmony tradition. Doo-wop reflected not only its current time but the complicated interracial history of America, with its economic inequity, social tension, and physical violence. As this music became more and more popular with white American youth, the racial double helix emerged in an unprecedented way.

The social crossing over began in concert venues where black and white young people, drawn together by attraction to new music, uneasily occupied a common space. Usually it was the black fans and performers who were most at risk when things got out of control. Even though it was an interracial audience, they knew they were the ones on foreign, possibly hostile, terrain. As Earl Carroll remembers,

> You came out on stage but you would face the [back] wall not the audience and sing the songs that you had to sing. But, I mean, you're on a tour and you wanna get paid for the gig. You had to go on and do it, and at that time we did 'cause we knew what we were up against. Nat King Cole came in right behind us, and that's his home, Birmingham [Alabama]. And he was just so polished, so together, with [the song] "Nature Boy" he had at that time, and all those beautiful love tunes he was singing. And I remember them [the white male audience members] getting up on stage and almost beating that man to death 'cause he was just so polished and the girls was swooning, and they just couldn't stand it.[65]

Along with the possibility of physical violence, crossing over also evoked a kind of economic violence. Even with the hostile white reaction to live performances, the independent producers and eventually the major record companies, which were white-owned and -operated, found ways to cash in on the undeniable popularity of this music.[66] As with jazz thirty years before, this exploitation initially took the form of co-optation by white musicians, this time best exemplified by what was known as the "cover version." Record producers, aware of the growing mainstream popularity of a song by a black group, would release a version by a white group, often before the original had an opportunity to gain real popularity, quashing the black group's one chance at success. Mercury Records released a version of "Sh'Boom" by the white Canadian vocal group the Crew Cuts that went to number one on the Pop chart in the same year that it was a hit for the Chords, consigning them to eventual one-hit wonder status. As far as Carroll was concerned, the covers were usually of inferior aesthetic quality: "Pat Boone ran in and tried to do "Tutti-Frutti on Rudy" by Little Richard. But he just didn't have that drive. He was kind of too clean with it."[67]

Moreover, "covering" wasn't limited to recordings. White artists also tried to emulate black stagecraft. Because of the close proximity of the first integrated tours in 1956, trade secrets were learned face to face. As

Carroll remembers, "Yeah, it would be two people sitting together on the bus, you know. And it was a lot of whites and a lot of blacks that were on the bus. I remember Paul Anka, he had just come out with his first big release, 'Diana.' He wore those big buck shoes and he used to follow me around, asking me different questions. 'What do I do when I go on stage, Speed?' and 'How 'bout this and how 'bout that,' you know?"[68]

Just as their audiences reflected a new degree of social crossing over, while backstage and traveling between venues, young black and white entertainers were interacting in unprecedented ways. Music making created a space for social crossing over, where the dream of integration began to be realized. But, according to Carroll, when night came, the reality of racial separation returned. "They would drop the white artists off into hotels in midtown, and then would take the black artists across the tracks to stay in hotels, you know. And then it was tough because the black hotels didn't have that many rooms, it was like a boarding house."[69]

The day-to-day realities of the road were experienced along with the dollars-and-cents realties of the music business. Still in their late teens and early twenties, the Cadillacs were traveling the country and earning money like few of their peers from their neighborhood could hope to do. Nevertheless, they had their suspicions that all what was not right with the business practices of their manager, Esther Navarro. As Bobby Philips remembers, "We had this driver named Rudy and he had the contracts in his briefcase. We ain't never seen the contracts. Now when he was out of the room, when we was at the Apollo, we broke into the briefcase. We looked at the contracts. She said we were there for $650.00 but the contract said $1,750.00."[70]

In the 1957 they split from Navarro for the first time and, though they would work with her again in less than a year, the seeds of mistrust had been sown. These episodes of social and economic violence, which the Cadillacs shared with many other black vocal groups in the 1950s, became interwoven with the positive and exhilarating experiences of traveling the country and performing their music for an expanding audience. For all who were involved—the performers, the business people, and the audiences, black and white—the good, the bad, and the ugly of doo-wop music making would accrue meaning in the coming decades.

ECHO AND HARMONY

Since the 1950s, doo-wop has come to signify sonically the time and place where it was born. Not only individual and collective memories but also something about the actual sound of the records evokes this association. Embodied in doo-wop's vocal style and arrangements, rhythm, and lyrics heard in the original recordings and contemporary performances are nostalgically affective allusions to earlier lives. The echo of the street corner is both a metaphor for a time gone by and an actual auditory experience.

Doo-wop groups found reverberant spaces to facilitate their music making, and, ultimately, the "echo" itself fostered their musical style. The acoustic spaces where doo-wop groups sang were all, to some extant, enclosed areas.[71] The degree of enclosure that exists in an urban environment, even in open-air locations like school yards, is much higher than in rural or suburban locations. The more enclosure there is, the higher the intensity of reverberation, on the metaphorical, social level as well as on the actual auditory, experiential level. The great numbers of people who are squeezed into dense, built-up cities create many more opportunities for both socially and sonically resonant experiences than can typically found in non-urban environments. Reverb contributes to, and metaphorically is, the continuity of experience. It is the continuation of a past event into the present and on into the future. The intentional use of reverb in the public rehearsals of doo-wop was a way of mastering this enclosed social space, a way of giving a sense of continuity and ownership to otherwise ephemeral everyday life events.[72]

There was an aural give-and-take with the enclosed physical space that was facilitated by reverberation. When a melody line is sung in a reverberant space, each note overlaps to some degree with the others, creating a kind of naturally occurring harmony.[73] This can inspire the singer to think and feel more harmonically. Also the quality, the degree or depth, of reverb that occurs in a particular space can influence vocal production. The porcelain tiles of a bathroom have resonant qualities that differ audibly from the bricks of the buildings that surround the school yard. The singers listened to how their voices bounced back to them in these spaces, and they would adjust their timbre, volume, and pitch levels accordingly.

This interplay facilitated a blurring of the boundary between the singers and their acoustic spaces. Their voices resonated both within and outside of their bodies. Street corner singers used their voice, both as sonic phenomenon and assertion of identity, as a way of literally sounding out, as in measuring or probing, their environment. Through this process their voices and the spaces were transformed through a vital symbiosis.[74]

The relationship of vocal production and environment existed within and contributed to the everyday sounds of the 1950s urban world—the

steady pulse of machines, traffic, factory noise, and subways were all aural components of city life and contributed as well to the singers' music
making.[75] Also in the urban aural mix were the sounds of other public
performers. There were blues singers who would accompany themselves
with guitars, percussion instruments, or harmonicas, and there was one
particular kind of street entertainer who, like the vocal groups, needed
no instrumental accompaniment. Called "hamboners," these were solo
artists who played their bodies like percussion instruments, slapping
their chest and thighs often in highly syncopated rhythms. Some hamboners would add to the rhythmic pattern by inserting vocal sounds, and in
between these sounds and over the body slaps would sing or chant verses,
often in a free-form style. Hamboners were not only influential on the
vocal groups who overheard them but were part of the black tradition that
would lead to rap and hip-hop.[76]

There are few better examples than doo-wop of the connection that
can develop in societies between geography and music. Music making is
not only a way of being in the world, it is a way knowing or understanding
the world. We use all of our senses to comprehend our environment, not
just sight, smell, taste, and touch: we also *listen* to fathom and become familiar with our particular place in the world.[77] Music making is a means
by which we can be both products and producers of our environment. In
the 1950s vocal harmony world, the sights and sounds of the city merged
with the singers' voices to create a complex soundscape. They infused
and inscribed the urban streets of postwar America with their sound
and, in the process, came to know that world in deep and meaningful
ways.[78]

Within this soundscape, metaphorically bouncing off the buildings
surrounding the street corner, was the prehistory of the 1950s urban
black experience. The new social experiences of the doo-wop singers—
including how this music was created, who took credit for its authorship,
who were the financial beneficiaries, and how it was received by the wider
society—added new layers of resonance to the trajectory that preceded
them. The places where doo-wop was created were more than just resonant physical spaces. They were also locations imbued with the psycho-
logical, social, and cultural heritage the singers brought to them.

Through vocal harmony, social frameworks were created in which individuals developed notions about social relations within an understood
and viable group dynamic. Although vocal groups were the more socially acceptable and less dangerous alternative, they often mirrored the

hierarchical structure and group ethos of the street gangs with which some singers were associated. An individual was required to sacrifice personal concerns and desires for the benefit of the group. This group ethos is reflected in the structure of doo-wop vocal arrangements in which, because of the lack of instruments, every voice was important to the success of the performance. However, not all vocal parts were created equal.[79] In the prototypical doo-wop arrangement the hierarchy is apparent: the lead vocal stands alone and is the most important part. Nevertheless, that part is absolutely dependent on the foundation provided by the other voices.

This group ethos not only reflects the 1950s urban black teenage social experience but presages things to come. These singers working together were the musical prophets of the coming civil rights and black power movements. Their music making provided a model of ideal behavior where sonic harmony and social harmony are part of the same equation, a glimpse of utopian communal cooperation and aspiration.[80] These groups constructed and occupied a complex sonic and social "place," a bridge between a past of oppression and migration and an imagined, though barely articulated, more harmonious future. The vocal groups were part of the larger emergence of black change that added a deeper resonance to a genre of music sometimes characterized as "simple" or "innocent." There is a difference between what is heard in this music on a purely surface or sensual level and what is more deeply felt when it is experienced from a fuller understanding of its context and history.

For example, the so-called nonsense syllables that compose the background harmony have a deeper significance than may be apparent. Because of the history of the use of such sounds in black musical tradition, these song texts resonate more deeply within the black community than simple combinations of consonants and vowels.[81] Perceived in this way, these syllables are always making some kind of "sense." Sometimes this sense is practical or utilitarian, as when the syllables are obvious imitations of musical instruments. Doo-wop groups took this musical practice to a new level, as percussive or hornlike patterns became more than just novel ways to fill the space between verses or secondary accompaniment, but the actual aural focal points of the songs. These onomatopoeic patterns would often overshadow the words and melodies.

Sometimes the "sense" the nonsense syllables make is in their emotional resonance. In the Cadillacs recording "Gloria," the lyrics tell the story of unrequited or lost love. The background vocals provide more than just accompaniment; the emotional state of the singer is underscored as well. This is accomplished not only through the use of the syllable "woo," a simulation of weeping or moaning. Because this syllable, or a close approximation of it, was used in so many vocal harmony ballads with similar subject matter, it became a convention of the style and a recognizable expression of a distinctive type of communal sorrow. It is a sound with a deeper meaning honed in the acoustic space of the street corner and social "place" of the urban black community of the 1950s.[82]

The Cadillacs' "Gloria" begins with Earl Carroll singing the name "Gloria" in progressively shallower reverb as if approaching from far away. The bass singer, Bobby Philips, intones three descending notes that lead to the opening chord, where the other singers join in with the "woo" lament. On this record, reverberation is more than just an acoustic phenomenon. It is a metaphor for the social and cultural emergence of the black forbears of doo-wop from the space and place they created and occupied into the national psyche. And doo-wop does not forget. The American vocal harmony tradition is encoded with the interracial and nostalgic history of the nation. Just as acoustic spaces absorb and reflect sound waves, so does a musical tradition its cultural and social context. In the 1950s, American vocal harmony acquired a new symbolic location, the street corner, a location that would begin, almost immediately, to accumulate nostalgic resonance and become another of the vocal landscapes of memory lingering in this nation's aural history.[83]

y the end of 1950s the vocal groups who had started recording and performing a half decade earlier were finding it increasingly difficult to put songs on the charts. The
Cadillacs, having broken up and regrouped, attempted
to mimic the style of one of the most popular groups of
the time, the Coasters, who were known for comic novelty songs about
teen life such as "Yakkity Yak" and "Charlie Brown."[1] The Cadillacs' foray
into the novelty song genre was short-lived and only marginally successful, but it eventually led to an important career move for their lead singer
Earl "Speedo" Carroll. The other Cadillacs were left to fend for themselves
in the changing popular music climate of the 1960s.

Even before the heyday of doo-wop was over, however, nostalgia for
this music was already burgeoning. Collectors, disc jockeys, record store
owners, and avid fans were beginning to seek out the by then often-obscure
45 rpm records of only a few years before, creating an aura of emotional
memory for a music era that had yet actually to end. At the same time, a
new generation of young male singers, now in predominantly white urban neighborhoods, were singing the street songs and rhythm and blues
records they had been hearing, added their own unique timbre and cultural influences to the continuing interracial legacy of vocal harmony
history.

A DIFFERENT STREET CORNER

The street song "Gloria" in the version recorded by the Cadillacs had returned to the streets almost immediately after its release in July 1954.
Even though the Cadillacs' record was never actually a big seller, it quickly
became the standard by which any vocal group's talent was measured.[2]
Maybe it was the opening solo intoning of the word "Gloria" which gave
an ambitious young lead singer a chance to shine before the rest of group
started singing; or maybe it was the fashionable falsetto break that was
intrinsic to the melody throughout the song; or maybe there was something about the word "Gloria" itself with its connection to the Catholic
mass that gave it a resonance beyond worldly romance and in a more

mystical or spiritual realm.[3] Whatever the reason, "Gloria" was popular not only in the black neighborhoods of New York but also, by the end of the 1950s, in the white, primarily Italian American, urban areas.[4]

In the South Beach section of Staten Island (home of the Elegants), in the Brownsville and Canarsie sections of Brooklyn (the Salutations' turf), on Belmont Avenue in the Bronx (after which Dion DiMucci's group, the Belmonts, was named), and in Ozone Park in Queens (home of the Capris), young Italian American men where staking out their public harmony territory just as their black vocal role models had done before them.[5] Many were second-generation Americans, children of northern Italian and Sicilian immigrants who had settled in working-class urban America and vied for jobs and resources with other newly arrived immigrant groups from Ireland and Eastern Europe as well as blacks recently transplanted from the South. Although they drew strength from their group identity in this competitive environment, the Italian American teenagers of the 1950s did venture away from their own culture at least musically. While they were listening to the Italian-language radio programs and idolizing and feeling pride in the Italian American crooners of the previous generation, such as Frank Sinatra, Tony Bennett, and Frankie Laine, they were also listening to rhythm and blues. Radio for this generation more than any previous was the great usurper of the physical boundaries that separated white and black; it was the medium through which both sides crossed over in an intimate way, yet at a socially safe distance.[6]

Like black singers, the Italian Americans received part of their musical education in school and in church, and sometimes it was there that the racial divide was crossed. Vito Picone, lead singer of the Elegants, was thirteen years old when he had such an experience, which ultimately led to the beginning of his music career. "I was always a clown in class. I said something I shouldn't have said. The teacher happened to be a West Indian who had just moved into our grammar school [which] was 99 percent Italian. And this woman when she turned to us and said, 'Hello class, my name is Mrs. McCullough,' I turned to a friend of mine and said, 'She looks like a different McColor to me.' As punishment, [the principal] made me sing in her choir. This was my first introduction to harmony."[7] Soon after learning the rudiments of harmony singing in Mrs. McCullough's choir, Picone formed the first of his vocal harmony groups, practicing in, among other places, the bathroom on the Staten Island Ferry. He would come to esteem rhythm and blues music over all other types of music and develop certain notions of authenticity that ironically conflicted with his own career ambitions as a singer.

Like other aspiring white singers, Picone preferred the original black versions of songs over the white covers that were often released very soon after. He went to the Apollo Theatre in Harlem and listened to radio stations that played black artists to hear his heroes Sam Cooke and the New York–area vocal group the Heartbeats. As he started to perform, he considered his interpretation of rhythm and blues more authentic than what was heard in cover versions by singers like Pat Boone. He was not unaware of the difference in racial reality between him and those he sought to emulate; the geographic and social boundaries were clearly drawn in the urban landscape. But Picone's learning to ornament his vocalizing like Cooke and to arrange his group's harmony parts like the Heartbeats was not about cashing in on a current musical fad as the major record companies were doing. It was rooted in his love and identification with the expressiveness of rhythm and blues. He made the music his own.[8]

The Heartbeats were a highly influential group from Jamaica, Queens, whose lead singer, James Sheppard, was known for his plaintive voice and skillful ballad writing. (He would record his biggest hit, "Daddy's Home," with his second group, the Limelights, in 1961.)[9] In June 1956, the Heartbeats' "A Thousand Miles Away" was released on Hull Records. In June 1958, the Elegants released "Little Star" on the same label, and the young Picone paid homage to his mentor Sheppard by quoting the Heartbeats' signature "rat-a-tat-tat-too" accompaniment.[10] Picone also incorporates a Sam Cooke–style embellishment at the beginning of the song, the "whoa" yodel most famously employed in Cooke's "You Send Me."

Sheppard was also influential in the life and career of Nick Santamaria, lead singer of the Capris, who until high school was not a fan of rhythm and blues. But that changed after a chance encounter with his fellow student Sheppard. "My first introduction to harmony was when I walked into the bathroom [at Woodrow Wilson High School in Queens] and I heard this group doing "A Thousand Miles Away" and that just blew me away."[11] In the Capris' best-known record "There's a Moon Out Tonight" (1961), the resemblance between Sheppard's phrasing in "A Thousand Miles Away" and Santamaria's smooth but expressive delivery can clearly be heard. Both songs are typical 12/8 ballads, a rhythmic meter with a slow three-note pulse; both rely on the familiar ice cream chord changes; and the song titles are located in virtually the same place in the verse melody. The difference, however, in the Capris' record is the prominent, nearly constant use of falsetto. This coupled with a unique (for vocal harmony of the time) and effective barbershop-style cascade or chime ending, make this record one of the best examples of how doo-wop incorporated old and new practices.

Picone's and Santamaria's testimonials suggest that one reason why Italian Americans, much more than other white ethnic groups, made vocal harmony their own was close physical proximity to African American youth in the 1950s. The historical coincidence of large influxes of blacks and Italian immigrants into densely populated cities made the social and cultural mingling of the two groups inevitable. One result was an intimate sharing of the vocal harmony tradition not seen before in American society.

There were also salient cultural similarities between these ethnic groups which predisposed urban teen males in the 1950s Italian American community to be receptive to black vocal harmony practice. Public music-making in the form of serenades sung by smitten young men under their beloved's bedroom window was a well-known tradition in the old country that was easily translated into group harmonizing by the sons of Italian immigrants. Also, many of them were involved in their own street gangs, whose social structure was amenable to vocal group formation.[12]

Young Italian American men brought their cultural and social lives to the 1950s city streets and also their own musical influences—Italian popular music they heard on the radio and the emotive styles of Tony Bennett and Frank Sinatra they emulated—which made their iteration of doo-wop much more than a mere imitation of the black original.[13] It was a new strain of vocal harmony altogether. Italian American doo-wop shows how complicated it is to delineate separate American "black" and "white" musical styles. A much richer analysis can come from regarding racial categories as social constructions and physical differences such as skin color as only one of many variables.[14]

One of the most famous venues for racial mixing in the 1950s, and where the Italian American presence was significant, was on the television show *American Bandstand*. In its first years, most of the white dancers on the show were teenagers from South and West Philadelphia, areas where, as in New York, Italian and black neighborhoods were adjacent. These were parts of the city that many of the other white ethnic groups had abandoned for the suburbs.[15] At Overbrook High, an integrated school in West Philadelphia, some white students admitted to learning dances from the black students, although many others claimed to have made them up themselves.[16] Viewers closely followed the personal lives of the dancers on *Bandstand* like characters on soap operas, and eventually the enterprising host, Dick Clark, began to recruit teen idol singing stars from the same neighborhoods to appear, to capitalize on the country's infatuation with Italian American youth.

The close proximity bred by their shared vocal harmony practice also exposed these young Italian Americans to the racism experienced by their black fellow singers on the road and in the record industry. Picone experienced this racism from an interesting perspective (for a white person), which he looks back on now with some humor.

> They gave them [the black entertainers] standing ovations at the concert, and the next day they wouldn't eat in the same restaurant [with them]. We would get off the bus and [they would tell us] "you have to go in this section [and] *you* have to go in this section." When they got to my guys they were undecided. We were Sicilian. We very dark, olive-skinned, dark-haired kids and there was prejudice, no doubt about it. But they did have to make a decision and for all intents and purposes we were not African American—but we *were* different.[17]

More usually, however, racial confusion stemmed from the music itself. Often, from their recordings, groups such as the Capris and the Elegants were assumed to be black, and their appearances at chitlin' circuit venues like the Apollo sometimes caused surprised, initially icy receptions. As Nick Santamaria recalled:

> It was the first time we were appearing at the Apollo, and Clay Cole [the MC] went out and he said, "Ladies and Gentlemen we'd like to bring you five boys from Mississippi. They have the number one hit in New York, the Capris." And we walked out onto that stage and everybody's jaw dropped. They expected us to be black. Nobody knew we were white. But to me that was a compliment because that was the sound [we admired].[18]

Italian American teenagers connected with the emotional and aesthetic power of doo-wop and also to the male bonding inherent to group harmony. The experience of doo-wop singers was made even more complex by the particularly resonant cultural aura that was beginning to adhere to the music they were listening to and making. The relationship between time and place that young urban blacks had established only a few years before, had already become a *past* time and place. The nostalgic aura, already encoded in the DNA of a century-old American vocal harmony tradition, was passed on from the black street corner to the Italian American street corner. Through these "addresses" doo-wop took a shortcut to the land of nostalgia.

RECOLLECTION AND RECORD COLLECTION

The origin of the oldies circuit that formed in the 1970s can be traced back to the late 1950s. But invoking the term "oldies" and reviving music of previous generations actually were not new in American popular culture even then. A similar phenomenon involving the big band music of the 1930s and 1940s and the people who experienced it in their youth had occurred in the early 1950s. Radio shows devoted to big band music were aired, featuring the original recordings from the 1930s and 1940s. The terms "perennial," "oldie," and "evergreen" can be found in entertainment publications as far back as the 1930s.[19]

The relatively short time between the "newness" and "oldness" of doo-wop, however, was unprecedented. The New York DJ Alan Fredericks, of WHOM, is credited with bestowing the "oldies" title on this music, when, instead of playing current releases, in 1957 he began playing songs, many of them doo-wop, from the period 1954 to 1956 on his *Night Train* show.[20] In 1960 Irving "Slim" Rose opened the Times Square Record Store in New York, where he featured vocal group records from the early to mid 1950s. A new generation of New York City teenagers, albeit only slightly younger than the original fans, had access to this music. The Cadillacs' recording of "Gloria" was no. 23 on the Times Square Records Top 100 in Sales list for January 1961.[21]

The airplay and the store also gave some records a second chance to become hits. The Capris' "There's a Moon Out Tonight" went virtually unnoticed when initially released in 1958. Then in 1961, a young employee of Times Square Records named Jerry Greene received a copy of it from a customer. Greene, who later founded Collectables Records, a company that reissues and distributes doo-wop recordings, brought the record to Fredericks, who played it on his radio show. The song became a favorite with listeners and eventually sold about 160,000 copies, reviving the moribund career of the Capris.[22] Several other records such as "Rama

Lama Ding Dong" by the Edsels, which also was initially released in 1958, owe their popularity to the enthusiastic employees of Times Square Records.

For a brief time in the early 1960s, there was a national revival of interest in doo-wop. Many new songs were written and recorded. This was self-conscious vocal harmony, aware of its history and signature qualities and aware of the latent nostalgic potency of the sound. The song "Those Oldies but Goodies (Remind Me of You)" written by Nick Curinga and Paul Leo Politi and recorded by Little Caesar and the Romans in 1961, with the requisite 12/8 time signature and the familiar I–vi–IV–V chord progression, was emblematic of the moment. On other records the characteristic street-corner vocalizations, including the bass introductions and interjections, the falsetto, and the nonsense syllables, which typically were economically employed in the past, were now often greatly exaggerated. The Edsels' "Rama Lama Ding Dong" (re-released in 1961), with its almost nonstop, rapid-fire background vocal parts, presaged this baroque, "neo-doo-wop" style.[23]

It was at Times Square Records in the early 1960s that the collector mentality toward doo-wop was encouraged and supported. Before Rose began to buy and sell these records, vocal group songs were ephemeral. The majority of the thousands of sides released saw scant radio play and then disappeared from the mainstream airwaves forever. The patrons of Times Square Records were able to see and hear doo-wop as a whole genre rather than just a collection of individual pop records. They realized that they had tapped into a rich vein in American music where understanding and appreciating the history enhanced the listening pleasure.

New York was not the only place where an intense nostalgic interest in vocal group music was taking root. In 1959 Los Angeles DJ and producer Art Laboe released the first cross-licensed compilation album, *Oldies But Goodies*, which included many of the most popular doo-wop songs of the decade. Eventually a series of fifteen volumes, these albums generally focused on the big hits, and for many that was good enough. But for the handful of avid fans, especially the ones who frequented Times Square Records—like Donn Fileti, who would go on start the Relic Record reissue label based in Hackensack, New Jersey—the Laboe series was a jumping off point into a deeper, more expansive, lifetime love affair with doo-wop.

The collecting, documenting, discussing, and analyzing of this music fostered particular ideas about what made a quality—or, at least, an authentic—vocal group recording. For Laboe, Fileti, and the other hardcore fans and record producers who were white, one important criterion for authenticity was that the singers be black. This did not mean that white doo-wop groups went unsupported (as the Capris' experience shows): an authentic sound also included a vocal arrangement as close to a cappella as possible and many of the distinctive vocal group characteristics such as prominent bass and generous use of falsetto. But if a group had black members it was often perceived as being that much closer to the real thing.[24] This notion was a key component of the purist strain of record collecting and vocal group historiography, and it exerts a strong influence in the doo-wop community today.

Although in the beginning it may have been motivated more by infatuation with a style of music and its history and culture than nostalgia, this birth of a record collecting cult laid the groundwork for the rise of a very powerful form of nostalgic recollection. These enthusiasts forged their identities, at least in part, in the crucible of vocal group music. Through it they cultivated a sense of self that set them apart from their peers, a belief in something the crowd could not or would not understand. (Ironically, this powerful imprint on their identities, while helping to create a sense of specialness, also fostered a desire to share the love of their music with others.)[25] For these collectors, the music was precious, important, and worthy of recognition and preservation. It was the symbol of an era they treasured both for personal and for collective historical reasons. The 1950s and early 1960s were the days of their own youth and—in the wake of victory in World War II, when America had gained undisputed status as the world's most powerful democracy—of the nation's youth.

One of the bibles of the record collecting world was *DISCoveries* magazine. By the end of the 1960s, the disciples of Times Squares Records and many other like-minded fans were enthusiastically promoting the music they had discovered.[26] Possibly the impetus for their initial enthusiasm in the early 1960s was a sense that change was coming, that a powerful, iconic moment in American culture and history was about to end.

RHYTHM CHANGES

The post–World War II era, roughly from the late 1940s to the early 1960s, can be looked at as both the end of the swing era and the beginning of the rock era. Rhythmically and formally the new popular music of the 1950s still closely resembled the popular music of the 1940s. The majority of doo-wop songs were in 12/8 or 6/8 time, which are meters that consist of four and two groups of three, respectively. In jazz or swing, *two* written eighth or quarter notes are played as the two outer notes of a group of *three*. This is what makes the music swing. The form of most doo-wop songs was based on the Tin Pan Alley model of the 32-bar AABA structure, from which the prototypical I–vi–IV–V chord changes were extracted.

By the mid-1960s, the signature characteristics of swing time and form had receded in contemporary pop music. The three feel (12/8) of doo-wop and rhythm and blues had been largely replaced by the gospel-influenced two and (by extension) four feel (4/4) of soul. Formally, as well, the verse-chorus ABAB gospel song structure predominated. The dances that went with the new music were also different and further propelled the change in popular music. Rhythm and blues was essentially swing music given a stronger back beat (the accent being on two and four in a four-beat measure), and the kids in the 1950s were dancing updated versions of the Jitterbug and Lindy Hop. In soul music, the back beat was accentuated even more, but with the switch to the two-feel rhythm came new dances like the Twist, the Mashed Potato, and the Watusi.

Vocally, the preference in black music was moving toward the more emotive, intense vocal style of gospel—a transition prefigured in the songs of the Dominoes and Sam Cooke. The background singers were now mostly relegated to singing "oohs" and "aahs" or supplying the second or third harmony part to the hook or chorus melody. Some vocal groups were able to make the stylistic transition. The Dells from Chicago had both doo-wop hits in the 1950s and soul hits the 1960s, and several of the soul groups and solo singers had their roots in doo-wop groups of the 1950s.[27]

These changes in musical style and form brought with them popularity for the "girl groups," whose emergence coincided with a shift in the way that vocal group music was created. Many of the girl groups had associations with up-and-coming record producers such as Phil Spector, for whom the audiotape was a blank canvas for creating aural pictures as opposed to just capturing a performance. Although many of the singers in these groups had begun their careers before getting signed to record deals, their "sound" was ultimately the creation of a network of publishers, songwriters, producers, and record company owners.[28]

In the late 1950s and early 1960s it had become a given in the business that "rock and roll was here to stay." The question was how best to make it a profitable enterprise. The most effective approach, adopted most famously and successfully by Berry Gordy at Motown, was the assembly-line strategy: the labor of producing hit records was divided among a handful of writers, arrangers, musicians, singers, and business people.[29] Instead of taking vocal groups more or less straight from the street to the studio, the music was often assembled by committee during the writing and recording process.

Some of the female vocal ensembles had actually been around for a few years and had stylistic ties to the street corner sound. One of them, the Shirelles, had begun harmonizing in their high school in Passaic, New Jersey, in 1957. Their biggest hit, "Will You Love Me Tomorrow" released in November 1960 (Scepter no. 1211, no. 1 on the Pop and R&B charts), was the product of the collaboration of the songwriters Carole King and Gerry Goffin and the producer Luther Dixon. Still, the song shows traces of the vocal harmony practice of the previous decade. It begins with lead singer Shirley Alston Reeves (née Owens) singing the first verse without background vocals and the title phrase supported by three-part harmony. In the second verse, the background singers (Micki Harris, Beverly Lee, and Doris Coley) provide a "sha da dop shop" rhythmic motif straight out of doo-wop harmony.

The racial makeup of the girl group "machinery" should be noted. In the case of "Will You Love Me Tomorrow" the songwriters were white and Jewish, and the singers and their record producer, Luther Dixon, were black. The girl group sound was mediated by the politics of racial interaction. Initially, the Shirelles were not pleased with the song. It was too mainstream, pop, and white for their taste and Dixon had to persuade them to record it.[30] Their relenting was a move that launched one of the most successful careers of any girl group. What is important to note is that Dixon's matching this song with this group reflected not only a desire to reach a white audience but also, as with Motown and the general integrationist zeitgeist of the time, the desire to enter and share in the fruits of mainstream American culture and society.[31]

With the arrival of the Beatles in America, their appearance on the Ed Sullivan Show in February 1964, and the popularity of the many other British groups following in their wake, doo-wop became finally, and irrevocably, a thing of the past. For many of the doo-wop singers, however, race was also a major factor in their demise. It had begun in the late 1950s when Dick Clark and others promoted the so-called teen idols, who were all white. The powerbrokers in the music business considered Fabian, Frankie Avalon, Bobby Rydell, and many others, like the much more popular Elvis Presley, to be an easier sell to the white teenage female fans who were spending their allowances on concert tickets and 45s. Although the teen idol phase was short-lived, it effectively crowded black artists, and especially the largely anonymous members of the doo-wop groups, out of the marketplace. When the Beatles arrived, there simply was very little room left for doo-wop, even though, ironically, the Beatles acknowledged a deep artistic debt to the music.[32]

LAYING ON THE AVENUE

As a young person, singing and dancing with the Cadillacs was the only real career Earl Carroll ever had. Carroll had dropped out of high school at age seventeen when his group signed to Josie Records. They had been a featured act in many of the seminal rock and roll concerts of the 1950s, released two albums, recorded more than sixty different songs in all, appeared in the Alan Freed movie *Go Johnny Go* (1959), and had met and performed with most of the biggest stars of the day, including Elvis Presley, Bobby Darin, Chuck Berry, Little Richard, and Fats Domino. The Cadillacs were polished performers. They could sing, dance, and act, carrying on the black vaudeville tradition taught to them by Cholly Atkins and nurtured in the theaters of the chitlin' circuit.

For Carroll, life in the mid-1950s was good. Before he became a full-time entertainer he had worked in New York's Garment district for about $32.50 a week. With the Cadillacs, his salary quadrupled and many other desirable amenities came with it. "We was making maybe $150 a week, maybe $200 a week. We had access to doctors. We could go to doctors for anything. We had our tailor, F & F Clothes, down in the Village. We had our own transportation. It wasn't mine, it was registered under her [Esther Navarro's] name, but we would drive in style all over the country. I could deal with that, from $32.50 a week to maybe $200 a week. You know, for a kid from the streets, I had a job. It wasn't too bad, you know."[33]

Even though Carroll had an income and a lifestyle he probably would not otherwise have had, he was still essentially a salaried employee under contract to his manager, Esther Navarro. He and the rest of the group never received any royalties for the thousands of records sold during their heyday. Carroll also found that he had fewer opportunities to move to other branches of the entertainment business than his white contemporaries had. "The young white artists in those days like the Frankie Avalons and the Fabians and what have you, they'd make one record and they would get movie contracts. So they didn't have to stay in the music business that long before they became actors."[34]

As the 1950s drew to a close, the Cadillacs were searching for a new style. The Coasters, a black vocal group from Los Angeles, was very popular at the time with a string of hits that appealed to the manic, playful side of American teen-dom. The Cadillacs released a handful of tunes in the same vein including "Peek-a-boo" (Josie No. 846; #28 on the Pop chart and #20 on the R&B chart) in autumn 1958,which would be their last hit record. In this song, vocal harmony was used primarily for comic effect, especially the bass, which played the role of the ominous voice of parental authority. The Cadillacs were adept at the playacting these songs required, as can be seen in their performance of "Please Mr. Johnson" and "Jay Walker" in *Go Johnny Go*.[35]

The Cadillacs' career as vocal harmony clown princes eventually ended, but not before Carroll's work came to the attention of the Coasters, who were looking for a replacement for tenor Cornell Gunter in 1961. It was an opportunity to use his skills as singer, dancer, and comedian.[36] Earl Carroll was lucky. He had a full-time job in the entertainment field, a profession for which he was well trained and which would sustain him for the next twenty years. By the time he joined them in 1961, the Coasters' major hit-making days were essentially behind them. But they had had such a hot streak in the late 1950s that their name would always bring them steady work.[37]

Other doo-wop singers were not as fortunate. Many returned to their old neighborhoods, where between infrequent gigs, as Cadillacs bass Bobby Phillips put it, they spent their time just "laying on the avenue."[38] This often included involvement in illegal activities such as the drug trade, and many singers occasionally encountered the criminal justice system as time went by. Drug and alcohol use were common in the performing world and carried over into their personal lives, especially when the gigs began to dry up in the 1960s. For artists used to the high of performing, the next best thing too often was getting stoned or drunk or even shooting up heroin.[39] The disappointment of suddenly being out of the limelight, of the telephone not ringing as it had only a few years before with calls from booking agents, coupled with the plenitude and relative affordability of narcotics led many well-known artists, such as Frankie

Lymon of the Teenagers, to descend into drug dependency and post-fame depression.[40]

Many of the singers, though, just got regular jobs. The Regals' Al "Diz" Russell made lenses for Sterling Optical.[41] The Capris' Nick Santamaria became a policeman. And many went into the military, voluntarily and involuntarily.[42] Bobby Jay, from the Harlem group the Laddins, began a successful career as a DJ while in the army in Augusta, Georgia, in the early 1960s. "It was there that I met a disc jockey, Billy Jean, the Wild Child, and I was very surprised to find out that he was non-black. And he said something to me that was the turning point in my life. He said, 'I know you miss singing, but you grew up in the business, you know the record business, you know the artists. You got a great voice. Have you thought of being on the radio?' "[43]

For many of the singers, there was something about that early musical experience that was hard to forget. Maybe it was the special male bonding that came from singing in a group. Maybe it was the feeling they had the first time they heard girls scream at one of their concerts and they opened their eyes to see that the girls were actually screaming for them. Or maybe, if they were lucky enough, it was the great thrill and satisfaction of hearing their record on the radio for the first time. That is why, even if they had day jobs or were otherwise hustling to survive, they kept making music.

Bobby Phillips performed and recorded on and off over the next twenty years with various incarnations of the Cadillacs and other vocal groups.[44] After they left the Josie/Jubilee label and Esther Navarro, the Cadillacs' name appeared on the rosters of Smash, Mercury, Lana, Roulette, Arctic, Capitol, and, finally, Polydor, which in 1970 released the last pre–oldies circuit Cadillacs record.[45] They were billed as "the Original Cadillacs." The song was called "Deep in the Heart of the Ghetto Parts 1 and 2" (Polydor no. 14031), a soulful, socially conscious recording like the Temptations' "Ball of Confusion." Phillips sang lead, pushing his bass voice into the tenor range, successfully imitating the raspy, emotional style of the Temptations' David Ruffin. The record shows the group's ability to make music that was contemporary both in style and subject matter.[46]

As is so often the case in the music business, the opportunity to make a hit and launch a second phase in their recording career was fleeting. When a legal problem arose, the Cadillacs' chance passed them by. According to Phillips, "Robert Spencer [a member of the group at that time] messed up, 'cause he was signed to another company. And when Polydor asked if anybody was hooked up he said 'No.' He lied, and when they found out they snatched the record in [withdrew it from distribution]."[47]

Meanwhile, Carroll was touring with the Coasters and experiencing some of the same racial tension he had encountered in the 1950s. Only now, because the Coasters had been so popular with white audiences, there was a different twist.

> I remember towns, when we'd go to the South they thought the Coasters was white. They didn't have the pictures. They just had the records "Charlie Brown," "Yakety Yak." I remember Myrtle Beach [South Carolina]. We came in. The joint was packed. We were supposed to be performing there, the Coasters. And the group came with the band and all that noise came right down to a hush. And then, I was looking at everybody, everybody's looking at us, and we go to put our stuff up on stage, and I hear this buzzing and some nasty comments. We said, "Take your stuff and let's get out of here as quickly as possible."[48]

DOO-WOP THOSE FIFTIES

As the original members of the Cadillacs were coping with changing musical tastes in the 1960s, there was a growing legion of fans who not only knew what the Coasters and Earl Carroll looked like but also deeply prized the music they had made in the 1950s. By the end of the 1960s, the support of this fan base would create new performance opportunities for these singers. Around 1969, what had loosely been referred to as rhythm and blues or vocal group music started to be called, simply, doo-wop.

Credit for the term's common usage is given to a particularly enthusiastic DJ on New York City's WCBS-FM, Gus Gossert. The vocal harmony of the 1950s and early 1960s had had an underground presence in the radio world since 1963 with *The Time Capsule* show on WFUV, the Fordham University station in the Bronx. Alan Fredericks and Irving "Slim" Rose had first revived interest in the music a few years earlier. But it was Gossert's presence on a major commercial radio station and his insistent, zealous proselytizing for the cause of the newly named doo-wop that served as the cultural tipping point for this music.[49] Doo-wop soon became the audio and visual symbol of 1950s-centric oldies music, and a new group of collectors and fans started magazines and radio shows and helped promote concerts.

The groundwork had been laid for a larger music revival, and one of its heroes is Richard Nader. Nader started out as a disc jockey and concert promoter in his native town of Pittsburgh and, by the mid-1960s, was doing the same in New York City. In 1969 he conceived of putting on the first big oldies concert in the Felt Forum at Madison Square Garden in New York. According to the disc jockey Bobby Jay, "Richard went to people on Wall Street and other investment people, and said, 'I have an idea of finding old singers and putting them together and taking it to Madison Square Garden. I think it'll sell.' Most of the groups on that first show in October of 1969 and subsequent shows through the early seventies hadn't sung together in years."[50] After the success of this seminal concert, Nader's Felt Forum oldies shows became annual events, and he moved on to other venues in the New York City area and beyond.

In 1972, WCBS-FM became the first twenty-four-hour oldies radio station in the country, featuring *The Doo-Wop Shop* on Sunday night, initially hosted by Norm N. Nite and then taken over by Don K. Reed, who, along with his eventual coworker Bobby Jay, would MC many oldies concerts. A plethora of doo-wop-oriented publications appeared for the first time, including *Bim Bam Boom* (1971–74), *Big Town Review* (1972), *Record Exchanger* (1969–83), *R & B Magazine* (1970–71), *Story Untold* (1977–86), and *Yesterday's Memories* (1975–77). The following decade saw the establishment of *Record Collector's Monthly* (1982) and *Echoes of the Past* (1987), both still in business. These publications included many invaluable interviews with singers who have since died.

In Clifton, New Jersey, Ronnie Italiano founded the United in Group Harmony Association (UHGA) in 1976. This organization, which would be the model for several similar societies around the country, was dedicated to the preservation of what it considered to be an underappreciated musical heritage, promoting concerts and inducting groups into its Hall of Fame for over thirty years. The word *doo-wop* is notably absent from the organization's name. A stronghold of the purist strain of vocal harmony appreciation that got its start at Times Square Records in the early 1960s, the UHGA looked with disfavor on the term.

An intense nostalgia for the era that had given birth to doo-wop was surfacing in the larger popular culture. The filmmaker George Lucas, who released *American Graffiti* in 1973, and the dramatists Jim Jacobs and Warren Casey, who premiered the musical *Grease* in 1972, drew on the era for artistic inspiration. *American Graffiti* spawned the popular television series *Happy Days* in 1974 and its spin-off, *Laverne and Shirley*, in 1976. In terms of ticket sales and viewership, the collective nostalgia represented by these films and television shows was unprecedented in American history.[51]

Why were so many people in 1970s nostalgic for the 1950s? Possibly one explanation lies in the events of the decade between and their effect on the national psyche. Many Americans who were teenagers in the 1950s found their identities—as members of their families, communities, and the larger society—questioned and disrupted by the social upheaval of the 1960s.[52] Although similar times of anxiety had occurred in American society, never before had there been such deep cultural transformation. From gender roles, sexual orientation, and race relations to the roles of government, family, and religion, practically every aspect of society was being reassessed.[53]

In 1973 one of the Richard Nader oldies shows was the subject of a documentary film, *Let the Good Times Roll,* which featured a veritable Who's Who of 1950s rock and roll including Chuck Berry, Bo Diddley, Chubby Checker, Bill Haley and the Comets, Fats Domino, Little Richard, Danny and the Juniors, the Five Satins, the Shirelles, and the Coasters with Earl Carroll. The film includes concert footage interspersed with photographs, newsreel footage, and television and film clips from the 1950s that focus on the teen rebellion and societal upheaval connected with the music, offering a counternarrative of sorts to the more placid *Happy Days* scenario. Perhaps the most revealing moments in the film are those when the performers are not onstage. In one scene, Bo Diddley comments on the racism encountered on tour. In another, Chuck Berry visits a broken-down school bus he had toured in and comments, "If it could talk, I imagine we could convict every band member I had." Earl Carroll is seen backstage as well, singing an impromptu blues number and chatting with Bo Diddley as Diddley fries some chicken on a hot plate.[54] By showcasing the non-glamorous side of these iconic artists' lives, the filmmakers provide a sobering look behind the scrim of nostalgia.

Songs that referenced 1950s culture were written in the early 1970s, such as Elton John's "Crocodile Rock" (1973) and, most notably, Don McLean's "American Pie" (1971), an end-of-the-innocence elegy for the postwar generation. The song's galvanizing phrase, "the day the music died," which refers to the airplane crash of February 3, 1959, that killed rock and rollers Buddy Holly, Ritchie Valens, and J. P. Richardson (aka

"The Big Bopper"), poignantly expressed the closing of a chapter in American musical and social history.

New doo-wop-style vocal groups emerged such as Sha Na Na, whose members, unlike the working-class singers they emulated, met when they were students at Columbia University in the late 1960s. Their big break came with an appearance at the Woodstock festival, where they stood in stark relief to contemporary rock acts like the Who, Santana, and Jimi Hendrix. Sha Na Na featured the doo-wop sound and but not the doo-wop look. With greased-back hair, tight blue jeans, and rolled-up sleeves, not the usual tuxedo, the group's bass singer Jon "Bowzer" Bauman embodied the stereotypical rock and roll rebel, the avatar of 1950s cool that by the late 1960s signified conservatism, not rebellion.

The young working-class urban Italian American males who once were on the outside looking in at the white American mainstream had now, because of their close association with early rock and roll, been elevated to the level of working-class heroes. Several members of Sha Na Na even adopted Italian-sounding stage names like Tony Santini, Gino, and Ronzoni.[55] In a way, the members of Sha Na Na were playing the role of musical reactionaries, members of a counter-counterculture who would often taunt the "hippies" in the audience with an aggressive, albeit performed, claim to rock and roll authenticity that was, ironically, cloaked in inauthentic garb.

Other groups who formed in the wake of the oldies revival include Flash Cadillac, who appeared in the prom scene of *American Graffiti,* and Manhattan Transfer, who recorded a version of "Gloria" in 1975.[56] This recording was very much a homage to the Cadillacs, with a prominent bass intro and blow harmony background vocals exemplifying the nostalgic turn in doo-wop performance in the 1970s. Stylistic innovation was superseded by reverence for and emulation of past practice. This was about trying to sound like they did in the "good old days." The revival in interest in the music of the 1950s also made it possible for old groups such as Earl Lewis and the Channels to re-release earlier recordings, including their 1956 version of "Gloria," which met with greater success in 1971.

The aging of the 1950s teenage generation and the rise in the entertainment world of many of that generation such as George Lucas fueled a resurgence of popularity for the music. At the center of this was the street corner doo-wop group, whose iconic status signified oldies music and nostalgia for the 1950s in general. The feelings evoked by the image of the street-corner singer were part of a historical nostalgia surrounding the long relationship between vocal harmony and race and place.[57]

From minstrel invocations of a black southern pastoral life and the mythologizing of the late-nineteenth-century white Main Street in the barbershop revival of the early twentieth to the nostalgia for the 1950s in the 1970s, vocal harmony is used as a vehicle for traveling back to an imagined past. Singing and listening to vocal harmony becomes a refuge inside a cultural cocoon where the vicissitudes of changing times can be, at least momentarily, avoided.

The male bonding inherent in vocal group experience also plays a role in the nostalgic resonance of vocal harmony. Changes experienced in young adulthood can create emotional chasms that music can bridge. Common, often traumatic, life transitions, like going off to war, or even simply adjusting to working outside the home, can create a deep need for nostalgic refuge. This emotional paradigm had a role in the 1970s doo-wop revival. Many of the audiences at the oldies shows were made up of formerly urban-dwelling white males who seemed to pine for the lost neighborhood street of their youth where they had had the free time to just hang out, if not actually sing.

It is important to highlight the "urban" and "white" part of this demographic, for leaving behind their neighborhood street was part of the larger "white flight" from U.S. cities in the 1960s and 1970s. For whites who grew up in urban America in the 1940s and 1950s, many of whom were Italian or Jewish, the changing racial composition of city neighborhoods in the wake of the African American Great Migration was the main reason for moving to the suburbs. Blacks were blamed for the overall decline in urban living conditions in the second half of the twentieth century.[58] Ironically, even though blacks were the reason whites abandoned the city, the music they shared was one of the reasons they missed it. As with the white-dominated barbershop quartet revival of the early twentieth century, the complex interracial heritage of doo-wop is often usurped or, at least, complicated by nostalgic reflection promulgated primarily by the white mainstream. This usurpation is never entirely successful. The interracial dialogue at the heart of the American vocal harmony tradition can be muted but never completely silenced. Doo-wop–induced white nostalgic longing will inevitably be laced with interracial remembering.

PERFORMING NOSTALGIA

Many of the songs sung by the barbershop quartet revivalists in the 1920s and 1930s were tunes that harked back to the old neighborhood and the lost community of youth.[59] Similar location-focused compositions were produced in the 1970s, including "Looking for an Echo" written by Richard Reicheg and first recorded by Kenny Vance in 1975. Vance was an original member of Jay and the Americans, a mostly Jewish vocal group from Brooklyn that reached the height of its fame in the 1960s but whose roots were in doo-wop harmony. Vance now performs on the oldies circuit with his group, the Planotones, covering many of the doo-wop standards, and his closing number is usually "Looking for an Echo."[60] The song contains the characteristic closing falsetto flourish, the four-part vocal harmony with a high tenor voice on top, ice cream change structure, and a slow 12/8 rhythmic meter. "Looking for an Echo" is a newly composed "oldie" which lyrically signifies the bygone teenage practice of singing in subway stations and bathrooms. The lyrics also pay homage to the influential black vocal groups the Moonglows, the Harptones, and the Dells. In doo-wop culture, "echo" is a means of making music, a way of being and seeking meaning in the world, and, in this case, an affective songwriting metaphor for remembrance.

At least one song written in the 1970s was a negative take on nostalgia for the 1950s and the experience of playing on the oldies circuit. Rick Nelson, who was a child television star on *The Adventures of Ozzie and Harriet* in the 1950s and who had many hits as a recording artist in the late 1950s and early 1960s, wrote "Garden Party" (1972) in response to getting booed for his long hair and new material at a Madison Square Garden revival show. The lyrics express the social dissonance performers would often encounter when confronted with the expectations of an oldies concert audience. Nelson was happy to sing his old hits like "Hello, Mary Lou" (1961), "but if memories are all I sing, I'd rather drive a truck."

At an oldies concert performers are expected to sing nothing but their hits, the songs that endeared them "way back when" to those who now have returned to see them. Nelson made the mistake of flouting this expectation by performing a cover of "Honky-tonk Woman," a hit at the time for the Rolling Stones.[61] For many oldies artists, it is a damned-if-you-do, damned-if-you-don't scenario when it comes to recording and performing new material. Shirley Alston Reeves, the lead singer of the Shirelles, left her group in the mid-1970s to pursue a solo career only to find that she was in the impossible place between nostalgic expectation and her desire to evolve as an artist. She, like many other still relatively young and ambitious recording artists, experienced the show business catch-22 of releasing new material in a contemporary style and being told that the new material will not sell because she is an oldies performer who has not a hit record in many years.[62]

Nonetheless the oldies circuit created a relatively lucrative market niche for those who had survived the financial exploitation and racism of the past, who still had the physical and musical wherewithal to perform, and who were willing to work within the boundaries of nostalgic expectation. By the end of the 1970s, the groundwork had been laid for a reunion of the Cadillacs, who were inspired to reassemble with their original lead singer, Earl Carroll, after a 1979 appearance in a popular Subaru commercial. In 1982, Carroll, weary from twenty years on the road with the Coasters, took a job as a custodian at P.S. 87 in Manhattan while continuing to work steadily on the weekends with the Cadillacs.

Carroll had rarely sung lead with the Coasters, and he was not an original member. The oldies circuit now gave him the opportunity to be, once again, the star of the show, and to front the group for which he was initially famous, albeit now on a part-time basis. This decision to return to his lesser-known but historically important first group put him in a position to receive some much deserved recognition and even financial restitution over the next twenty years. He was the subject of a spot on the television show *20/20* about his dual life as singer and custodian; he was inducted into the United in Group Harmony Association Hall of Fame; a 3-CD sixty-song Cadillacs box set was issued by Collectables Records, for which he receives royalties; and the Cadillacs received a Pioneer Award from the Rhythm and Blues Foundation, which included generous grants for Carroll and original bass singer Bobby Phillips.

In 1999, the group also appeared in the record-setting PBS fund-raiser *Doo Wop 50*, evidence of the continuing regenerative popularity and profitability of doo-wop. This show was the most lucrative fund-raiser in the network's history, garnering more than $20 million in pledges nationwide, and it initiated a slew of oldies-oriented PBS fund-raisers.[63] For PBS, it was a historic move away from its long-standing target audience. Classical music, ballet, and opera had always been the entertainment stock-in-trade of public television. When PBS needed money, they targeted the generally more affluent demographic group that supports and consumes those exemplars of high culture. Before *Doo Wop 50, The Three Tenors,* featuring opera stars Luciano Pavarotti, Placido Domingo, and

Jose Carreras had been the most successful fund-raising tool for the network. The success of *Doo Wop 50* revealed that there was another relatively affluent and most likely larger demographic group that was willing to support PBS, this time in the name of popular culture. These people were middle-aged or retired, primarily white, and mostly from working-class backgrounds who had entered the middle class. They wanted to reconnect with the music of their youth, and they now had the financial means to pay for it.[64]

The resounding success of *Doo Wop 50* meant more "oldies" PBS fund-raisers put together by executive producer T. J. Lubinsky, a vocal group music enthusiast in his early thirties at the time and the grandson of Savoy Records founder Herman Lubinsky. Bobby Jay remembers his first encounter with the younger Lubinsky: "I met him when he was sixteen. He came up to CBS to interview Don K. Reed and myself. He was doing a documentary for school on vocal groups and things like that and he just never stopped. He just kept on going and the next thing I know he's telling me he's working for PBS. He had an idea that he pitched to PBS. It went through the roof. In New York alone I think it made three million dollars the first night. It gave a new shot to the genre."[65] Subsequent shows included *Doo Wop 51, Doo Wop 52,* and an expansion into later musical genres with *Rhythm Love and Soul,* and *Superstars of Seventies Soul Live.* As of this writing, over thirty nostalgia-oriented, popular music–focused PBS fund-raisers have aired around the country.

These television shows have produced financial windfalls for the artists. Videos and DVDs of *Doo Wop 50* and subsequent shows, after their initial use as fund-raising premiums, have been packaged and sold alongside CD reissues of original doo-wop recordings. The groups were paid only AFTRA scale for their appearances on the shows, but they do receive royalties for CD and DVD sales. Moreover, the national exposure has given many of these groups a much-needed career boost, with new performance opportunities being offered beyond the home regions where they normally gig. Even though the Cadillacs' national fame had never been on the level of the bigger groups of the 1950s, post-PBS they have received invitations for shows in the Midwest, on the West Coast, and in the Southwest. They also appeared on the QVC home-shopping cable network in November 2000 to help sell the *Doo Wop 50* products.

The trajectory of the Cadillacs is representative of the journey of doo-wop as it took a shortcut from the street corners of its birth, with a brief sojourn of laying on the avenue of cultural insignificance, to the mysterious land of

Nostalgia, USA. The Cadillacs were a black group who emerged from Harlem in the early 1950s during doo-wop's first period of popularity. At the beginning of the following decade their music was emulated by white singers, including their ballad "Gloria," which at same time was becoming the object of nostalgic consumption. Starting in the 1970s and continuing to the present, the Cadillacs have been the beneficiaries of the advent of an oldies circuit that has provided numerous performance opportunities with the support of an active doo-wop community that continues to foster an appreciation for the pioneering vocal group sound of the 1950s.

1. *Publicity photo of the Cadillacs from the mid-1950s*
with Earl Carroll (top left), Bobby Phillips (bottom left), Lavern Drake (center),
James "Poppa" Clark (top right), and Johnny "Gus" Willingham (bottom right).
(Photo courtesy of Showtime Archives)

2. Publicity photo of the Cadillacs from the 1959 film Go, Johnny, Go! *featuring (from left to right) J. R. Bailey, Earl Carroll, Bobby Phillips, and Robert Spencer. (Photo courtesy of Showtime Archives)*

(opposite top)
3. Earl Carroll at the taping of the 2005 PBS special at the Sands Casino in Atlantic City. (Photo courtesy of Julius "Juice" Freeman)

(opposite bottom)
4. Bobby Phillips at the Sands taping.
(Photo courtesy of Julius "Juice" Freeman)

5. Gary Lewis at the Sands taping.
(Photo courtesy of Julius "Juice" Freeman)

*6. The Cadillacs performing "Speedoo" at the Sands taping.
(Photo courtesy of Julius "Juice" Freeman)*

7. *Earl Carroll singing "Speedoo" with Gary Lewis dancing behind him, Sands taping. (Photo courtesy of Julius "Juice" Freeman)*

8. Bobby Phillips singing "Speedoo"
with Earl Carroll looking on, Sands taping.
(Photo courtesy of Julius "Juice" Freeman)

9. *The Cadillacs and the author with Jerry Blavat (holding microphone)*
at a 2007 Rhythm & Blues Foundation event, Philadelphia.
(Photo courtesy of Julius "Juice" Freeman)

T he doo-wop community today is a social network that comprises four subgroups, who are affected differently by certain endemic issues. For *the singers* recognition and reconciliation, which encompass both financial recompense and artistic and historical appreciation, are extremely important—in a word, they want respect. The *mediators* (the intermediaries—from promoters to record collectors—between the singers and the audience) and *the audience* are usually quite willing to show this respect, but for many in these two interrelated subgroups, respect for the artist is complicated with nostalgic remembrance relating to their own personal circumstances (or, for a younger generation of fans, nostalgic tourism). Also integral to this community are the members of *the band,* most of whom are at least one generation younger than the singers, the mediators, and the traditional members of the audience. For them the steady work they have found in the doo-wop community must be balanced with their own notions of musical authenticity, nostalgia, and their personal lives. All of these people, for whatever reasons, economic, nostalgic, or musical, are sharing a territory, and their continuing interaction has helped to define and transform that territory.

THE SINGERS

At the center of the doo-wop community are the singers, the members of the vocal groups who perform on the circuit, many of whose careers began more than fifty years ago. Most are in their sixties and seventies. There are just as many white as black groups, and several integrated groups. Black or white, men make up the majority of groups, although there are several notable female groups and female members of otherwise male groups such as the Platters and the Skyliners from Pittsburgh (known for their 1958 hit "Since I Don't Have You").

Many singers have told me that they are happy with the work on the oldies circuit. Eddie Jones, the former musical director for the Cadillacs and a longtime vocal group singer and arranger, described to me what it was like to be an oldies circuit performer: "Suddenly, it seemed, we were getting more respect. They realized that there was good money to be made and they were willing to share it with us. They were now giving us our money up front. Also the audience had more respect. They knew who we were already before the show. We didn't have to prove ourselves."[1] The singers feel more in control of their lives; the days of managers making shady deals behind their backs are more or less over. According to the Cadillacs' bass singer, Bobby Phillips, "We mostly control our own bookings and stuff. We're more aware of what's happening now."[2] Most groups are making more money than they did in their youth, earning anywhere from $3,000 to $25,000 per group per show depending on the name recognition of the act, the venue, and the type of show. Corporate and private-party gigs can often pay twice as much as theater or arena shows.

Oldies shows generally use the package or revue format of the 1950s Alan Freed and Apollo Theatre tradition. There are usually five or six and sometimes as many as ten acts on an oldies bill. Some singers do not like the revue format. As Nick Santamaria, the Capris' lead singer, relates: "Unfortunately today, if you have five or six or seven acts on the show, you're kind of limited in the amount of time you can do. It's very difficult as a performer when you have twelve minutes to get your personality across, because you come out and you're maybe only able to do, tops, four numbers. And I find it's an integral part of the performance to be able to communicate with the audience; to be able to spend a minute to show them that you share the same values that they do, your love for the music, your gratitude for them supporting you."[3]

These performers' professional lives have been extended by a profound nostalgic impulse in American culture. But they still want to be viewed as vital artists even if they are doing the same material night after night. Their music making occurs in the present, even though the events are usually framed as evocations of the past. Despite its limitations, the typical oldies concert format has proven to be a successful structure for presenting multiple doo-wop group performances. It has made it possible for more groups to be involved, many of whom would not have enough material to sustain an entire concert on their own.

When doo-wop groups venture beyond the familiar oldies circuit, they do not always encounter comprehending and sympathetic audiences, at least initially. After the Cadillacs played a blues festival in the Netherlands in 1997, one reviewer recounted a not entirely enthusiastic reception. "[They were] identically dressed, even down to having just the second and third jacket buttons of their startlingly identical green suits fastened.

Choreography with a capital 'C' led to murmurs of 'Las Vegas showbiz' from certain parts of the audience."[4] Outside of the doo-wop community, the Cadillacs' performance practice, typified by their flashy, matching tuxedos and their well-rehearsed vocal choreography, lacks the historical context necessary for full appreciation. Flamboyant attire and choreography are part of the long African American musical tradition that the Cadillacs experienced and participated in at the Apollo in the early 1950s. All the other performers on the festival bill were traditional blues acts. Although they and doo-wop groups have overlapping musical ancestries, and fifty years ago blues musicians like Muddy Waters and B. B. King easily shared a stage with the Cadillacs and other vocal groups on the chitlin' circuit, today most concert promoters consider these genres separate if not incompatible.

Backstage, as the Cadillacs were about to go on in their matching green suits, there were a few derisive snickers from some of the denim and leather–clad blues musicians. The Cadillacs had to win over the crowd and their fellow entertainers and prove they had a right to share the stage. After all, the jump-blues of songs like "Zoom" and "Speedo" represents just another, more flamboyant, side of the blues tradition. The group brought an unexpected energy to the show. Right after they left the stage, the MC, a white American from New Orleans named Ready Teddy, came on and was inspired to do a series of backflips. As the reviewer noted, the following act "had the daunting task of following the mayhem left in the Caddy's wake."[5]

Even in the New York area, the Cadillacs must continue to prove themselves as musical artists and not just "Las Vegas showbiz" performers, especially when critiqued by non-oldies publications. A preview in *Time Out New York* of a show at Radio City Music Hall referred to the Cadillacs as "the Harlem *loons* who introduced the *loopy* 1956 anthem 'Speedoo.' "[6] The Cadillacs themselves do not necessarily mind the "Las Vegas" or "loon" label. They, like many of the oldies acts, consider themselves entertainers first and foremost and are happy to have a chance to prove themselves as such. What matters most to them, in addition to being properly compensated, is putting on a good show and connecting with the audience.

Within the nostalgic frame, cognitive dissonance between the musical evocation of the past and the realties of the present, heightened by the emotive power of the music, often engenders a complex social experience for the group members. Memories of past injustices and inequities persist and play out in interesting ways in the doo-wop community. In the dressing room at a December 2, 2000, show in Wallingford, Connecticut, the Cadillacs and I watched the PBS fund-raiser, *Doo Wop 51*. A white group, the Diamonds, and a black group, the Gladiolas, were singing the song "Little Darlin'" in tandem. The Diamonds had recorded a much more successful cover of the song soon after the Gladiolas released the original recording in 1957, but no mention is made of the fact in the introduction to the joint performance or of the issue of cover versions.[7] The show's producers obviously wanted to honor Maurice Williams, the lead singer of the Gladiolas and the writer of the song, but also they wanted to maintain an air of good feeling and "harmony" between the performers and with the audience. For many who were witness to the performance, however, the underlying tension was discernible.

Dave Somerville, the Diamonds' lead singer, has worked steadily on the oldies circuit for many years. He is surely aware of his legacy as the front man for a white group best known for their covers of black songs—and the racial and economic consequences of that legacy. His approach, however, is similar to the one taken by the producers of the PBS show: he tries to lighten the heavy issues of racial encounter in the marketplace and on the road.

Well, by the end of 1957 the Diamonds were eight hits deep. We were actually still four blue-eyed, semi-virgin white guys from Toronto in brown, three-button suits and we were about to get a terrific education. We were invited to join rock and roll's first major touring show and for sixty days of one-nighters, we barnstormed North America with a dozen pioneer jukebox giants. We traveled in a Greyhound with Fats Domino, Chuck Berry, and the Drifters. I think we did sixty shows in sixty days and it was exhausting. We weren't educated the way Americans are about the history of the country and what discrimination was all about. There were no black people in Canada at that time. I mean I didn't meet a black person until I was in my late teens. And so it was interesting to be on the bus with black folk and see how they were treated. We were just observers. All the black people sat in the front of the bus, by the way. We of Caucasian persuasion took up the back half. The reason was explained to me by Phil Everly [of the Everly Brothers]. He said, "When we get into the South we're going to have to stay in separate hotels." And I don't know if you know this about Rock and Roll, but from a musical, technical standpoint, the accent is on two and four, and that's what puts the rock in the roll. But with the audience sitting on two sides and with the trained headlight coming at you, you couldn't see, but I always knew where the white kids were sitting, because they were the ones clapping on one and three.[8]

Somerville uses the same patter in his stage show. For many vocal group members, interviews are performances too, and they often rely on a well-practiced version of their biographies. Somerville emphasizes his youthful innocence in the 1950s, especially concerning racial matters. He carefully does not to refer to his group's well-known reputation for making cover records, which most of their "eight hits deep" were. After a brief comment about southern segregation, he ends his reminiscence with a comical take on racial difference ("the accent is on two and four").

The year before, another sequence was staged for *Doo-wop 50*, in which the Cadillacs sang "Gloria" along with three groups who had covered the song. (Sometimes when the Cadillacs do a show, one of the other groups who recorded "Gloria" will be on the same bill. This is a common occurrence on the oldies circuit, since many of the groups do each other's songs, and often some sort of compromise is worked out.) The singers in the *Doo-wop 50* scenario were, in order of appearance, Earl Lewis of the Channels, Jimmy Gallagher of the Passions, Vito Balsamo of the Salutations, and Earl Carroll of the Cadillacs. They all seem to be just having some fun with the implied competition, as each singer elaborately crooned the opening phrase of "Gloria." However, by putting Speedo last and allowing him to sing the first verse by himself, they were acknowledging his primary role in the evolution of one of the most important songs in the doo-wop canon. While those outside of the doo-wop community may not have fully understood what was happening, those on the inside, the performers and the serious fans, surely were aware of this attempt to give respect where respect is due.

THE MEDIATORS

This subgroup consists of the promoters, disc jockeys, support organizations, magazine and fanzine writers and editors, record collectors, managers, booking agents, lawyers—in short, those who mediate between the singers and the audience.[9] They are mostly white, male, and in their sixties and seventies. They are usually not musicians or singers, although there are notable exceptions.

Promoters put together most of the package shows in venues ranging in size from high school auditoriums to casinos and large arenas. Oldies radio stations advertise the shows, and their DJs are often the MCs. (In recent years, most commercial oldies stations have updated their formats to target a younger audience, and doo-wop now gets airplay primarily on college radio specialty programs such as the *Group Harmony Review* on Fordham's WFUV and, increasingly, on Internet stations.)[10] Record *collectors* come again and again to the concerts and have their own fanzines and Internet organizations for buying and trading rare records.[11]

Preservation societies such as the United Group Harmony Association in Clifton, New Jersey, raise money to present shows and honor pioneer performers. Some, like the Rhythm and Blues Foundation, which is not exclusively for doo-wop, give small grants to needy or underappreciated group members as well. These organizations also produce fanzines, maintain websites, and sponsor shows. For many years one important New York–area organization was Oldies Forever, which published a quarterly comprehensive oldies concert calendar. Buyers, sellers, and collectors of non-musical 1950s memorabilia and "classic" automobiles like the '57 Chevy have ancillary but visible presence in the community. Concerts are sometimes presented in tandem with car shows, and audience members will dress up in 1950s vintage garb. Record companies such as Rhino have bought the master tapes of many of the original doo-wop recordings and have successfully reissued the material on CD. Lawyers have successfully sued record and publishing companies, or the companies that bought them, for royalties due the artists. Managers and booking agents keep groups working on the revival circuit.

Concert promoters are the most visible of the mediators.[12] Their names often appear on the concert marquees alongside those of the artists, and many have been working the oldies circuit since it began. Pioneer oldies promoter Richard Nader (whose company has been run by his wife, Deborah, since his retirement), often doubled as MC. Using nostalgia as a rhetorical device, one of his favorite ways to frame an event was as a "reunion" where "our music" will be heard. He would refer to the assumed ages of the audience members to connect them to the music they were about to hear. "How many people here are over fifty years of age and really remember these songs?" he asked at a concert in Madison Square Garden in New York. "[Loud applause.] How many are under the age of thirty-five and don't know what they are doing here? [Scattered laughter.] You know how lucky I am? How lucky we are! Our music is still around.

Now we're . . . we're getting on. But our music is still here and I think it's richer and better than ever."[13] (Nader also took the opportunity to note the longevity of his own contribution to the continuing popularity of the music. "You know we've been doing these things since 1969. I went back through all the advertisements from all my shows. I'm talking about fifteen hundred shows. By the way, we sold out the twenty-thousand-seat main arena of Madison Square Garden twenty-one times between 1970 and 1978. Which was an all-time record until Elton John broke our record in 1996. I'm very proud of that.")

Nader had certain notions of authenticity when it came to his oldies shows. As a rule, groups had to contain at least one original member, a fact that he highlighted throughout the revue: "The originals . . . originals . . . let's hear it one more time for the original Moonglows!" Whether a group has original singers or not is a key issue for mediators, particularly those in the promotional end of the business. What is more important, authenticity or entertainment? Should the concerts be framed as events for the recognition of the singers' historical importance or nostalgia for its own sake? What brings people to the shows, the members of the groups or the songs associated with particular group names?

Even if a promoter chooses to favor authenticity over nostalgia, it is not always so easy to determine when a group contains original members or not. The instability of group personnel has been a defining characteristic of doo-wop culture from the beginning, consigning many of the singers of the most famous songs to relative anonymity and opening the door to a plethora of so-called fake or imposter groups. Many of these contain members who have no relationship to the originals. But in other cases, there may be debatable lineages, given the splintering process endemic to American vocal harmony. The Ink Spots were one of first groups to splinter into several different groups; in the 1990s, over forty groups in the United States and abroad were performing under the Ink Spots moniker.[14] The splintering process tends to be an exponential one, especially with the more popular and long-lasting groups such as the Ink Spots. As replacements of the original four or five members come and go, all involved may try to claim group-forming rights, and then new members in these subsequent groups can do the same, and so on.

It then often becomes an issue of who owns the trademarked name of the group. After doo-wop's initial fade in the early 1960s, many group leaders sold the rights to their group name to their managers or other people in the business. These new trademark owners then capitalized on the oldies circuit marketability of the name by assembling new Drifters, Coasters, and Platters, often composed of singers obviously too young to be original members. Group leaders sold the name rights for a variety of reasons, but the most common is that singers who had begun their careers in 1950s had simply moved on to new musical situations or had left the business altogether and did not see the value in a name associated with a past time and style.

As a result, many original members have not legally been able to advertise their performances using the group name, a situation that many in the doo-wop community, such as Nick Santamaria, find abhorrent. "It's disgraceful when an original artist cannot perform a song that they recorded. I think it's disgraceful when the public is duped. You can see a thirty-year-old Coasters group, and they'll go on stage and they'll say 'back in 1961 we recorded this song.' You'll get four guys going out as the Coasters one night and the following night they'll go out as the Platters, and if they shave their legs they'll go out as the Shangri-Las [a female group]."[15]

Even if singers are not legally prohibited from using their name, often they will find themselves in competition with groups using the name operating in other parts of the country. Gary Lewis remembers encountering another group of Cadillacs in 1996 at the Rhythm and Blues Foundation Pioneer Awards ceremony in Los Angeles: "This man had a nerve to drive up in his van, and 'The Cadillacs' was written on the side." Bobby Phillips adds, "And he came to Speedo and said, 'Ah, man, I didn't know y'all were still together.' And I looked at him and Speedo looked at him and I just walked off. He knew damn well we were still together."[16] One of the reasons the group is referred to as "Speedo and the Cadillacs" is so the public will know that they are the group with the original lead singer and not either a splinter group featuring someone who had a less significant relationship with the original group or a fake group with no connection to authenticity.

Issues of group authenticity and name ownership are common to both black and white groups. Vito Picone recalls that "on the cover of the *Philadelphia Inquirer* were three black guys and a white girl who are 'the Elegants.' In the article it says how years ago they recorded 'Little Star' and because they were black they were not able to go out on the road and perform, and so the record label found these white kids and put them out on the road to become the Elegants." Picone realized the value of owning his group's name relatively early but did not understand the complexity of the legal process. "I didn't know at the age that we were that there was such a thing as a federal trademark. So what happened was we incorpo-rated the name. I didn't know that incorporating was only good in the state that you incorporate in. I found out that there's this federal trademark. So I went to go trademark the name. This was only, maybe, ten years ago and I was turned down by the Department of Commerce, because there was a band in San Diego, California, called Los Elegantes."[17] Eventually, with the help of his congresswoman, Picone was able to secure the trade-mark, which he must renew periodically. What he discovered was an im-portant facet of oldies circuit life, one that a handful of people in the business had known for many years.

Battles over name ownership pitting singers against mediators also plagued the Drifters. In 1969, after CBS-FM radio in New York proposed a partnership with *Rock Magazine* to reunite old singing groups in live con-certs, Larry Marshak, a *Rock* editor, contacted several former members of the group, including tenor Charlie Thomas and bass Beary Hobbs, who signed an exclusive management contract with him. In 1971 Faye Treadwell, wife of the group's original manager, sued Marshak but the suit was dis-missed two years later, with the court finding that she had willfully de-faulted on the use of the name in the United States when she moved her operation to the United Kingdom. In 1976, Marshak convinced his Drift-ers to trademark the group name and then assign their rights to him. Unhappy with the power Marshak had over his livelihood, Charlie Thomas later broke with Marshak and started his own Drifters group—against which Marshak has brought suit several times over the past thirty years. After Hobbs's death, Marshak continued to use the Drifters moniker with whatever members he put together. One of these groups is known as the "Beary Hobbs Drifters."

"Cornell Gunter's Coasters" is also a Marshak group. Gunter was one of the original members who left the group in the early 1960s. He, along with the other originals, was given part ownership of the trademark by Lester Sill, the Coasters' manager. When Gunter died, his portion of the trademark went to his sister Shirley Gunter, who made a deal with Mar-shak in 2000 to put out a Coasters group. Marshak defends his business practices and claims that for most oldies audiences, original members are not important. "I can understand why somebody who's not benefiting by the groups I have is unhappy, but that's the law. I really doubt anybody could think these are original members when the records were made in 1952. It's almost like Les Miserables. The talent is right out of Broadway shows, and when they get a job and go back to Broadway, we replace them. It's no longer dependent on any individual."[18]

A Platters group recently active in the Las Vegas area was owned and operated by The Five Platters, Inc., a company founded by manager Buck Ram and Jean Bennett in 1956. According to Bennett, unlike most of the other groups of the 1950s, each member had a 20 percent interest in the Platters name, which they sold back to the company when they left the group. Buck Ram died in 1991, but Bennett, now in her late eighties, continues to manage this Platters group and license the name to several other companies.

Because of the existence of groups run by Marshak, Bennett, and other trademark holders, some original members have been barred from using their group name to promote their shows. To remedy this, in 1998 a draft of the Truth in Rock Bill was proposed in Congress by Representatives Dennis Kucinich (D-Ohio) and Charles Norwood (R-Georgia). The bill, aimed at amending the Lanham Act of 1946 which regulates trademarks, in the case of a performing group defines the product and service as inseparable from the original performer. Eventually its main proponents decided to wage the battle on a state-by-state basis. In January 2006, Pennsylvania became the first state to pass the renamed Truth in Music Bill. As of this writing, the bill has been signed into law in thirty-three states and has begun to substantially curtail the income of Larry Marshak and other promoters.

The Chairman of the Truth in Music Committee at the Vocal Group Hall of Fame based in Sharon, Pennsylvania, who has traveled throughout the country over the last few years promoting this legislation, is Jon "Bowzer" Bauman, the former bass singer and leader of Sha Na Na. He explains the bill this way: "'Truth in Music' says you need to have at least one member of the group that made the hit records in the group that's on stage that night, unless you have a darn good reason why you don't. There are really only two of those darn good reasons, 1) that somehow the group has a valid federally registered trademark for the group name, or 2) that the show is clearly advertised as a tribute or a salute in a manner that is not so confusingly similar to the actual group name that it would tend to deceive the public."[19]

Because of this bill, for the first time, one need not own the trademark to a group name to be allowed to use it, as long as one is an "original" recording artist associated with that name. But who is an original? One problem with the bill is that, while it defines the terms "sound recording" and "recording group," it does not define the term "hit record." Sonny Turner replaced Tony Williams as the lead singer of the Platters in the early 1960s. He made several records with the group but not any of the ones for which the Platters are best known. He is considered an "original member" by some promoters because he has been a performing member of a Platters group for over forty years. Others consider the original bass singer, Herb Reed, to be the only true surviving original Platter.

Another problematic phrase refers to a member of a performing group having a legal right to use the group name so long they have not "abandoned the name or affiliation with the group." This stricture means that, for example, Shirley Alston Reeves, the lead singer of the Shirelles on their early 1960s hits such as "Will You Love Me Tomorrow" and "Soldier Boy," cannot perform under the Shirelles name because she officially went solo in the 1970s. The only other surviving member of the group, Beverly Lee, owns the trademark.

Jean Bennett believes that the supporters of the Truth in Music Bill unfairly stigmatize trademark owners like herself. "What happens when they all die? When Herbie Reed is gone and no one can use it, that's it? The legacy should go on legitimately through whoever maintains that name and owns it through an early connection."[20] Harvey Robbins, a Boston-based oldies show promoter who founded the Doo-Wopp Hall of Fame in that town, agrees. "If you see the Boston Celtics, who's playing? Bill Russell? Larry Bird? They're not there because time has taken a toll. If a group has a legal trademark, owns the legal rights, and has represented the music of the original recordings in a proper fashion, that group should not be disallowed from representing themselves as the group by name."[21]

Todd Baptista, another promoter who works in the New England area, had a dispute with Robbins when he tried to mount a doo-wop show in New Bedford, Massachusetts. He hired the Flamingos featuring original guitarist and second tenor Terry Johnson, whose falsetto can be heard on their big hit from 1959, "I Only Have Eyes for You." The owner of the Flamingos name, however, is J. C. Carey, who inherited the trademark on the death of his father, Jacob Carey, the original bass singer of the group. Robbins, on hearing of Baptista's show, advertised his own show with Carey's group by billing them as "the only trademarked official Flamingos group performing in the world in an exclusive area appearance!" Baptista contends that "having a trademark or copyright doesn't mean the public is getting what they paid for. [Robbins] has argued that the Boston Celtics no longer contain Larry Bird but are still the Celtics. But the team is not advertised as the '1986 Championship Winning Celtics' when you buy tickets for a 2006 game."[22] Because the Truth in Music Bill gives equal protection to both trademark owner and original performer, disputes among promoters are sure to persist.

Equal protection is a welcome change for performers like Herb Reed. One of the Platters' biggest hits was "The Great Pretender." For Reed, ersatz or even tribute groups are the marketplace manifestations of the Great Pretenders, the equivalent of identity thieves. "They are destroying my legacy by being as bad as they are. There are so many phonies out there. It's like the plague."[23] Historical recognition and the integrity of their music are important to original members. So is being properly compensated. As Veta Gardner, the wife and manager of Carl Gardner, founding member of the Coasters, says, "In the early days, these guys didn't make any money, and here it is, they should be on the Mediterranean somewhere getting big royalties in a nice yacht, and instead of this, someone is stealing their money."[24] For these singers and their families, the hope is that the enforcement of the Truth in Music law will address these inequities in a substantive way.

THE AUDIENCE

Another subgroup in the doo-wop community social structure is the concert-going, radio-listening, and record-buying audience, mostly in their fifties, sixties, and seventies and a fairly equal mix of male and female fans. The core oldies audience since the late-1960s has been white, many of them Jewish or Italian Americans who grew up in urban areas and then relocated to the suburbs. The shared political sentiment of this core audience plays an important role in the dynamic of the doo-wop community. They are, in large part, those members of the white working-class traditionally aligned with the Democratic Party who, over the last forty years, moved their political allegiance to the right.[25] They were the teens or pre-teens of the 1950s who did not identify with the progressive or countercultural politics of the 1960s. The differing political views of this conservative fan base and those of the black performers, many of whom identify with the progressive politics of the last forty years, create divisive issues that are usually submerged beneath the nostalgic surface. What is unspoken, however, is not invisible.

At the December 2, 2000, oldies show in Wallingford, Connecticut, I surveyed ten audience members, five women and five men, during intermission. All were white, and they ranged in age from fifty-five to sixty-five.

Their professions, from which some had retired, were either blue-collar or low-level white-collar jobs including warehouse manager, nurse, legal secretary, transit worker, school teacher, and computer consultant. They all had been listening to doo-wop since their early teens, and nine said they attended at least one doo-wop concert a year. In a attempt to measure the importance of nostalgia versus authenticity, I asked each interviewee to rate on a scale of one ("not important") to five ("very important") the importance of having groups with original members. The average was three, indicating that authenticity as I was defining it was moderately but not overly important. This conclusion is supported by the fact that although all of the respondents could rattle off the names of their favorite groups and their favorite songs in quick succession, very few knew the name of even one member of any of the groups—either black or white.

When asked the question "Why do you like doo-wop?" the majority of their responses involved identifying with the time and place of the music's origins. The 1950s were simpler and happier times not only for them personally but for the nation as a whole. Several of the interviewees had grown up in New York City, which they seemed to take pride in, even though they had moved to the suburbs many years ago. As Shirley B., fifty-eight years old, responded: "Although I now live in Connecticut, I am a native New Yorker from Manhattan's Lower East Side. New York fifties groups were and always will be the greatest artists. It's people like them that make me proud of the era and the place I grew up in."

From the interviews of these ten audience members, whose age, race, and gender profile is typical for the oldies shows I have played for the past two decades, one can draw certain conclusions about the doo-wop fan base. They are a group that has had a life-long relationship with music. They share certain demographic characteristics including race, class, and an urban-to-suburban migration history. Most significant, although there is an intense identification with the music, because the singers remain more or less anonymous, there is less of an identification with the artist than is found in other genres where the performers' names and personal details are well known. The identification with doo-wop singers is more symbolic than personal.

This begs the question of what the circumstances would be if the majority of doo-wop audience members were black. Why is there seemingly no contemporary African American audience for doo-wop? Some writers have pointed to a tendency in the black community to be forward-looking in terms of expressive culture. In the early 1960s, this theory maintains, soul changed the style that would dominate black taste in popular music for the entire decade. Doo-wop was left by the wayside.[26] But this perspective reads the African American community as a monolithic group. And it is refuted by the evidence of a sizable, though still minority, black audience for doo-wop and other styles which I have encountered on the oldies circuit. The race of the promoter and the location of the show can dictate the racial makeup of the audience. At venues such as Boys and Girls High School in Brooklyn and the Apollo in Harlem the audience is almost entirely black. My interviews with people at these concerts revealed that nostalgia for the music of one's youth is not the exclusive province of white America; blacks also feel reverence for past musical practices.

I asked a sixty-two-year-old black woman at the April 4, 1998, concert at the Boys and Girls High School, "So why did you come to the show tonight?" She answered, "Because I grew up in the time of this music and I can relate to it and I love it. I grew up in the doo-wop era. It has a message clearly understood. They say just what they want you to hear. There's no sex in it, there's no 'goin to bed,' none of that. You have to imagine, and I think there's something in the mystique of imagination." Doo-wop was an important part of the soundtrack of this woman's adolescence. Her phrase "mystique of imagination" eloquently counters what has often been criticized as the simplicity of doo-wop lyrics. She implies that doo-wop songs, in what they do not say, can offer space for the imagination to muse about past and present life.

At this point I had yet to develop my survey for interviewing multiple audience members at a show (and, unfortunately I never had another opportunity to use it at a predominantly black-attended show), so I cannot systemically compare the black audience members at this concert with the white audience at the Wallingford show two years later. Possibly the singers are individually anonymous to black fans as well. The urban to suburban migration demographic characteristic of white fans most likely does not apply to the black audience, which I observed to be in the fifty-five- to seventy-five-year-old age range. Boys and Girls High is located in Bedford-Stuyvesant, a predominantly black section of Brooklyn, and, unlike Madison Square Garden, is a local venue whose shows are not heavily advertised outside the immediate vicinity. So assuming that a large proportion of the audience lives nearby, the characteristic white nostalgia for the old neighborhood would not apply. Many of the doo-wop singers still live in their old New York neighborhoods, so a stronger personal connection between singer and audience could be assumed, even if the names of the singers are not familiar.

The racial composition of the audience can also affect how a show is presented. The audience at the October 17, 2000, concert in Madison Square Garden was almost entirely white. The promoter and MC, Richard Nader, acutely aware of the social history of doo-wop, was careful not to make any distinctions in the performance styles of the various groups, who were almost equally divided black and white. At the November 18, 2000, show at St. John's University, Bobby Jay, the black MC, shared an inside joke with the predominantly black audience. After Shep's Limelights exited the stage, knowing that a member of the current group, Clarence Bassett, was an original member of the Videos and the writer of their hit "Trickle, Trickle" (which the Limelights had just sung), Jay commented: "And, of course, you heard they sang the lyrics right? Not like . . . you see I love [the white vocal group] Manhattan Transfer. I love them personally. But they sing the wrong lyrics. 'Ronnie, please lend me your show.' You see, when we were growing up, a short was a car. And if you were talking about a long short you were talking about a Cadillac. [Many in the audience say "yeah."] It's 'Please lend me your short.'" Jay, before a comprehending audience, was making his case for authenticity. By closely critiquing the white Manhattan Transfer on the detail of their performance of a song originally recorded by a black group, he was subtly but publicly reclaiming ownership of his cultural heritage.

Just as race is not a singular determinant of the doo-wop audience, age is not necessarily a defining factor either. Since creating a website for the Cadillacs in 2004, I have received several emails similar to this one from Kevin of Altoona, Alabama, which indicate that the popularity of doo-wop is cross-generational: "I am 29 years old and my parents raised me on great music from the 1950's and 1960's and I prefer music from yesteryear instead of most of today's music because the words were pure and the beats were great." This may be even more true outside the United States. Over the past fifteen years or so there has been a steadily growing American 1950s culture–based performance circuit centered primarily in Europe. At events such as the Screamin' Festival near Barcelona, Spain, the Rhythm Riot in Sussex, England, and the Summer Jamboree in Senigallia, Italy, Europeans, most a generation or two younger than the original teens of the 1950s, dress up in period-specific clothes and listen to performances of music from the American postwar era. Long-standing fanzines like *UK Rock & Roll* keep track of the festival circuit, which also has included annual events in North American cities such as Montreal.

Most of these groups are rockabilly bands, usually featuring a musician playing double bass (instead of electric bass), big hollow- or semihollow-body electric guitars, and stripped-down drum sets sometimes consisting only of a snare drum and crash cymbal. Most of the musicians are amateurs or semiprofessionals playing for the love of the music and to hang out and dance to the other bands. Usually a handful of professional acts, rockabilly legends like Billy Lee Riley or Dale Hawkins, top the bill, and festival organizers also try to hire at least one doo-wop group. The Cadillacs played the Screamin' Festival in Spain in 2006 and 2009. Both times the group was given the royal treatment, fans twenty to forty years younger clamoring for autographs and pictures. As young as they were, many of these fans knew the Cadillac catalog including the more obscure songs. The respectful reverence mixed with youthful exuberance was a combination the Cadillacs had not experienced in many years. This was an audience engaged in *nostalgic tourism*. Doo-wop was not the music of their youth. It was solely an aesthetic choice, a historical tourist destination they would choose to return to again and again.

THE BAND

The *band* is the fourth subgroup in the doo-wop community. Typically comprising a drummer, a bass player, a guitarist, a keyboardist, and saxophonist, the band accompanies or backs up the singers. There are both black and white musicians, and often a mix in the same band.[27] The majority are male. Most bands have a distinct hierarchy. A musical director (MD), often a long-time veteran of the circuit, is in charge and gives the other members musical cues and advice on how the songs should sound. The MD often doubles as musician contractor, the person who hires the different players for each show.

In the 1950s, some groups had singing members who were also their MDs, such as Raoul Cita in the Harptones, who also helped facilitate the recording and performing process.[28] These individuals would often wear many hats: producer, arranger, manager, songwriter, and MD. Jessie Powell was the MD, arranger, and occasional songwriter for the Cadillacs. Like many MDs in the 1950s, Powell got his start playing in big bands and small jazz ensembles in the 1940s.[29]

Carl Vreeland is a white multi-instrumentalist in his mid-forties who has been a contractor and occasional MD for Shirley Alston Reeves.

I have seen him play every instrument in the backup band except saxophone. He has been working with Reeves since the late 1980s—her group was his first oldies gig. He auditioned to be her guitarist, and two weeks later, when the position suddenly became vacant, he became her musical director as well, so he "had to learn the ropes fast."[30] At that time, Reeves, like other oldies acts, was working five nights a week on average and kept a steady group of musicians. In the last few years, oldies circuit singers have been working fewer gigs and are unable to provide the steady employment that would keep musicians dedicated to a single group.[31] This makes it advantageous for vocal groups to have a musician who is familiar with their show who can rehearse new members and lead the band. As Vreeland tells it, "I had to train Shirley into trusting me to work with a circle of guys. They all would learn the show and sometimes you gotta break in new guys. I have a book of musicians that I hire."[32]

Vreeland's job as MD and contractor includes making sure that all the musicians have the itinerary for the show and the proper equipment. He also accompanies the singers on "fly dates," or out-of-town shows where, because of the cost of airline tickets and hotel rooms, it is only feasible to bring the MD. In these circumstances, Vreeland has to rehearse the local musicians hired by the promoter in the afternoon and then lead them through the show that evening. In addition to Shirley Alston Reeves, Vreeland has also been MD and contractor for the Tokens and the Crystals. He juggles his various employers this way: "The key is to please everyone and make sure the dates are covered. And how I do it fairly, for instance, if Shirley is offering me five nights in Vegas, and the Tokens are offering one night, I have to go with the quantity and they understand that."[33]

The current pay scale for band musicians ranges from about $150 to as high as $300 or $400 a show, depending on the prominence of the act, the musician's years of service with the act, and whether or not he is also an MD or contractor. The money is good compared with a typical jazz club date, which can pay less than $100 per night, but the money is not the only reason oldies gigs are attractive to musicians. Unlike at a wedding, which might actually pay more than an oldies gig, the audience has come primarily to hear the music. Since the music is not just aural wallpaper for eating or drinking, the oldies show is usually a more satisfying musical, if not financial, experience. According to Vreeland, "The oldies shows are concerts really. The audience is there to hear the music. You're not background music like at a club. Maybe the oldies circuit doesn't lead to things, but you learn a lot from these artists about the business. With wedding bands you're more like a carpenter. You're just doing a job and you're playing other people's music. With this, you're playing the artist's music."[34]

There are also less club and wedding dates than there used to be. Jim Wacker, a white keyboard player in his mid-fifties who started working on the oldies circuit in the mid-1980s, believes there is just less work in general for musicians these days. "The oldies acts are the only ones who work steady. The Holiday Inn doesn't have live music anymore. In the U.S., live entertainment is a thing of the past to a large extent."[35] Wacker's history is representative of how musicians develop relationships with oldies acts. His first gig was with Chubby Checker in 1985. Before that he had had an eclectic career playing "just about anything" including country, top forty, rock and roll, punk, disco, and heavy metal. A friend was the guitar player with Checker's band, and Wacker auditioned along with many others at a rehearsal studio in Manhattan. There were no chord charts, so the players had to learn Checker's set, which was quite extensive, by ear from a cassette tape. "There was no reading on the stage. Chubby was a band. He didn't change personnel that often [so he expected his musicians to know the show by heart]."[36]

Checker, like many oldies acts performing in the 1970s and 1980s tried his best to resist the "oldies" label but eventually succumbed to the allure of the better money and steadier work of the circuit, a transformation that Wacker witnessed.

> When I joined it was almost a heavy metal band, we were wearing leather and chains and everything. They had a record just released in 1982 with all new material that was getting some airplay. It was in the rider [an addendum to a performance contract] that the word "oldies" was not allowed to appear anywhere in the promotion. But that got phased out after a while as their hits were more and more in the past. When I joined, the sound of "The Twist" [Checker's big hit] wasn't anything like the 1960s version. It was more like [the punk rock band] the Ramones. But now they've gone a little more towards the original and his price has gone up.[37]

In the last several years Wacker, like most band members, has split his time between many different acts, including the Cadillacs, the Tokens, the Platters, the Drifters, the Shangri-Las, and Gary US Bonds. He has also played with one of the Marshak Drifters and remembers when two sets of Drifters showed up for the same gig. For him working with one of the "fake" groups is akin to backing-up an Elvis impersonator. It is just an accepted part of being in show business.

A few musicians have been with the circuit almost from the beginning, but most band members are at least a generation younger than the original singers. Some of them were initially unfamiliar with many of the doo-wop acts. Although they may have heard some of the songs on the radio when they were growing up, their first love was the popular music of their teen years. Bob DesJardins, the current bassist with the Cadillacs, who is white and in his mid-fifties, grew up listening to Motown, the Beatles, and the Rolling Stones. He modeled his playing on that of Jack Bruce, the bassist for Cream. Anthony Vigliotti, a white drummer in his mid-forties, had similar musical influences in his youth. His first oldies gig was with the Marvelettes in 1986, and he went on to work with the Elegants (a fake group first, then Vito Picone's group) and eventually more steadily with Shirley Alston Reeves. He learned to play her hit "Will You Love Me Tomorrow" differently from the original version. As he remembers, "Most of these groups' songs I had to learn on the fly. I'd never listened to their music before. I didn't listen to the records, I just learned from the group. I learned the Shirley gig from a live tape. We've never done it the original way. We've always done the country feel. I didn't know this until later."[38]

Paul Page, a white bassist in his mid-forties, was also introduced to the oldies circuit via Reeves's band.

In the fall of 1985, I was playing in a top-forty band and that business was falling off, drinking ages were being raised, and so forth. A guy in the band had a connection to a booking agency and management company that represented [sixties-era British singer] Bill J. Kramer. In the eighties when the oldies circuit was raging, the plan was for him to move to the U.S. We were hired to be the Dakotas [his backup band]. So it encouraged me to study that music. They tried to avoid the oldies circuit as long as they could [by performing new material]. [But] on that tour we bumped into the oldies circuit, it was inevitable. On one of the package shows we backed up Shirley, in March of 1985. At the time she had a steady band, which she wanted to replace. Billy's thing ran out of gas. Shirley didn't really have charts so we adjusted her style to our band. Those early years, 1986, 1987, we were doing more than 150 dates a year. Throughout the summer we would work five days a week.[39]

For Page, like many of the other white musicians raised on sixties and seventies rock music, working with Shirley and the other acts on the old-ies circuit was like going to rhythm and blues college. "That's when I really learned to read chord charts and to play all the different group styles. We backed up Shirley, Ben E. King with the 'Stand by Me' re-release. Then I was with the Tokens. That was about 200 dates a year. I backed up over 50 groups that had a hit at some time. Playing oldies has taught me great bass-playing from other genres. I'll be with an original band and use what I've learned. It adds authenticity to these contemporary singer-songwriters' work. The oldies circuit is like a classroom for younger musicians."[40]

Page, like Vreeland and Wacker, is also an evolving creative artist and the oldies format, playing the same songs night after night, can become stifling. He tries to strike a balance. "I kind of burned out from the pace and I tried to play with more contemporary acts in New York. But the lure of the money got me back into it. Since 1988, I've been freelance. It's al-lowed me to make a living. I don't play jazz standards, club dates or wed-dings. So as a side man and self-taught rock musician I can make a liv-ing. I pay my rent with oldies acts and [that also allows me to] play with less lucrative contemporary acts."[41]

Another musician who has witnessed the changing fortunes of the old-ies circuit and lifestyle of the oldies band member is the black bass player Cleveland Freeman. Freeman, in his mid-fifties, hails from the musically fertile Jamaica section of eastern Queens.[42] He began his oldies career in the early 1980s working with Arlene Smith of the Chantels and, soon af-ter, with Shirley Alston Reeves. In that decade, he would often go on bus tours with Reeves for weeks at a time. In the nineties, like the other mu-sicians, he started playing for whoever would hire him for the evening. Unlike Vreeland, Wacker, and Page, however, Freeman has always had a day job as a truant officer for the New York City school system and has adjusted his lifestyle accordingly. "Saturday morning I'm getting up at 7:00 a.m. to do a show in Boston with the Cleftones for the Doo-wop Hall of Fame at Symphony Hall. Monday at 8:30 a.m. I'll be back on the job."[43]

Unlike the white musicians, Freeman was a frequent visitor to the Apollo Theatre in his youth and was quite familiar with the vocal groups who are the mainstays of the oldies circuit, especially the black groups. As he says, "This is the music I grew up with and so I met my heroes."[44] Greg Woods, a black keyboard player also in his mid-fifties had a differ-ent relationship with the rhythm and blues of the previous generation. "I didn't grow up with doo-wop. But I did grow up with gospel, the blues, and jazz. Doo-wop was an easy transition. I can see the common roots. By the time I arrived in high school, we had the Temptations. The Mills Brothers and Platters were ancient history. The Cleftones and the Teenagers were old. By the time I was dancing, we had the Delphonics and the Stylistics. Doo-wop had evolved into silky soul. But the history is still remembered."[45] So for Freeman, Wood, and other black musicians there was less of a cultural divide to cross when they started working the oldies circuit. As Woods remarked, "I knew the records. Black folks had their own underground network in terms of music and most of this is out of the black experience."[46]

Both Freeman and Woods have worked as MDs and contractors on the oldies circuit and like Vreeland they have an extensive list of musicians at their disposal. "You gotta have two or three guys in every spot," Freeman explained. Almost as important as musical facility is the ability to work with others with the minimum of personal conflict. "They have to leave their egos at the door. The whole is greater than the sum of its parts."[47] Because there were, and still are, so many doo-wop groups on the circuit, all of these musicians have had to learn how to provide appropriate instrumental support for the genre. As Vreeland told me, "You really have to think of yourself as accompaniment, staying out of their way." When he's breaking in new musicians, "I tell them keep it simple and stay in the groove."[48] Keyboard players like Wacker and Woods must become proficient at playing 12/8 time right-hand triplets for the familiar four-chord ballads and, as Woods says, "keep the songs [harmonically] simple, nothing more than a 7th chord."[49] As a bassist, Page has a special problem particular to doo-wop: "I find it challenging to play with a bass singer. When do you double [the singer's part]? When do you lay out [not play]? It opens your mind up to different things, working with a non-instrumental source."[50]

In addition to reconciling differences of race, age, and musical background the band members must also wrestle with conflicts in their personal lives rooted in class difference, which I define in terms of occupation rather than socioeconomic status.[51] With this in mind I think of the band musicians as belonging to a *musician class*. One element that defines this class is how time is spent. When is leisure time? When is work time? Musicians usually work at night, which means they, like others on the night shift, stay up later and wake up later than the norm, even when they do not have a gig. Because their schedule is different from the societal norm, professional musicians have a kind of outsider status that both binds them together and creates tensions with the non-musicians in their lives.[52]

One prime example of a source of such conflict is Saturday night. For many households, Saturday night is the time many people are likely to go out and *hear* live music. It is also the main gig night for most musicians. Their work time is leisure time for others, including the musicians' partners. A Saturday "night" gig can actually begin in the early afternoon, especially if the musician is a member of the "house band," which will be backing-up most if not all of the acts on that evening's show. The house band must be there to do the sound check and rehearse with all the groups, usually well before showtime. As one musician remarked to me, the "work" is the traveling to the show, setting up the equipment, rehearsing the groups, and waiting to go on. "The show is free."[53] According to Page, "For all-day gigs, hopefully you get as much information ahead of time as possible. I've got a book of charts and tapes on everybody I've played with. Every act is different. Some have a music director who will hand the books around. You'll rehearse the heads and tails [the beginnings and ends of songs]."[54] These all-day gigs result in more time away from family and non-musician friends and can add tension to domestic relationships.

Just before we go on, Freeman likes to remark, "Well, it's just another night with the fellahs!" This comment reveals his awareness of and fondness for the musician class he belongs to. The longevity of the oldies circuit has meant that, like the singers, the band members have created bonds within their subgroup that go back years. Backstage at a February 7, 2002, show in Wilmington, Delaware, I listened as Freeman and Woods rattled off name after name of professional musicians they have come to know over the past thirty years. The oldies circuit is a memory-saturated environment on many levels. Common personal history coincides with common musical canon. Often during rehearsals Freeman will boast, "Just call it!" daring Woods and others to name any song and he will prove that he can play it. With these phrases, he is defining the social territory of the band member, by celebrating the lifestyle as male bonding and by calling attention to intragroup competence.[55]

Another important defining aspect of the musician class is the fact that it is generally a freelance profession, which engenders a particular attitude toward work. With the freelance lifestyle comes the fear of the consequence of not taking a gig, which may result in losing favor with the contractors or the artists themselves. Musicians know that if they turn down too much work, the phone may stop ringing. Because of the anxiety of dropping out of the circuit, the "next gig" is always the priority in the working musician's life. According to Freeman, when he gets a call for a job, it is never a matter of whether he *wants* to do the gig, just if he *can*. So he simply asks, "Where, when, and how much?"

The steadily dwindling performance schedules of the oldies performers have added to this "next gig" anxiety, making the careers of musicians like Paul Page less predictable. "Physically they [the oldies performers] are slowing down and there just isn't the market. I've had my ups and downs. I have to be more proactive as a freelance musician."[56] This uncertainty and pressure can cause conflict in a musician's personal life, and is a reason why many musicians choose to be single. An alternative is having a partner who is also a musician or in some other entertainment profession. Katrina Ruiz, the wife of Richard Ruiz, the main drummer for the Cadillacs for many years, sings full-time with a wedding band. Since they both work primarily on weekend evenings, both are home during the day, and that is when they spend time together and share domestic duties.

The doo-wop community has a deep, musically suffused relationship with time, personal memory, and history. The long, relatively stable history of this community and its connection to a deeper historical interaction of music, race, and nostalgia that predates doo-wop result in a dynamic performance environment filled with discourses both musical and nonmusical. By labeling this aggregation a "community" I do not mean to imply that there is a unified front or consensus of opinion regarding music, race, and nostalgia. All the members of the various subgroups have their own agendas, which are often in conflict with others'. It can be argued, however, that there have been changes for the better in terms of financial restitution and historical recognition. The take-away message that can be inferred from oldies performances, where blacks and whites are seen sharing the same space and singing in harmony, is "Racism—Bad; Pluralism—Good." Given the history of racial injustice associated with doo-wop, this message can certainly be construed as a conscious attempt at righting a past wrong.[57]

Nevertheless, traditional paradigms of power relations, although cloaked in new language, persist. New images of racial interaction may be supplanting old ones, but whatever images are represented are still directed by the people in charge. He who produces the show calls the tune.

The representation of race relations has been revised, but this does not necessarily solve the problems of appropriation and exploitation. The sound and image of "harmony," both musical and social, sells, and ultimately selling is the engine that drives whatever social transformations may or may not be taking place.[58] The interplay between the exigencies and demands of the marketplace and the yearning for political, social, and cultural transformation will always exist. What is unique, and fascinating, about the doo-wop community is that its longevity and the continuity of social relations at its heart have provided opportunities for the kind of slowly evolving dialectic necessary for real change. Behind the spectacle of the oldies show this complex dialectic continues to play out in the lives of oldies circuit performers.

CHAPTER 5 **THE OLDIES CIRCUIT**

began playing on the oldies circuit in 1987 with Speedo and the Cadillacs, and then twelve years later I started working with Shirley Alston Reeves, the former lead singer of the Shirelles. My relationship with both groups, on both the professional and the personal level, has grown steadily deeper ever since. Being on the stage and making music has always been the first order of business, but certain experiences compelled me to take a closer look at the social network I was involved in.

One such experience occurred backstage on December 2, 2000, at the Oakdale Theatre in Wallingford, Connecticut. The conversation turned to stories of being on the road in the 1950s and 1960s. Present in the dressing room were Cadillacs Earl Carroll, Bobby Phillips, and Gary Lewis, and musical director Eddie Jones. Also present were three members of the band including me, the only white person in the room.

CARROLL: You know how long it was before a black act could sleep in Las Vegas?

LEWIS: A *long* time.

CARROLL: I mean the stars, I mean, Nat King Cole, Pearl Bailey, all of them. They had to go through the kitchen.

LEWIS: You're talkin' about the fifties, now.

CARROLL: They couldn't get one of them rooms. You had to go across the tracks.

LEWIS: Uh huh.

CARROLL: That boy, Cal Green, man. Played with the Midnighters? He got caught for a roach [a partially smoked marijuana cigarette] and got fifteen years.

LEWIS: In Vegas?

CARROLL: No, through the South. That was days of that Emmett Till shit.[1]

LEWIS: Yeah, yeah.

CARROLL: What they did to that poor boy was so sad.

PHILLIPS: Oh, yeah.

CARROLL: You know that got to be the devil, man.

PHILLIPS: Mm hm.

CARROLL: And they are still doing that shit today.

PHILLIPS, LEWIS: Yeah, man.

CARROLL: They dragged that man in back of that truck.

PHILLIPS: Yeah, yeah in Texas.[2]

LEWIS [looking at me, smiling]: You better watch them devils.

[Laughter all around]

CARROLL [laughing and pointing at me]: Yeah, John, looked up and said, "What, has we got one in here?"

In this exchange Lewis and Carroll took a deeply serious subject and injected it with humor, by putting me on the spot, in a light-hearted way. Carroll claims I was trying to blend in, not be white, pretending that I had a surprised look on my face, as if to say "Who me?" I knew I was being teased, but I appreciated their comments because I felt they were trying to include me in the conversation—it would have been worse if they had pretended I was not there. Nevertheless, it reminded me that racial difference was not going to be overlooked, at least not in the Cadillacs' dressing room. Color blindness was not an option.

This is a common scenario backstage at a Cadillacs show. Remembrances of past racial confrontations are mixed with interpretations of current affairs, which can evolve into performative events laced with comedy or infused with pathos depending on who is in the room. Also intertwined is commentary on the inevitable aging of the doo-wop community. The subjects of memory, race, money, and aging circulate under the rubric of group harmony singing, which provides the cultural context and social space where these stories can be told. This is life on the oldies circuit, a world I became much more deeply involved in during fall 2001.

BECOMING A CADILLAC

Currently the vocal group Speedo and the Cadillacs consists of three African American men: leader and first tenor Earl "Speedo" Carroll, born November 2, 1937; bass Bobby Phillips, born January 28, 1935; and baritone Gary Lewis, born February 4, 1942. Lewis, like the others, is a long-time veteran of the vocal group scene. He was born and raised in Boston and demonstrated a love of dancing at an early age (in 1960 he and his partner won the Harvest Moon Ball Dance Contest in the Couples Lindy Hop). He was also a fan of doo-wop, especially the groups like the Cadillacs known for their dancing. In 1961 he joined the Crests and later became a member of the Drifters while also teaching choreography to other vocal groups.[3] He joined the latter-day Cadillacs in 1981.[4]

A fourth man, Eddie Jones, also black, who died in 2007, was, until 2001, the Cadillacs' pianist, MD, and second tenor. He was born in 1934 in Los Angeles. His father had been musical director for the Delta Rhythm Boys and for the Lamplighters (with whom the younger Jones also sang in the mid-1950s).[5] In 1951 Jones moved to New York, where briefly he was the lead tenor with the Solitaires. Later he was lead tenor in the Demens, for whom he wrote "Take Me as I Am," which was released on Teenage records in 1957.[6] It was his work as vocal arranger and MD for many of the groups of this era, including the Bobbettes, the Chantels, and Little Anthony and the Imperials, that established his reputation in the doo-wop world.[7] And it was this reputation that led Carroll to enlist Jones's services as MD in 1981.[8] When I joined as guitarist in 1987, there was another singer with the group, second tenor Johnny Brown, also African American and of the same generation as the others.[9] This lineup gave the Cadillacs a four-part harmony sound with Carroll, Phillips, Lewis, and Brown in front of the band displaying the signature group choreography. In 1998, I arrived for a show to find that Brown had not only suddenly left the group but abruptly left town. He died in Seattle in 2004. After this, Jones sang second tenor from behind the piano.

In August 2001, Carroll, upset with Jones for what he and the others considered a serious drinking problem that would often negatively affect the shows, offered the second tenor spot to me. I had mixed feelings about this turn of events. Jones had become a good friend over the years along with the rest of the group, and he was also important in my research. But here was an opportunity not only to sing with the Cadillacs but also to gain access to another realm of the doo-wop community. I had to weigh my allegiance to Jones as a friend against my interests as a performer and a researcher. This was not the first time Carroll had threatened to replace Jones as a singing member of the group, and so, knowing that there was the distinct possibility that Jones would be fired whether I took the job or not, I accepted Carroll's offer. Jones retained his job as MD.

On the evening of August 27, 2001, I had my first rehearsal with the Cadillacs at Public School 87 on the Upper West Side of Manhattan, where Carroll worked as a custodian during the day. The rehearsal is a rich site for exploring any musical culture, and doo-wop is no exception. The intimacy of harmonizing allows singers to really get to know one another's voices in both a musical and a social sense. Working out song arrangements and harmony parts requires close listening and a commitment to cooperation.[10] At the first rehearsal, it was just the five of us—Carroll, Phillips, and Lewis, with me on guitar and Jones at the piano—in the school's music room. In addition to the lyrics of the songs, including the right background syllables, I had to learn to blend my voice's timbre with the others. I had some difficulty at first, and Phillips said, "You better be careful Speedo don't turn around on you in the show." He was referring to Carroll's literally stopping the show on several occasions to turn around and yell at Jones for making a mistake. Everyone, including Jones, laughed, and this moment of levity helped smooth my entry into the rehearsal environment.

A week later we had another rehearsal, but this time without Jones, and I learned how much the group depended on him for their notes, even after so many years of singing the same songs. Jones was one the few musicians on the oldies circuit who could be both MD and vocal arranger. The vocal arranger has always played a vital role in doo-wop practice, providing pitch references and instrumental accompaniment. In the present day, someone like Jones, who had done this kind of work since the 1950s, also serves as a cultural standard-bearer, the one whose responsibility it is to remember and relay the distinctive harmonic practice of doo-wop. I use the word "practice" because learning to sing the Cadillacs' repertoire involves more than just memorizing a fixed vocal line that your predecessor may have sung and your successor may sing. One must learn the doo-wop style, the range of options that work within the genre. In my first rehearsals with the Cadillacs I discovered that their approach is less rigid than I had expected. There is flexibility in choosing harmony notes, within the agreed–on parameters. Doo-wop singers make music in a flexible creative process with an understood but by no means fixed set of options.

My first rehearsals with the group were for a show in Honolulu on September 15, and I was getting nervous. Would I be able to sing my part and play the guitar at the same time? Then on September 11, 2001, life was thrown into complete disarray. Jones lived near the World Trade Center and although he and his family and their building were unharmed, he would live with the sight, sound, and smell of the tragedy and its aftermath for months. His drinking increased.

Having yet to receive word that the upcoming show was to be cancelled, we rehearsed on September 13. Jones began to fine-tune my technique. He corrected my articulation on the background syllables for the song "Zoom" ("Bong, sha-dooby-dooby, bong, bong, bong"), instructing me to "snatch the notes," meaning give it a sharper attack. On "Speedoo" (where Jones sang a fifth part), he showed me how to simulate a muted trumpet for the high second tenor part by tightening my lips into an oval shape and placing the "wah, wah" syllables at the top of my mouth or hard palate, resulting in a closed nasal timbre. Jones also instructed me to slide into the note, carefully listening to the other vocal parts for the right pitch location to "land" on after the slide.

The next day we learned that the gig had been postponed until October 6. We took a couple of weeks off, meeting again to rehearse on October 3. Somehow in the midst of all the trauma and upheaval, we were able to continue with my training as second tenor. Jones showed me how to lead the other singers in an a cappella section toward the end of "Gloria" where the background singers hold an E minor seventh chord on the syllable "ooh" over which Carroll sings "Glo-ri-a" in a metrically free style. As soon as he finishes singing a triplet turn on the syllable "a," I sing, just slightly ahead of and thus leading Lewis and Phillips, the last two notes of a triplet in answer to Carroll. We all then hold an A13 chord until we feel our breath running out, simultaneously inhale, and then sing the notes of the tonic D major chord, during which the tempo of the song is reestablished by the MD's count. This is a subtle and intricate maneuver that took me months to master.

At this rehearsal I began to get feedback that, although cast in musical terms, seemed to address my social position in the group. Phillips said I was "just a little too tender" or tentative on the "Speedoo" harmony part. Jones told Carroll, "[John] just sings a different way. I guess that's the way it's going to be. He needs more roundness and he's just not loud enough." Carroll eased some of the tension by saying, "He'll get it. He's just got to learn to blend." Although his comment ostensibly referred to my singing, I could not help but think about how "blending in" with the Cadillacs was actually a complex case of learning to harmonize both musically and socially.

I was a younger, college-educated white man from a small town in New Jersey who had learned to sing by emulating the white rock singers of the 1960s and 1970s. Now I was spending time with an older generation of African American men with grade school educations (except Lewis, who had gone to college for a short time). Carroll and Phillips had dropped out of high school when the Cadillacs made their first record, and they had lived most of their lives in the New York City area, where they were nurtured in the rhythm and blues singing tradition of their youth. Yet we were not strangers to one another. I had spent much of my adult life performing with these men, and they had witnessed many of my ups and downs. They had become more than just professional colleagues or mentors. They were my friends. The "blending" that we were attempting to do at this time, while facilitated by our preexisting friendship, still involved the negotiation of generational, racial, educational, and musical differences.

Complicating matters further was the issue of my replacing Jones as second tenor. Backstage at the Honolulu gig, I had a chance to talk with him, and told him I had mixed feelings about the situation. He shrugged it off with, "Don't worry about it. You gotta do what you gotta do," and that was all he had to say. I thanked him for his generosity and understanding and said I looked forward to continuing to work and learn from him in the future.

However, the groundwork for Jones's departure from the group was laid at the Honolulu show. He had been drinking and had not had a decent night's sleep since 9/11. By showtime he was in pretty bad shape. We had to use a local house band unfamiliar with our music, so the MD's job was particularly important. Jones started the first song in a tempo that was far too slow. He completely flubbed the beginning of the second song of the night, "No Chance," and I turned around and restarted the song quickly after it fell apart. Before the next number, I looked at him to ask whether he or I should start it. He nodded toward me. I assumed this responsibility for the rest of the show and later that evening I wondered if I would be doing this for the whole show in the future. Indeed, by the following March Jones was out and I was now guitarist, second tenor, and MD for the Cadillacs.

THE BIG FIVE

The typical Cadillacs show, what they refer to as *The Big Five*, follows the same format each performance: five songs—the group's big hits—with standard introductions, the same updated Cholly Atkins choreography, and comic routines between numbers. This between-song patter, which I have watched the Cadillacs develop over the past twenty-three years, is integral to the show. Stage patter—"jiving" or talking and kidding onstage—has a long history in African American vocal harmony. It was common with secular vocal groups of the 1930s, and a similar practice has also existed among gospel quartets.[11]

The *Cadillacs' Big Five* format is structured as follows:

"Peek-A-Boo" (1958); Coasters-style, comic, up-tempo tune

Patter about "love" and "nose"

"The Girl I Love" (1956); first ballad

Patter about "the Fifties"

"Zoom" (1956); first jump-blues tune

Patter about "baby brother"; "Birds, Bees, Fleas"

"Gloria" (1954); second ballad

Patter about "rock and roll"

"Speedoo" (1955); finale, second jump-blues tune

The set begins with the Cadillacs creeping on stage in afraid-in-a-haunted-house fashion to the opening notes of their song "Peek-a-Boo," a novelty tune from their Coasters-influenced period. They make funny faces and gestures to portray the comic elements in the song. When the first song ends, the spoken part of their performance, the patter, begins. Depending on the racial make-up of the audience, the patter and how they deliver it can have an evocative resonance peculiar to the oldies circuit. To the opening chords of the ballad "The Girl I Love," Carroll says, "I don't know how many of you out there in the listening audience really relate to the fifties, but if you do, you know in the fifties every rock 'n' socker I knew was hope-to-die in love, including myself. I had a young lady that had my nose so wide open you could run a freight train through it. Oh, I was in love." His reference to his nose usually does not get much of a reaction from white audiences, but black audiences typically laugh and clap their hands in recognition. "Having your nose wide open," Carroll has told me, was a common expression in his old Harlem neighborhood for being sexually aroused.

By invoking this phrase, Carroll is engaging in an insider racial discourse. In the 1950s, black male singers often could not directly face their white audiences, much less make sexual references, lest the perceived interest of white female audience members provoke violent reactions from the white males in the audience. The kind of racially specific signifying exemplified by Carroll's patter is certainly no longer as dangerous a gesture as it once was. But because such subjects usually remain unarticulated at oldies shows, the repression of this complex racial history infuses such a moment with a subtle but palpable resonance. Intentionally or not, Carroll is continuing a discourse unique to the doo-wop world which references the historical relation of race and popular music performance.

Before the next song, "Zoom," an up-tempo jump blues, the patter turns again to the 1950s, but without racial inference. This time the topic is growing old, a typical trope for doo-wop performers, which draws attention to and reaffirms the nostalgia that frames their world.

> CARROLL: Moving right along, here's a tune we had the pleasure
> of recording way back in nineteen fifty [wipes his hand over
> his mouth].
> PHILLIPS AND LEWIS: Wait a minute, wait a minute. Watch it, Earl.

As we begin to play the next song, "Gloria," Carroll introduces the Cadillacs and then the band, which he has called on various occasions "The Fleetwoods," "The All-stars," and "The Hubcaps." He then points to me and says, "And the young man on guitar right back here, that's my baby brother over on my daddy's side." Phillips chimes in, "Oh, no wonder."

I have learned to play along with the routine, always acting surprised by the comment and then smiling and nodding at the audience as if to say, "Yeah, right. Don't you believe it.." Usually white audiences laugh as much as black ones. Carroll wants to bring something to our attention. He is, in effect, saying, "Look how this young white guy is up here making music with—and working for—these aging black men. There's something unusual about this, right?"

But below the surface of this performer-audience exchange echoes the racial history of the music, the complicated memory of the decade in which the music was born, when such a thing would have been impossible. Beneath the surface also is a subtle commentary on the current social structure of the doo-wop community. Part of what goes on at doo-wop shows is the performance of a certain utopian dream of racial harmony. By indirect or nonpolemical means we are encouraged to imagine a different, more desirable way of being in the world.[12] The doo-wop stage is a performance space where white and black musicians participate in a tradition forged in racial interdependence.

The artists slip in and out of awareness of these utopian inferences. This allows them just to enjoy making music for its own sake and making a living. And when it suits them they can look at what they are doing from a wider angle. Carroll's "baby brother" commentary both subverts and supports an ideal, integrated society our presence together imagines. He is playing with the utopian dream, offering it for contemplation while keeping it safely cloaked in humor for those who would rather not dig too deeply.

Carroll usually introduces, "Gloria," this way: "This next tune is something like the national anthem of the doo-wops. But we're very proud to say we're the first one to put this one on the map. That's right. Well, it was recorded by "the Birds," "the Bees," "the Trees," and "the Fleas." They all recorded it. But I'm kind of proud to say we're still the first ones that did it." By rattling off band names (fictitious and not), Carroll is sardonically commenting on the multiplicity and diversity of voices and groups that comprise the history of this song, whose very authorship is disputed—and again his remarks are infused with racial resonance.

"Gloria" has passed though many hands on its way to the oldies circuit: written by the New Orleans mixed-race Creole record company owner Leon Rene in 1946; recorded in the late 1940s by black artists Charles Brown and the Mills Brothers; transformed on the streets of early 1950s Harlem into a doo-wop ballad by the Cadillacs; copyrighted in its new form by their white Jewish manager Esther Navarro on its release in 1954; covered in the late 1950s by Italian American groups like the Passions and the Salutations; and then elevated to nostalgic icon status in numerous performances by white and black groups on the oldies circuit since the early 1970s. When Carroll closes his eyes and sings the familiar, sweet falsetto-lifted line "Gloria, it's not Marie, it's Gloria," he is doing more than just singing about lost or unrequited love. He is also reasserting his ownership of the long, racially mixed legacy of this song and what it has come to represent.

Carroll and many other black performers have a particular way of speaking to each other which melds life backstage, in rehearsal, and on the road with onstage performance, transferring the energy of the stage to the other realms of show biz life. When Carroll sees an old friend before the show and enthusiastically greets him with, "Well, whaddaya know you rascal? How they treating ya?" and replies to "How you been?" (in a way that everyone in room can hear) with "Well, you know, chicken today, feathers tomorrow," there is a continuity between behind-the-scenes talk and what is said in front of concert audience, and the doo-wop gig experience is enriched as a result.[13]

Another favorite phrase of Carroll's expresses the ambivalence an old-ies singer can have about performing. Although he is always grateful for the work, at Carroll's age it can take a lot out of him. So right before we go on, he will say something like "Let's get this over with so we can blind 'em with ass!" (i.e., finish and leave so quickly that all the audience will see is our backsides). While on the surface it may just mean "let's get out of here and go home," on a deeper level the phrase reveals the feeling of wanting to escape or separate oneself from an uncomfortable situation—understandable, considering the racial history of this music. (Also, the phrase speaks about the nature of show business, where dazzling the audience with sexually provocative gestures is stock-in-trade.)

Before the last number of *The Big Five*, the exuberant up-tempo jump-blues "Speedoo," Carroll connects the energetic timbre, tone, and sentiment from his backstage performance to the show itself: "Are you ready to rock and roll? [He waits for a response from the audience.] I said are you ready to rock and roll? [Once again, he waits for the response.] Well then, I guess we better rock and roll!" Phillips intones the first three notes of the bass line, which cues the band to start the song. As the music begins and we sing the background vocals, Carroll picks up his cane and dons his top hat just like his childhood idol Bill "Bojangles" Robinson would do. Soon the group is in their high-stepping glory, promenading across the stage and into the audience in an extended vamp that can last for ten minutes or more. During the onstage portion of the vamp, Carroll does his version of a dance called "the Itch," also known as "the Heebie Jeebies," made famous in the 1920s and 1930s by the African American dance duo Butterbeans and Suzie.[14] While Phillips and Lewis stand to the side and clap their hands, Carroll turns his back to the audience, extends his backside, and commences to "scratch" that and other parts of his body in time to the music. What he said backstage right before we went on is now part of the show. This song and *The Big Five* end with the three Cadillacs marching off stage as Carroll tips his hat one last time.

JOINING THE SHIRLEY ALSTON REEVES BAND

Shirley Alston Reeves was born Shirley Owens on June 10, 1941, in North Carolina and moved to Passaic, New Jersey, at a young age. It was at Passaic High School in 1958 that she began singing with the other members of the group that would eventually become the Shirelles. They had two number one pop hits on which Reeves sang lead, as she did for most of the Shirelles' records: "Will You Love Me Tomorrow" (1960) and "Soldier Boy" (1962). Because in the 1970s she went solo and relinquished any rights to the group name, Reeves must advertise her shows as "Shirley Alston Reeves, former lead singer of the Shirelles," and not simply under the group moniker, even though she performs with two other women as a vocal group act (at the time of this writing her singers were Iris Lammers, who is Hispanic and in her forties, and Tanya Alexander, a black singer in her thirties).

Critical to any discussion of Reeves's career is her long-time MC, body-guard, and valet, Ronnie Evans, who died in July 2004 at the approximate age of seventy-seven (his birth year has always been a closely guarded secret). I was fortunate enough to join the group in fall 1999 when Evans was still part of the act. Evans was a gay black man well over six feet tall, extroverted and flamboyant, whose nickname was "Diva." He would go onstage at the beginning of the show announcing, "They'll make your back crack, your liver quiver, and your knees freeze. And if you don't dig that you've got a hole in your soul. So let's give a big warm welcome for my gal, your gal, everybody's gal—the fabulous Shirley Alston Reeves!" After the group came on he would stay and play the maracas, occasionally interjecting comments and exhorting the crowd. Offstage Evans had many stories to tell about life in show business, and as a gay black man his point of view was different from the one usually heard on the oldies circuit.

Unlike Earl Carroll, who had a day job as a custodian for twenty years and usually performs only once or twice month, Reeves's sole career has been as an entertainer. She works primarily in the Northeast, though she does perform in the rest of the country as well. For the local New York–area performances she usually brings her own band, of which I had been an occasional member. I discovered before too long that Reeves has been one of the most reliable employers of band musicians for over a quarter century. Many a guitarist, bassist, drummer, and keyboardist have passed through her ranks. When Reeves is one of several acts on an oldies ticket she usually plays just the Shirelles' hits, in this order: "Mama Said" (1961); "Baby It's You" (1961); "Everybody Loves a Lover" (1962); Tonight's the Night" (1960); "Foolish Little Girl" (1963); "Will You Love Me Tomorrow" (1960); "Soldier Boy" (1962). Often, however, she's the only act in a show and will have to play for as long as ninety minutes or more. On these occasions she performs other girl group numbers such as Martha and the Vandellas' "Heat Wave" (1963), the Dixie Cups' "Chapel of Love" (1964), the Bobbettes' "Mr. Lee" (1957), and the Crystals' "Da Doo Run Run" (1963) and a medley of tunes by the Drifters as well as songs by Little Richard, Chuck Berry, Fats Domino, Sam Cooke, and the Teenagers.

Reeves prefers that her musicians not read from chord charts when they perform, and I was amazed at how many musicians had memorized her arrangements. Because everyone in the band must know these songs by heart, new members are expected to study the chord charts and listen to a tape of Reeves's show before their first gig with her. According to her veteran band member Cleveland Freeman, Reeves thinks that it looks unprofessional when her musicians "have their heads buried in the charts."[15] Another reason this no-chart approach is important to a Reeves performance is that often the song order, especially for longer shows, is not decided before show-time. The MD for the evening is expected to anticipate the song order, and so the other musicians need to be paying attention.

In my time with the group the MD was either Greg Woods or Carl Vreeland. I learned through observation and eventually confirmed by interviewing Vreeland how the sequence of songs is subtly strung together as the show progresses. Reeves prefers a certain sequence of Shirelles songs, but before and after those numbers she likes to "feel her way through," depending on what she thinks will work with that particular night's audience. There is no discussion or hesitation onstage. The appearance of a preconceived song order is accomplished by Reeves and her MD communicating through cues embedded in her between-song patter. Communication can be further complicated if both Woods and Vreeland are on the gig so there are two potential MDs present. As Vreeland describes it, "Sometimes not only can I sense what song she wants to do, but sometimes she'll give me a cue no one else will notice. After 'Blueberry Hill,' I might guide her into 'Mama Said' [by leading the band in the opening chords]. Sometimes she may ignore our cue and she'll say something over the mike to cancel. Once Greg wanted to do 'Heat Wave' [and the band was about to follow him] when Shirley said 'It's time to go way back' meaning 'Mr. Lee.' "[16] All of this happens very quickly, and even when there is the occasional miscommunication, rarely is it obvious enough for the audience to notice—a sign of both the competence of the individual musicians and the overall coherence of the ensemble.

This is a group of musicians who take pride in their work and appreciate the opportunity to be entertainers that working with Reeves affords them. As Woods wrote in an email he sent to other members of the band after a show, "No slackers in this organization. I respect all you guys as musicians. And as time goes on, I respect even more how special what we have going on is. I was telling someone that working with Shirley is more like a family outing than a gig. It is great that we enjoy what we are doing. And I am not surprised that so many other artists have raided the pool [of Reeves's musicians] for their own shows."[17] Once I had memorized Reeves's entire repertoire and understood the onstage communication, I, too, became a member of the family, at least on a part-time basis.

VOCAL BEHAVIOR

As my research deepened, I decided to break down my experiences on the oldies circuit into discrete categories based on where the experiences occurred and what happened there. The three primary locations where I performed my research were *offstage, onstage,* and *in the audience.* Three kinds of *vocal behavior* occurred in these locations: *speech, stage speech,* and *singing.*

Offstage sublocations included *backstage* before, during, and after the show; *rehearsals; the meeting place* where we waited for the transportation to the show; *the ride* to the show, which can be train, plane, or automobile; and *interview sites,* where the roles of ethnographer and informant are more clearly delineated. *Speech* is the main vocal behavior in all these sublocations except at rehearsals, where *singing* is generally the dominant modality. In addition to *singing* their songs, *onstage* the performers engage in *between-song patter,* a form of *stage speech. In the audience* sublocations are the *theater,* where both *singing* by the audience and *speech* takes place, and in the *lobby,* where *speech* occurs before the show, during intermission, and after the show.

One can consider *speech* and *singing* discrete domains of human behavior with different contexts and functions. Because of the common dominator of physical vocal production, one can also perceive *speech* and *singing* as two endpoints on a continuum.[18] Two criteria, *range of tone* and *rate of improvisation,* can be used to delineate the kinds of vocal behavior arranged along the continuum. At one end of the continuum a *narrow range of tone* and a *high rate of improvisation* characterizes *speech. Stage speech,* which is at the midpoint of the continuum, features a *wider tonal range* and a *lower rate of improvisation,* by comparison. *Singing,* the third category at the other end of the continuum, has a *very wide tonal range* and, because in doo-wop shows the songs are usually performed the same way each time, the *rate of improvisation* is low.

A second semantic continuum runs parallel to the vocal-production continuum, with *rationality* corresponding to the speech endpoint, and *emotionality* corresponding to the singing endpoint. The degree to which meaning is acquired from the unheard, non-sonic context delineates rationality from emotionality. Speech acquires greater meaning from the people, places, and things to which its sounds refer than from the sounds themselves. It engages more actively the intellectual or rational realm of the psyche. With singing, by contrast, the heard, sonic experience is a semantic end in itself. It connects more directly to the emotional realm of the psyche.[19] On the semantic continuum stage speech belongs somewhere between normal speech and singing. While still recognizable as speech to the listener and experienced on a rational level (acquiring meaning from its unheard, non-sonic objects), it also can be experienced on an emotional level (acquiring meaning from the sound itself) not only because of its wider tonal range and less improvisatory character, but also because of its being situated onstage in a musical performance.

While certain locations have expected modes of vocal behavior, the nature of this behavior should not be assumed to be static or predictable. There may be rules or expectations, but the "actors" within these "performance" settings have a certain amount of freedom to create and improvise. Improvisation can lead to revised or new perspectives on the rules and expectations of these locations and in turn lead to revised or new future "performances."[20] Sometimes a state of self-awareness on the part of the actors is achieved within a particular location, which leads them to take certain behavior with an accepted meaning and make it mean something else. This is analogous to a change of key in a musical performance such as shifting the tonal center of a song from B-flat major to C major.[21] When Earl Carroll refers to me as "baby brother," he is transcending the normal band introduction and "changing key" to a subtle commentary on race and generational difference.

By delineating vocal behavior in this way I want to draw the reader's attention to how members of the doo-wop community use their voices in different ways to achieve different results. If a doo-wop group is singing well on-stage, the audience may be moved to tears or may give the group a standing ovation. This response could lead to more gigs, although not necessarily to the sale of new recordings by the group. If, during their stage speech, the group makes a joke about how they have sold millions of records but somehow are not millionaires, they have raised a serious issue in a lighthearted manner which may or may not make the audience a little more sympathetic to their situation. Or if offstage after the show the leader of the group makes an impassioned speech about how in the past he had a number one hit from which he made little money and now he has made a new record which few will buy because they are only interested in the number one hit from which he still makes little money, those listening may be moved to take action. Or maybe the group will add another joke about it to their show. Or maybe they will try to slip the new song into the act. There is a feedback loop—a circuit within the oldies circuit—between what is experienced offstage, onstage, and in the audience which, over time, can inform and transform the performances contained in those locations.

These locations are also influenced by interactions with external forces. The promotion of and commentary about doo-wop and oldies circuit shows in the print, broadcast, and online media can infiltrate and infuse the vocal behavior. The history of doo-wop and the oldies circuit as remembered by the community, together with their personal histories, flows through the inner circuit as well. In a world where nostalgia is king, pasts are always present. The vocal behavior found in these locations is the means the doo-wop community uses to navigate, comprehend, and transform their world.

In spring 2003 I played a show on the oldies circuit nearly every weekend. Between March 13 and June 13, I did ten shows. Five were with the Cadillacs and five with Shirley Alston Reeves. All were in the Northeast, from Boston south to outside of Washington, D.C., in venues ranging from small catering halls such as Masso's in Williamstown, New Jersey, on April 11 to large arenas such as the Kimmel Center in Philadelphia on April 19. In the second through the fifth show in this sequence, from March 29 through April 19, I paid close attention to the experiences, organizing my data according to the vocal behavior framework.

Familiar issues surfaced, like echoes within the socially reverberant spaces offstage, onstage, and in the audience. A definition of *echo* is "to send back or repeat."[22] When something echoes, a relationship with a past time is assumed. A past experience is being reexperienced in some way in the present time. Echoing at the heart of the doo-wop community is a deep historical relationship between race, nostalgia, and vocal harmony, and the members of this community are engaged in an ongoing process of harmonizing these elements.

Shows on the oldies circuit are framed as nostalgic events. Nostalgia is a means for connecting the present with the past by creating an experiential bridge that usually passes over dissonance or conflict to create the illusion of a more serene personal and collective continuity.[23] Vocal behavior in the doo-wop community also addresses discontinuities, especially concerning issues of money, race relations, and recognition. The metaphorical echoing of past experience in the present can disrupt the aura of continuity and undermine illusions about received history and social relations surrounding this music. When such cognitively dissonant echoes of the past surface, present circumstances can be augmented and even transformed. Doo-wop discursive practice includes the reconciliation, transcendence, and transformation of these discontinuities.

50 PERCENT OF SOMETHING

On the way from Penn Station in Newark, New Jersey, where I frequently met the Shirley Alston Reeves entourage, to a March 29, 2003, concert at W. J. Clarke High School in Westbury, New York, our van broke down in a heavy rainstorm on the busy Staten Island Expressway. We were stranded for almost forty-five minutes until AAA came and towed us to a nearby gas station, where we left the van. We hitched a cramped ride with the drummer, Anthony Vigliotti, who fortunately lived on Staten Island.

While we were waiting in the van for AAA, the conversation turned to the subject of music lawyer Chuck Rubin, who had created the New York–based Artists Rights Enforcement Corporation in the 1980s to recover unpaid royalties for many of the artists from the early days of rock and roll. The topic had come up because of a recent ruling in a major lawsuit for several million dollars, in which Rubin was involved, brought against Phil Spector, the legendary girl group producer, by his former wife and protégé, Ronnie Spector. She, along with the two other Ronettes, had filed for breach of contract, loss of earnings, and part ownership of the Ronettes' master recordings.[24] In October 2002 the New York State Court of Appeals ruled in Phil Spector's favor, stating that the Ronettes were not entitled to master recording ownership, which denied them access to the lucrative synchronization rights to the use of their music in movies, television, and advertisements. The court did rule for the plaintiffs that they were owed for performer royalties. Chuck Rubin, the Ronettes' lawyer, called it "a mixed decision."

Mixed decisions and compromise are par for the course in oldies litigation. The Ronettes' case was one of several that followed a landmark 1991 Sixth U.S. Circuit Court of Appeals ruling, also involving Rubin's organization, which stated that two Nashville record labels owed $1.2 million in back royalties to several performers, including the original members of the Shirelles.[25] Such settlement figures can be deceptive, because often a large portion of the settlement is paid to the attorneys involved. During our conversation on the highway that night, Reeves used the phrase that has come to be associated with Chuck Rubin: "50 percent of something is better than 100 percent of nothing," referring to the fact that Rubin's fee is 50 percent of the settlement. For Reeves as for many of the oldies performers and songwriters who have turned to Rubin for help, these were acceptable terms.

Another such artist is William "Prez" Tyus, the original manager and songwriter for the Students, whom I have known since the late 1990s.[26] Tyus wrote the group's most famous song, "I'm So Young" (1958), which, because it was covered by the Ronettes, made Tyus one of the coplaintiffs in their lawsuit against Spector. For Tyus, not only was the "50 percent of something" arrangement acceptable, it was the best financial turn of events he had experienced in many years. On May 7, 2005, Tyus was the keynote speaker at a fund-raiser for Bridges, a New York City–area homeless outreach organization that had helped get him off the streets in the early 1990s. It was from Tyus's poignant speech that I learned in detail about the hardship of his homelessness and was able to put his receipt of unpaid royalties into true perspective.

Others feel that the Rubin arrangement is a Faustian bargain. Rubin was hired by the Coasters in the early 1990s to sue Atlantic Records for back performance royalties. Earl Carroll, who was a member of the Coasters from 1961 to 1980, was included in the suit, but thought Rubin's 50/50 deal was unsatisfactory and decided to work with a different lawyer, who asked for a smaller percentage. The other three Coasters involved in the suit, Carl Gardner, William "Dub" Jones, and Billy Guy, fearing that they would end up with nothing if they did not all work with Rubin, tried unsuccessfully to change Carroll's mind. Eventually each of the four settled with Atlantic separately, with differing accounts as to who had made the best decision.

The "50 percent of something" arrangement continues to be debated on the oldies circuit as artists seek reparation and recompense, a process that inevitably involves compromise. For most of the artists, the vanguard portion of their careers, when the music they were making was culturally "new," crested when they were very young, and the business decisions they made, or did not make, at that time have had a crucial impact on the rest of their lives. Artists who have had longer careers who also made early business missteps do not need to depend so much on rectifying the past. John Fogerty, the former lead singer and main songwriter for Credence Clearwater Revival, signed away the publishing rights to his songs to his manager in the early 1970s. Fortunately, he went on to write and record popular new material in the 1980s and 1990s, so his early mistakes were somewhat mitigated by later success.

Because the hit-making days for many oldies acts like the Ronettes, the Shirelles, and the Coasters are in the past, that part of their life still looms large. Past business mistakes can resonate more deeply and make the quest for reparation a more urgent and emotionally vexed one. That Rubin is Jewish like so many of these groups' first record company owners and managers, regardless of whether he is perceived as helpful or hurtful, adds another layer of resonance to this issue. The money, or, at least, access to the money, is perceived as still being in "white hands." Although the balance of power is not the same as it was when the artists were young unknowns, music business can still involve uncomfortable interracial relations.

OFFSTAGE ENCOUNTERS

The discourse about racial interaction is inescapable on the oldies circuit, whether the subject is past practices or present circumstances. We arrived at W. J. Clarke High School late but still in time to perform. The show was well attended by a mostly white middle-aged audience. Reeves was the only black act on a bill that also included the Duprees from Jersey City, New Jersey, whose big hit was "You Belong to Me" (1962); Lennie Coco and the Chimes from Brooklyn, known best for "Once in a While" (1960); the Happenings from Patterson, New Jersey, of "See You in September" (1966) fame; the Long Island group the Chaperones, known for "Cruise to the Moon" (1959); and the oldies cover band Risky Business.

The concert was promoted by Long Island DJ Micky B., who was in Tico and the Triumphs, Paul Simon's early 1960s doo-wop group.[27] It is notable that the advertisement for the show featured a white Elvis Presley–type singer with a guitar even though all the acts were vocal groups, one an African American girl group. The promoter chose to emphasize the nostalgic component of the concert rather than showcasing the actual talent by using photographs of the various groups, as is commonly done. Advertising the show with this particular piece of well-known oldies iconography—the Elvis Presley lookalike—may have erased the racial history underlying this music, but behind the scenes the usual doo-wop discourse continued.

I was offstage in a classroom with two musicians in the Reeves backup band, who were both black.[28] One of them sat down at a piano and started playing and singing "I Don't Want To Cry" (1961), a song first made famous by the soul singer Chuck Jackson. Two members of one of the white groups on the show walked into the room and said they used to perform the song in the 1960s with a vocal arrangement of the string part in the bridge of Jackson version. They sang their version with the Reeves band member accompanying them, in a spirited and facile performance. Afterward everyone clapped and reminisced about hearing Chuck Jackson's version for the first time, and how they fell in love with the song. Then the conversation evolved into a comparison of music making in the 1960s and today. One of the white singers said music was more tasteful in those days, not vulgar and crude like rap, which showed how the world was "more civilized" back then.

Soon the discussion moved to the World Trade Center attack, the fear and anger that it had catalyzed, and how the attack was representative of the demise of civilized life. Then the white singer made a strong statement in favor of the Iraq War, commenting on what he thought was the barbarity of the Muslim religion, asserting that Muslims "were just animals." The two black musicians fell silent for a moment, then said they had to get dressed for the show. Our impromptu interracial music making abruptly came to an end. The Reeves entourage and I had talked about the war while we were stranded in the van and later after we had arrived. The two black musicians involved in this scene were decidedly against the invasion and had made a joke about how "at least America won't be blaming black people for their problems anymore."

The incident illustrates how white and black artists can join on a musical level but can still be divided on social and political issues. The black musicians in no way condoned the World Trade Center attack, although they did in some way identify with newly racially profiled Muslims, as fellow outsiders in American society. The doo-wop community has made it possible for people of different races to occupy the same physical and sonic space, be it on stage or off, but disparate views on politics, culture, and society can still clash.

When the participants in an offstage discourse are all black (or the white person involved is someone like me whom they have become more socially comfortable with), there is a noticeably different, less tense, less emotionally inhibited kind of behavior than in a racially integrated setting. At the next oldies concert I played, this time as a member of the Cadillacs' band, on April 5, 2003, at The Showplace in Upper Marlboro, Maryland, I was witness to an all black (except for me) backstage interlude.

Carroll, Phillips, Lewis, me, three members of the black group the Dubs, and the Cadillacs' drummer for this show, Reggie Barnes, were in the Cadillacs' dressing room before the show. Barnes is a veteran of the vocal group scene, having been a singer in the late 1950s and early 1960s with versions of the Cadillacs, the Fi-tones, the Solitaires, and other groups. The Dubs are a New York–area group who, like the Cadillacs, formed in the early 1950s. Everyone in the dressing room except for me had known each other for a very long time.[29]

Carroll, a self-professed "ham," realized he had a captive, familiar audience and began to tell ribald stories about his youthful days "uptown" in Harlem. He described, in graphic and comic detail, a sexual liaison with a married woman and having to hide from her jealous husband on a balcony. Everyone, especially Barnes, laughed loudly and encouraged Carroll to continue. The more everyone laughed and carried on, the more animated and descriptive Carroll became, repeating the particularly funny parts several times in a row. He realized that Barnes was practically falling off his chair in uncontrollable spasms of laughter and so he zeroed in on him, making comments like "Reggie knows what I mean. Yeah, Reggie's been there, haven't ya Reg?"

I have been witness to such scenes many times in my years with the Cadillacs. The offstage storytelling and commentary on matters past and present can evolve into full-blown performances if the audience and the mood are right. What makes them right is invariably the level of familiarity among the actors in these private, behind-the-scenes productions. These interludes, like the performance about to take place onstage, involve expected, well-practiced ways of speaking and reacting to speech. It is a kind of ritual behavior that contributes to an atmosphere of good feeling and fun, which is then carried over onto the stage, as it was that evening.[30]

Billed as *The Sounds of Doo Wop V,* the Showplace event was promoted by the black company WLF Productions. Their CEO was Wilber Fletcher, who in the 1960s had been a singer and drummer with a regional family group called the Fletcher Gospel Singers (who later became the Soulmakers). After the group broke up Fletcher left the music business, but he returned in 1994 as a concert promoter. In addition to the Cadillacs, there were several other black acts on the show including the Dubs and a fake Platters group, which was pointed out to me by Earl Carroll, who did not recognize any of the members. As far as Carroll knew, only original member Herb Reed, who was not present, was allowed to use the group name, and he expressed surprise and dismay at how fake groups persist. Also on the bill were the Five Keys, originally from Newport News, Virginia, with three original members, all well into their seventies. Despite their age, their harmonies were very tight and their show surprisingly energetic. The Teenagers were there with former WCBS-FM DJ Bobby Jay on bass and a new lead singer, Timothy Wilson, who handled Frankie Lymon's high tenor lead part with great skill.[31] The Fabulous Hubcaps, a white oldies show band who performed material by a variety of artists, were on the bill as well. Although they were not an original group, several of their members looked as old as the other acts on the bill. Rounding out the show were the Valadiers, one of the few white Motown groups, who had a couple of minor hits in the early 1960s.

The lineup on the *Doo Wop V* show was almost a reverse racial image of the Reeves show from the previous week. The Reeves show had a white promoter with one black act on an otherwise white roster playing for a mostly white audience. The majority of the audience for the *Doo Wop V* show was black, with a white representation of about 25 percent. This mirrors the demographics of Greater Upper Marlboro, Maryland, which is 75 percent "Black" and 20 percent "White Non-Hispanic."[32] This example supports my point that the racial make-up of doo-wop concert audiences has as much to do with who promotes the show and where the show is located as it does with white and black musical preference.

WE HEARD YOU UP THERE

The April 5, 2003, Upper Marlboro show was in an equestrian center the size of an airplane hangar memorable for an overwhelming, music-enveloping reverb that created a rather muddled sound. As I walked through the audience it literally hurt my ears to listen to the show. On-stage with the Cadillacs I had a lot of trouble hearing the other musicians and singers, which made it difficult to carry out my duties as MD. As I played the set I worried about whether my vocal part was in balance and in tune with the others, which detracted from my ability to lead the band. We ended the show with the song "Speedoo" and, surprisingly, during the closing vamp (a repeating harmonic sequence) all of the other acts joined us on stage and danced along with the Cadillacs. Surprisingly again, after the show, the lead singer of the Dubs complimented my singing and said, "We heard you up there. We were watching you." I realized that I had come a long way since my first show as second tenor a year and a half before. I now had a more audible and visible presence in the Cadillacs show and in the doo-wop community. With the job of MD came increased responsibility and possibly greater performance anxiety, but also the opportunity for greater recognition.

The next show was with Shirley Alston Reeves on April 11, 2003, at a catering hall called Masso's in Williamstown, a small town in southern New Jersey. Here I had a chance to compare my experiences as MD with that of two veteran oldies circuit MDs. On this show Reeves opened up for Charlie Thomas's Drifters. In the long hit-making epoch of the Drifters from the early 1950s through the mid-1960s there was a succession of great lead singers including Clyde McPhatter, Ben E. King, Rudy Lewis, and Johnny Moore on songs such as "Money Honey" (1953, McPhatter), "Save the Last Dance for Me" (1960, King), "On Broadway" (1963, Lewis), and "Under the Boardwalk" (1964, Moore). Charlie Thomas joined the group in 1958 and sang lead on the minor hit "Sweets for My Sweet" (1961). Because of his fifty-plus-year tenure with the group he has as good a claim to authenticity as any of the singers currently performing under the Drifters moniker. In the old days he was a tenor, but now he has a somewhat raspy but soulful baritone, which he uses to sing all the Drifters favorites including an show-stopping arrangement of "Up on the Roof" (1962) that playfully incorporates the theme from the 1950s private-eye television show *Peter Gunn.*

His MD was Barry Gregory, a heavy-set white-haired white man with glasses in his late sixties. Gregory has had a varied musical career, which began with playing drums and leading bands in the U.S. Army from the early 1960s until he retired from service in the late 1970s. He then went on to have some success as a singer in the Christian music field in the early 1980s. These vocal talents he was quite willing to share during the sound check before the show. Usually, the MD just goes over the heads and tails, or beginnings and ends, of the songs with the vocal group and the band. On this occasion, Gregory rehearsed with the Drifters and then, after they went to the dressing room, he proceeded to sing the entire set himself with the band, turning the sound check into an off-the-cuff private performance. For Gregory, this gig was made more enjoyable by getting the chance to sing, albeit for a small audience, all the great Drifters songs he listened to as a young man.

The drummer for this band was Carl Vreeland, who was also the drummer and co-MD for Reeves on this night. He found Gregory's full-song approach to the sound check unnecessary and rehearsed just the heads and tails of Reeves's numbers. Vreeland can play guitar, bass, keyboard, and drums proficiently. Because he was also the musician contractor for both of the acts on the show he was able to choose his instrument for the evening. He told me in the car on the way to the show that he has been putting himself on more gigs as a drummer because that was the first instrument he learned to play. Playing drums connects him with the sense of fun he had when he first discovered music as a kid. Being the MD and musician contractor, two roles that are often combined on the oldies circuit, gives him both the power to vary his musical experience in a performance environment where the show format rarely changes and, in this case, the chance to connect with a past self.

For the band musicians in the doo-wop community the past can echo in the present just as it does for the stars of the show, and opportunities can arise for reconnection with former inspirations and aspirations. These are generally more personal experiences, whereas for the stars of the show, like Shirley Alston Reeves, personal memories are often commingled with public representations of their legacies.

PERFORMANCE RIGHTS AND REPRESENTATIONS

In the dressing room before the Williamstown show I was sitting at a table with the Reeves entourage and mentioned that I had seen *Why Do Fools Fall in Love,* the 1998 Hollywood biopic about Frankie Lymon, the lead singer of the Teenagers. The story centered on the legal battle over the rights to his estate between his three alleged wives and the owner of his record company, Morris Levy. Lymon became addicted to heroin soon after becoming a teenage star in the mid-1950s and eventually died of an overdose at the age of twenty-six. Reeves and the others felt that the story had gotten the "Hollywood treatment," overemphasizing the sex and violence in the story, and did not do justice to Lymon and his talent. Reeves then talked about her experience with biographical filmmaking. She said she was working with a writer who told her that "she wouldn't recognize herself" in the movie because her story needed to be "spiced up," just as Lymon's biography had been. Reeves found the untruthful treatment distasteful and was unsure whether she would go forward with the project.

The screenwriter did not want to include one of the more interesting aspects of her life story. Florence Greenberg, the Jewish owner of the Shirelles' record company, Scepter, who was also the group's manager, had had a long-running affair with the younger, black songwriter and producer of the Shirelles, Luther Dixon. Greenberg was the first women to run a major record company. The Shirelles, who had gone to Passaic High School with her daughter, were the first successful act on a Scepter roster that also included Dionne Warwick, Chuck Jackson, the Isley Brothers, and Maxine Brown. Greenberg was jealous of the Shirelles when Dixon was with them, so she would often lavish expensive gifts on him. As Reeves put it, "a lot of Shirelle money ended up being driven or worn by Dixon."

The screenwriter felt this interracial relationship was not an important aspect to the story, but for Reeves the dynamic between their record company owner and their producer, who was also the artist and repertoire director, inflected every aspect of her experiences at Scepter. A similar situation existed for the Cadillacs in the 1950s, whose Jewish manager, Esther Navarro, had an affair with their black music director, Jessie Powell. These liaisons reveal another facet of racial interaction in the 1950s vocal harmony world, one that is now only beginning to be integrated into the popular culture depictions of that time.

The Williamstown show was a fund-raiser for the local school board, and there was a predominately white audience of about two hundred people in attendance. Their age was much younger than the norm for an oldies concert, with many couples who looked to be in their thirties and forties. The occasion felt more like a party where the Reeves and Thomas groups were dance bands than an oldies concert where they were stars on the bill. When Reeves's group was introduced, the response was not as enthusiastic as she normally receives at a concert. However, people seemed to be familiar with the music and able to dance the right steps to "The Twist," and "The Stroll." Many of the women in the audience also imitated the girl group choreography of Reeves and her background singers. At the end of her set, Reeves invited a parade of men and women to come up onstage and sing the chorus of "Will You Love Me Tomorrow," which everyone seemed to know well.

This gig reaffirmed my belief that, in the doo-wop world, the songs travel across generations more easily than the artists do. Other aspects of oldies music experience, including the dances, hairstyles, and clothes, are apparently familiar to younger generations as well. This is why there is still an interest in making movies about the period and why the surviving artists, whose stories are at the core of this bygone era, continue to negotiate and contest the various attempts at media representations.

The memory of one particularly contested representation was revived at the next oldies show I played with the Cadillacs on April 12, 2003, at the high school in Hauppauge, Long Island. The show was promoted by LAR productions headed by Rob Albanese, who had promoted a show the Cadillacs had played about a year before at another venue on Long Island. That was the show at which much of the video *Life Could Be a Dream*

(2002) was made, an experience still invested with much bitter feeling. *Life Could Be a Dream* was a documentary taped by the Canadian company Dramarama which incorporated many interviews with members of the doo-wop community, including Earl Carroll, Bobby Jay, and Don K. Reed, as well as clips from the Long Island concert. The filmmakers offered no payment or royalty arrangements, claiming that it was a low-budget production for the Bravo cable television network which would not be for sale. Within a year of the taping, however, VHS and DVD versions were on sale in Tower Records, the now defunct chain store, and it was aired on the New York–area PBS station WNET. Some of the exploited parties, including Ron Albanese and MC Bobby Jay, tried to put together a lawsuit, but it ultimately proved not to be worth the time, effort, and money.

According to Jay, who was featured prominently in *Life Could Be a Dream*, not getting paid for the use of his image and words would not have been such an injury if the video had not been so well made and had not so sympathetically featured the artists in their current lives as oldies circuit performers. The documentary is an effective portrayal of the doo-wop community highlighted by a wonderful offstage interlude in which Jay along with Carroll and many of the other performers in the show spontaneously gathered around a piano in one of the classrooms and began to sing. The excitement increased as, one after another, singers entered the room and joined the music making.

The video crew was notified and soon after the cameras were rolling. In the background were five recent graduates of the New York High School for the Performing Arts, all in their early twenties, whom Carroll had hired for the evening to be the Cadillacs' horn section. Even before the cameras arrived, they were dancing and singing along, absolutely surprised and overwhelmed by how much fun they were having at a gig where many of the artists were old enough to be their grandparents. I was seated behind the singers gathered around the piano and in front of the young horn section, singing along but smiling a little uncomfortably, acutely aware of being in the middle of a very special, deeply resonant fieldwork and life experience. All this was captured on video, as good as any informal, spontaneous backstage moment represented in the media. The surprise marketing of *Life Could Be a Dream* was deeply painful for its stars. Just as in the 1950s, when so many of them were exploited by the entertainment business—ironically, a subject addressed in depth in the video—their rich, music-infused lives had been commodified and distributed with no financial compensation for them.

Like the show featured in *Life Could Be a Dream*, the Hauppauge High School concert was sold out to a mostly white audience. On the bill was a mixture of black and white acts including the Cadillacs, the Flamingos featuring Terry Johnson, the Chantels, and the Brooklyn Reunion, which was made up of members of the Passions, the Mystics, and the Classics. Also on the show were solo singer Jimmy Clanton, the Teenagers, the Del Vikings, the Excellents, and the Students. The Flamingos were one of the premier black vocal groups of the 1950s with hits like "I Only Have Eyes for You" (1959) and were led by Johnson, who had been with the group since 1956 as tenor, guitarist, and vocal arranger. The Chantels, one of first female groups of the doo-wop era, had an all-original line-up except for the lead singer. Their original lead, Arlene Smith, had relinquished the rights to the Chantels name when she went solo and now performs with her own vocal group.

The Brooklyn Reunion is representative of a recent trend in doo-wop performances of bringing together the lead singers of various (in this case, white) groups, resulting in enhanced star and hit power and also lower total artist fees for the promoters. Jimmy Clanton is a white solo performer, one of the early 1960s teen idols, whose big hit was "Venus in Blues Jeans" (1962). The Teenagers group on this show was the same as the one in Maryland a couple of weeks earlier. The Del-Vikings, whose big hit was "Come Go with Me" (1956), were from Pittsburgh and were one of the first racially integrated groups. The Excellents are a white group from the Bronx known for a version of "Coney Island Baby" (1962). Finally, the Students of "I'm So Young" (1958) fame, featuring original bass singer Richard Johnson, were making a rare East Coast visit from Cincinnati.

IN FRONT OF AND BEHIND THE MUSIC

This Hauppauge show was part of two-day event that featured more than thirty groups. In this format each act has only ten to fifteen minutes for their show, time for about three or four songs. This tight format leaves the performers little time to warm up, "get into the groove," or overcome any technical difficulties, and these shows tend to be a hit or miss. The Cadillacs did not think their appearance was their best performance, a miss they attributed to not rehearsing the week before and displeasure with their drummer's work. In his defense, he had not played a Cadillacs gig for several months and, because we had arrived late, we had had no sound check before the show. Because their choreography calls for intricate interplay with the drummer, who provides rhythmic accents in sync with the group's hand and leg movements, the Cadillacs consider him the most important member of the band. On this evening, our drummer remembered very few of these accents (which are not written on any chart), and, consequently, the Cadillacs' performance lacked cohesion and flair.

Nevertheless, the audience apparently really enjoyed the show, giving the group a standing ovation during the end of "Speedoo." One person exclaimed to me afterward, "The Cadillacs have still got it!" Sometimes there is this kind of disconnect that one can experience performing on the oldies circuit. What the group perceives as a subpar show can garner a surprisingly enthusiastic response. One explanation is that the show is experienced differently by those onstage and those in the audience. The performers hear it primarily through their monitors while the audience hears it through the speakers that are facing them. The two sets of speakers often have the various instruments and voices mixed at different levels. The disparity in perception of a concert is also due to the fact that the performers have experienced the show hundreds of times and have higher expectations and standards than the audience, for whom the show is a special occasion. While the audience may be less attuned to gaffes or inconsistencies, the performers may be acutely sensitive to deviation from the norm—because of over familiarity, they are cognizant of every little nuance.

Furthermore, within the nostalgic oldies circuit frame, the audience may be hearing and seeing more than the performance onstage. They may also be hearing and seeing the memories the concert evokes. For the audience, the echoes of the past are part of the total experience, and mistakes or subpar performances are forgiven or go unnoticed. Performers certainly are also attuned to the nostalgic frame, but they must also concentrate on the possibly strenuous, present time concern of putting on a show. The most typical response I have received from oldies audience members is how the music "takes them back," whereas performers are concerned with the professional level of their present-day performances.

Mediating between performer and audience onstage at oldies shows are the MCs, who are often well-known oldies personalities and performers in their own right. Jerry Blavat, the MC for the April 19, 2003, show I played with the Cadillacs at the Kimmel Center in Philadelphia, is a veritable institution in the Philadelphia oldies world. Blavat began his career in that city as one of the original teenage dancers on *American Bandstand* in the 1950s and eventually became a DJ in the Philadelphia area, where he still hosts various syndicated oldies radio shows in addition to emceeing local concerts. For these concerts, Blavat's name and image are the most prominent aspects of the promotion, overshadowing the performers.

On this show, Blavat did more than just introduce the acts. He danced and sang with them at the beginning and end of their sets, and for each new act he changed his shoes. Cheering him on from the first row as Christine, the production manager told me, were "his legions from South Philly," the Italian and Jewish neighborhood of his birth, mirroring the mix of his own white ethnic lineage. It was the third Blavat oldies show of the season and, like the two previous, had practically sold out the 2,500-seat hall.

There was a fairly even mix of black and white acts on the bill, including the Cadillacs, Johnny Maestro and the Brooklyn Bridge, the Angels, Eugene Pitt and the Jive Five, the Tokens featuring Jay Siegel, the Cleftones, and Baby Washington. Johnny Maestro was the white original lead singer of the interracial Manhattan group the Crests known for "Sixteen Candles" (1958), and he later led the Brooklyn Bridge, whose big hit was "The Worst That Could Happen" (1968). The Angels are a white girl group from Orange, New Jersey, whose big hit was "My Boyfriend's Back" (1963). The Jive Five are a black Brooklyn group known for "My True Story" (1961). The Tokens, a white group from Brooklyn recorded "The Lion Sleeps Tonight" (1961). The black group the Cleftones formed in Jamaica, Queens, and had a hit with "Little Girl of Mine" (1956). Baby Washington, a black solo artist from Harlem, is known for the song "That's How Heartaches Are Made" (1963).

The continuing existence of racial tensions, even in what appears to be a mixed concert environment was made clear to me when one of the black singers saw a member of one of the white acts on the show, which evoked moment of the past for him. Right before all the groups were to go back onstage for the finale, this singer related how many years before, after an argument, the white singer's wife had said to him, "All you niggers are the same." This past racial animosity became conflated with current business practice as the singer went on to talk about how the white groups, as he sees it, are favored by the white promoters. He recalled how he had recently received an advertisement for an oldies boat cruise on which there were no black acts, remarking that he routinely looks at the roster of performers on oldies shows and does a "racial inventory."

Several promoters have told me that the reason the Cadillacs are not on more shows is that they ask for too much money. As they see it, the group did not have the number of national hits to warrant the price they

demand. To Carroll and other black performers, however, the white promoters are being hypocritical. Many of their reputations are built on honoring the pioneering black vocal groups, yet they book few of these groups
for their shows or do not want to pay what the groups believe is a fair
price. When asked about this, some promoters invoke the maxim "it's
just business, nothing personal." But for many black artists in the doo-
wop community, with its particularly vexed racial history, business invariably is a personal matter.

The Cadillacs opened this Philadelphia show, a rare occurrence. Because of the energy generated by their dynamic choreography, especially
in their closing number "Speedoo," they are considered a tough act to follow on the oldies circuit. Even when better-known groups are on the bill,
the Cadillacs are often slated to close the show. Since this means staying
later than everyone else, the Cadillacs commonly bemoan this fate and
often try to convince other acts to change places with them, but I have
often felt that the complaining about going on last was a bit of backstage
playacting, For even though waiting all night to go on can be tedious,
being a tough act to follow has also been a point of pride for the group.

Not surprisingly, then, being asked to open the Philadelphia show,
instead of making the group happy, caused them to speculate about
whether their stock as performers was going down. Ultimately they rea-
soned that their placement in the line-up probably had more to do with
their being from out town and less familiar in the area than the other
acts. Their reasoning seemed to be confirmed by Blavat's introduction,
during which he said that he knew Esther Navarro at the Shaw Booking
Agency and referred to her as the songwriter of "Gloria" and "Speedoo." It
would be a rare New York City–area MC who would display such a patent
lack of knowledge about the disputed authorship of these songs. While
Blavat was rehearsing during the sound check, Carroll looked at Phillips
and they both smiled wryly.

In spite of our place in the line-up, it was one of the group's best shows
in a long time. All the parts worked. Reggie Barnes, our drummer for that
evening, played the accents for the choreography to perfection. The group's
comic timing was right on and the overall sound of our ensemble, augmented by a large horn section, was full and powerful. The Cadillacs
have big-band horn arrangements for all their songs, which were written
by Curly Palmer, long-time guitar player for the Coasters. The Cadillacs'
1950s recordings were a link to the big bands like Count Basie's, for whom
Jessie Powell, the Cadillacs' MD in the 1950s, had played. Palmer's jazzy

arrangements (with their 9th, 11th, and 13th chords) vividly illuminated the historical connections and created an impressive sound not usually heard on the oldies circuit.

Personally, it was the most satisfying oldies show I had ever played. I felt relaxed and connected to the audience. In part, this connection was due to the design of Verizon Hall, with a balcony encircling the entire theater, creating an unusual intimacy between performer and audience. But architecture was not the only factor. I must confess that since becoming more integrated into the Cadillacs show I recognize myself to be a bit of a ham, just like my rhythm and blues mentor, Earl Carroll. I especially enjoy participating in the group's between-song comedy routines. On this night, because of the first-rate sound system and excellent acoustics, it was very easy to cue the heads and tails of the songs, and I had a chance to try something I had seen the Cadillacs' former MD, Eddie Jones, do for many years. Palmer's horns charts for "Speedoo" have nothing written for the extended vamp at the end. So I created a "head," or unwritten, arrangement, telling the horn players each to choose a note in a D7 chord and then play a one-bar "hold that tiger rhythm," and to play this pattern for three measures and rest in the fourth while the tenor sax plays an improvised fill.

This four-bar sequence was repeated once and then the same approach was applied to a B minor chord. We alternated between the D7 and B minor sequences, creating a sixteen-bar overall structure that we repeated the entire time it took the Cadillacs to finish their routine, including their march across the stage and through the audience. As Jones had, I went over to the horn section and told them all this on the fly, at the beginning of the vamp section, while Carroll and Phillips traded verses. It worked like a charm, an exhilarating moment of impromptu music making that was one of the highlights of my many years of playing on the oldies circuit.

In the van ride from New York to the Philadelphia show, Carroll had become agitated about Randy Gilmore, who had recently written new horn arrangements for a smaller five-piece ensemble for the Big Five. Gilmore, a black saxophonist in his late forties and a long-time member of the Cadillacs' band, had at that time decided to give up music and sell his horn. Carroll thought it was a shame and told Gilmore, "You just don't give up, you just keep playing." He could not understand how Gilmore could stop after putting so many years into his career.

For Carroll, the doo-wop revival circuit is also a survival circuit. It is your duty to exploit, for all they are worth, whatever talent you have and whatever breaks you get. Andy Warhol's adage about everyone having fifteen minutes of fame is particularly apt for doo-wop singers. Fifteen minutes is about the total length of three or four singles. Depending on luck or business acumen those fifteen minutes may or may not add up to a great deal of money over the long term. Even for the many artists on today's oldies circuit who were not lucky or did not understand the music business in their youth, that small sliver of time has still provided enough fame for steady if moderately paid work for the past forty years and helped facilitate a degree of survival in the music business. You just have to hang in there.

The survival instinct has made it possible for Carroll and his contemporaries to create and maintain a long-lived and reasonably stable musical community where the negotiation, reconciliation, and harmonizing of past and present life are common practice. Oldies shows are not meant to be history or social studies classes and non-musical issues such as race relations and economic reparation are not the official order of business. Yet, such issues pervade the proceedings, in conversations offstage, in the audience, and even in symbolic gestures and veiled commentary onstage. These forms of communication are located on a continuum of revelation that has public overt forms such as between-song patter at one end and more private forms such as backstage signifying at the other. What is said and how it is said in each of these settings is determined by who is speaking and who is listening and what is at stake economically, socially, and politically.[33]

The format for most shows is quite rigid. The acts are expected to perform only their hits in a style consistent with 1950s practice. Over time, most of them have developed a standard set list and between-song patter. But a broader analysis encompassing both "the show" itself and its historical and ethnographic context reveals a more dynamic and vital performance milieu. Transformative conversations about race, commerce, and other important social categories have echoed beneath and sometimes above the surface over the decades. There may be the illusion of stasis.[34] But the vocal behavior circulating throughout the intimate inner circuit within the larger oldies circuit can help keep the lives of those involved vital and evolving. Music is the catalyst for this process. It creates a sonic space where all can re-experience the fun and connection to body and soul they had as young people, with room available for a more dynamic style of nostalgic musing.

Vocal harmony is a way of being in the world, a particular way of connecting with the past, present, and future. It creates a soft place on which to lay the sensitive issues of racial strife, masculinity, economic hardship, and the vulnerability of maturity. T. S. Eliot said that "humankind cannot bear very much reality."[35] Because the doo-wop community members have the opportunity to process the past, present, and future through this sonic filter, they have access to a special way of experiencing, and re-experiencing, life, in which, because it is sung, and sung with others in a familiar, comforting form, reality can be rendered more bearable. Doo-wop helps bring meaning, order, and beauty to the seemingly chaotic events and emotions of human experience.

The reason these groups have this longevity is because the songs were great. These songs will live forever. The Marshak groups are a case in point. None of those groups have original members and people don't care. That's what interests me most about that era. The sentiment of doo-wop really pene-trates a lot of people. There's something genuine about those songs and per-formances. It was before MTV, it was about the performance. A lot of the records were performances captured on record as opposed to today which are so produced. The doo-wop songs had a feeling to them. It's just about the song and the performance. It's more down to earth and real.[1]

hese opinions expressed by oldies circuit band member Carl Vreeland explain well the continuing appeal of doo-wop. Recording music straight to the hard drive of a computer where it can be digitally edited has become common practice. In a time when popular music is increasingly the product of such a process, there is an appreciation of the more "down to earth and real," the more human quality of the doo-wop records. One hears the flaws in the performance and production, the flat notes, the distortion, the badly balanced ensemble recording. But these are aspects that re-mind us that music, in the words of the ethnomusicologist John Blacking, is "humanly organized sound"—or disorganized, as the case may be.[2] Music making, especially singing, is an activity in which most of us, regard-less of socioeconomic status or musical background, can partake. Doo-wop fans identify with the human, flawed, and real nature of their favorite records because they can indulge in the fantasy that, with maybe just a little practice and courage, they could also be doo-wop singers.

Vreeland's words also illustrate the tension between the "lives" of the doo-wop songs and the lives of the singers who initially made those songs famous. The advent of relatively inexpensive technology of CD burners and MP3 players and accessibility of the vast cultural reservoir of the Internet have made it possible for the classic doo-wop recordings to find new audiences well beyond the doo-wop community. Ironically, how-ever, this wider digital availability has coincided with the disappearance of the genre from the airwaves. Mainstream radio, presided over primarily by two corporate behemoths, Clear Channel and Infinity, has systematically phased out the music of the 1950s and early 1960s, pre-Beatles era, from the programming of their stations. Songs from the latter part of the 1960s, the 1970s, and the 1980s now dominate the playlists of "oldies" radio.

The doo-wop songs linger on, but the doo-wop singers cannot. The aging original members of doo-wop groups are less able to endure the rigors of performing. They also must compete with the succeeding waves of oldies performers from the subsequent decades, from the 1960s to the 1980s. The rock-era nostalgia circuit has become a very crowded field indeed. Many of the acts from these later decades are being hired by the same promoters, such as Richard Nader's organization, that have been booking the doo-wop groups for so many years. In the 1970s, these promoters laid the foundation for an oldies circuit that catered to nostalgia for the 1950s, and now they and new generations of promoters and performers are doing the same with more recent musical styles. The eternal return of popular culture in this postmodern age of seemingly infinite cultural availability provides a perpetual resource for the revival circuit, where everything oldies is, eventually, news again.

Most doo-wop singers accept that there are only so many performing venues, only so much radio airtime, and that, eventually, older entertainers must make room for the young. But the music business can be merciless when the time comes for a change. In New York, the initial warning sign came in August 2002, when WCBS-FM DJ Don K. Reed's long-running Sunday night show *The Doo-Wop Shop* was suddenly canceled. Soon after, a large crowd of the show's supporters rallied in front of the Viacom building, home of WCBS-FM's parent company, but their protests fell on deaf ears. Then the final blow came. A June 4, 2005, *New York Daily News* article told the tale.

> Oldies radio is dead in New York City. After more than three decades as the top oldies station in the country, WCBS-FM (101.1 FM) abruptly scrapped its format yesterday for a concept called Jack. As Frank Sinatra's "Summer Wind" trailed off at 5 p.m., a voice intoned: "Why don't we play what we want? There's a whole world of songs out there." The move stunned longtime listeners. "I came home and I turned the radio on and it was not there," said Pamela Hall, who lives in the Bronx. "I thought I was going to faint. I really am sick. Part of my family is

gone." "This is the largest, the biggest abandonment of a loyal market segment in the history of New York radio," said listener Howard Bailen, of Manhasset, L.I. But officials at Infinity Broadcasting, which owns the station, said the new format was right for New York. No personalities will be heard on the station at the start. The Jack format blends hits from the past four decades, creating what the company claims is the "most expansive" play-list heard on radio.[3]

New York Newsday quoted other doo-wop fans who expressed similar sentiments: " 'For 30 years, I've listened to it and all of a sudden [it's gone],' Bobby Pace, 51, said Saturday. 'That's not nice. Everything is geared toward the younger generation. There's nothing for our age,' Denise Gallo, 45, of Howard Beach, said Saturday. 'The doo-wop is gone. It's the end of an era.' "[4]

Fans of the station were not the only ones shocked by the sudden programming change. Some oldies circuit musicians, like Greg Woods, feared that the shutting down of such a powerful and long-standing supporter of their music would have a negative impact on their livelihood: "The ripple effect is obvious. There will be less advertising for oldies gigs, which may mean less work for musicians and support personnel."[5] Jay Traynor, the original lead singer of Jay and the Americans, took the news even more personally: "I felt like I was taken hostage by some 20-year-old music research terrorist and sentenced to death. It's bad enough getting old but to be slapped in the face for it is sickening. Their day will come. I'm not stopping. We'll find other outlets, satellite, etc. Gather the troops and CHARGE!"[6]

Other outlets do exist for doo-wop and other types of 1950s popular music, including Internet and satellite radio shows and many specialty terrestrial radio programs, mostly on small-market, AM, and college radio stations. Doo-wop's presence in the big-market mainstream, however may be all but vanishing. But, as Jay Traynor expressed, the doo-wop community is not going down without a fight. The use of the Internet by community members to communicate their feelings shows a willingness to adapt to the changing technological landscape to maintain their musical culture.

Doo-wop singers will continue to perform and to circulate their musical heritage through the orbits of the airwaves, cyberspace, and concert circuits while living with the ever- accumulating obits of their fellow oldies circuit members as well as the mainstream radio programs that once played their music. Oldies concerts may be framed as nostalgic events or as opportunities for the recognition of the historically underappreciated, but in the process these shows are also musical monuments to perseverance. These shows are the ritual honoring of musical elders, many of whom were never big stars, who have nevertheless withstood the vicissitudes of time and changing cultural tastes as band member Paul Page attests, "A lot of them are not household names. Maybe they had one hit. Some just have regional appeal. I think it's a testament to them that they made a living in relative obscurity."[7] And if you listen closely, you will hear in the voice of those singers an emotional resonance and wisdom that only many years of singing and surviving can yield.

Voices mature and mellow, too. As Cleveland Freeland, a member of Shirley Allston Reeves's band put it: "So many of the groups have gotten better with age, their voices have gotten more full. I think Shirley's voice sounds better now than in the 60s, it's really rounded out."[8] Earl Carroll was seventeen years old when he recorded "Speedoo" in 1955 in the key of F major. The energy and optimism of youth was evident in the lightness and bounce of his delivery. In 1996, at the age of fifty-eight, forty-one years later and a minor third down, he re-recorded "Speedoo" in the key of D major. His voice, though still recognizably a tenor, was deeper and more soulful, his approach a little more thoughtful and deliberate, reflective of many years spent singing rhythm and blues. This re-recording was one of the cuts on *Have You Heard the News?*, the Cadillacs' first album of newly recorded material since the 1950s (Millrose Music No. 0444). The title song (which I co-wrote with Carroll and two other band members) hailed Speedo and the Cadillacs' return to the spotlight:

> Have you heard the news?
> Speedo's back in town
> Man, we're gonna rock this joint
> We're gonna dance the ceilings down
> Years have come and gone
> You know we've paid our dues
> But we never lost that soulful sound
> Brother, have you heard the news?[9]

Inspired by this experience I began to write songs in classic rhythm and blues style. By the summer of 2003 I had enough material for an album, and I approached Carroll with the idea of making another Cadillacs CD. We spent the next year arranging, rehearsing, and recording the album.[10] What I had suspected was borne out: Carroll, Phillips, Lewis, and Eddie Jones (with whom I co-wrote one of the songs) still had it.

Many doo-wop groups have made new recordings over the past forty years since the advent of the oldies circuit—collections of cover versions of classic vocal group songs or recordings in contemporary styles like soul, disco and funk.[11] My idea was to make an album of newly composed doo-wop. I used many of the characteristic elements of the style, the slow 12/8 rhythm in the ballads and the I–vi–IV–V progression, the ice cream changes, and modeled a few of the songs on old Cadillacs tunes. The eventual title cut, "Mr. Lucky," was based on "Speedoo," with its up-tempo use of a variant of the blues progression and percussive background vocal arrangement ("Bop, bop, shoo-be-doo bop shoo-bop" for "Mr. Lucky" as opposed to "Wah, wah, shoo-be-do" for "Speedo"). The first song on the CD, "Better than Ever," was also an up-tempo jump-blues number, which employs the ice cream changes instead of the blues progression as its harmonic foundation and features an active bass part just like the Cadillacs' favorite "Zoom." The lyrics for most of the songs on the album deal with current issues of the doo-wop community, including survival ("Mr. Lucky") and musical maturity ("Better than Ever").

Would the doo-wop community accept and support a recording of new material from an oldies group? Our first attempt at radio play on one of the many specialty doo-wop programs in the New York area was a revealing one. The DJ, Johnny Z., who has a Sunday night show on WFAS in White Plains, New York, just north of Manhattan, was eager to have the group on as guests but was hesitant at first to play the new CD ("We probably can't much play from it; it's strictly a doo-wop, street-corner show. But we will play their golden oldies.")[12] When we showed up for the interview, we learned that he had listened to the CD over and over again and was happy to play several cuts.

Overall, response to the album has been both hesitant and enthusiastic. An employee of Collectables Records, the current distributor of the Cadillacs back catalog, thought *Mr. Lucky* was not "doo-wop enough" for his company to issue it with the group's older records. There was not enough background harmony on the songs (Carroll, who was the primary vocal arranger, preferred the sparser approach), and the company were worried that their customers would claim false advertising if a Cadillacs record was not "classic vocal harmony."[13] In contrast, several DJs, including Bob Porter at WBGO in Newark, New Jersey, and Christine Vitali at WFDU in Teaneck, New Jersey, were quite enthusiastic in their support and played the CD numerous times on their shows. The response that per-haps best matched my expectations was Steve Percy's, DJ on WAIF FM in Cincinnati, whose *Time Machine Show* bills itself as "the only show in the area devoted exclusively to the playing of the sounds of the 50's, Rock 'N' Roll and Rhythm 'N' Blues with a special emphasis on the group harmony sound." According to Percy, the voices on the CD are "just like fine wine."[14]

Whether we can consider the project a success is still unclear. (Recover-ing our modest financial investment would be the first step.) On the whole, the doo-wop community was quite supportive of the release of *Mr. Lucky*. New York–area oldies record stores such as Clifton Music in Clifton, New Jersey, and Whirlin' Disc in Farmingdale, New York, stocked the CD, and several Internet radio and doo-wop websites played songs from it. Beyond the doo-wop community, however, there has been less support. I was able to convince most of the (now-defunct) New York City–area Tower Records, to take the CD on consignment, but only after pointing out that the Cadillacs already had a slot in their record bins. The *New York Post* was the only major area newspaper that would review the record, and al-though the review was generally positive, the majority of it focused on the Cadillacs' backstory, not the CD itself. For many doo-wop groups their reputations are both a blessing and a curse: they may open some doors professionally, but they may also overshadow any attempts at new career moves.

Like many band members, I have benefited greatly from the musical mentorship of the doo-wop singers who have employed me. The lesson that has had the greatest impact on me is appreciating the relationship of art and entertainment inherent in doo-wop. The Cadillacs, Shirley Alston Reeves, and others have taught me that much of the value and meaning of music is to be found in its performance: a real and vital connection between artist and audience. Because my musical background was in the white album-oriented rock of the 1970s in which art was often valued over entertainment, I had a much more distant relationship with an audience than I would eventually experience on the oldies circuit. I have learned to include the people for whom I am performing in the music making pro-cess and to enjoy my dual roles as entertainer and artist.

The modern dance choreographer Garth Fagan once observed that "in dance, as in every other art form, you grow with age: when you're a more mature painter, a more mature poet, a more mature dressmaker, you know more things, better things. But we still need the youngsters to jump around."[15] In exchange for the education that I have received, I have been able to contribute my younger energy and perspective to the music making of my mentors. I have had the opportunity to work in an inspiring and inclusive multigenerational network, which likely will not exist in the future.

The day will come when there will be no original doo-wop group members working the oldies circuit. If the music is to survive, a younger generation of singers will have to be in place. In the big band world, organizations such as the Duke Ellington Orchestra and the Count Basie Orchestra still continue to perform. Most likely, vocal groups called the Drifters, the Platters, and, possibly, even the Cadillacs will be entertaining the nostalgic masses. Just as Earl Carroll was willing to use my younger voice to fill in the harmony in the Cadillacs, other group leaders are increasingly filling their ranks with younger singers, giving a new generation the opportunity to experience the rich musicality of doo-wop and pass on the American vocal harmony legacy.

NOTES

Introduction

1. "Doo-wop is so submerged in caricature and deprecation that shadings of Rodney Dangerfield color its very name." Marvin Gottlieb, "The Durability of Doo-Wop," *New York Times*, 17 January 1993.

2. David Hinckley, "R-E-S-P-E-C-T," in booklet to *The Doo Wop Box: 101 Vocal Group Gems from the Golden Age of Rock 'N' Roll* (Los Angeles: Rhino Records, 1993), 17.

3. The influence of doo-wop singers such as Nolan Strong of the Diablos and Sherman Garnes and Frankie Lymon of the Teenagers has been acknowledged by Motown singers Smokey Robinson of the Miracles, Melvin Franklin of the Temptations, and Ronnie Spector of the Ronettes. Ibid.

4. Anthony J. Gribin and Matthew M. Schiff, *Doo-Wop: The Forgotten Third of Rock 'n' Roll* (Iola, WI: Krause Publications, 1992), 8.

5. Stanley Sadie and John Tyrrell, eds., *The New Grove Dictionary of Music and Musicians* (New York: Oxford University Press, 2001).

6. Jeffrey Melnick, "'Story Untold': The Black Men and White Sounds of Doo-Wop," in *Whiteness: A Critical Reader,* ed. Mike Hill (New York: New York University Press, 1997), 134.

7. Bob Hyde, Compiler's Notes, in booklet to *The Doo Wop Box,* 29.

8. Robert Pruter, *Doowop: The Chicago Scene* (Urbana: University of Illinois Press, 1996), 250–52.

9. Robert Pruter, "A History of Doo-wop Fanzines," *Popular Music and Society* 21, no. 1 (1997): 23.

10. "It is through expressive modes such as music that cultural symbols are maintained and manipulated as a source of power in a social context, within the economic and political constraints of particular historical situations." Stuart L Goosman, "The Social and Cultural Organization of Black Group Vocal Harmony in Washington, D.C., and Baltimore, Maryland, 1945–60" (PhD diss., University of Washington, 1992), 8.

11. Their music was "a source of power that afforded the singers some measure of control in the face of social adversity and the day to day sameness of repression." Ibid., 3.

12. The 1950s was an era of "expanding affluence" often perceived now as "orderly" where, nevertheless, "social ferment" was bubbling beneath the "placid surface." David Halberstam, *The Fifties* (New York: Fawcett Columbine, 1993), ix–x.

13. "The Frenzy or "Shouting," when the Spirit of the Lord passed by, seizing the devotee, made him mad with supernatural joy." W. E. B Du Bois, *The Souls of Black Folk* (New York: Penguin, 1995), 215.

14. "The evangelical success of revivalism was not limited by race. Worshipers at Cane Ridge [in Kentucky] commented often on the degree to which black and white southerners participated in the services and were the recipients of God's grace." James R. Goff, *Close Harmony: A History of Southern Gospel* (Chapel Hill: University of North Carolina Press, 2002), 19.

15. George Lipsitz, *Time Passages: Collective Memory and American Popular Culture* (Minneapolis: University of Minnesota Press, 1990), 120.

16. "'Oh, they were so sharp it hurt,' recalled Ben E. King, 'the Cadillacs had the best clothes, the best steps.' 'All the quartets sang louder when the Cadillacs cruised Brooke Avenue [in New York City],' wrote poet David Henderson." Brian Ward, *Just My Soul Responding: Rhythm and Blues, Black Consciousness, and Race Relations* (Berkeley: University of California Press, 1998), 48.

17. Lipsitz, *Time Passages*, 124.

18. Primitivism is an essential subtext of Modernism and "a return to first principles through the discovery of some elemental and vitalizing energy observable in pre-industrial societies, and particularly in peasant, tribal and folk repertoires. . . . Characteristically, Primitivism tends to connote those tribal or folk expressions which carry the suggestion of the unaffected and the unstudied, the powerful and the essential." Glenn Watkins, *Pyramids at the Louvre: Music, Culture, and Collage from Stravinsky to the Postmodernists* (Cambridge, MA: Belknap Press of Harvard University Press, 1994), 63–64.

19. Lipsitz, *Time Passages*, 64.

20. Fred Moten goes so far as to claim the "essential blackness of American radicalism." This quote was taken from a lecture that he gave in his course Black Performance: The Construction of a Research Project, which I attended in the Fall of 1998 at New York University.

21. "Popular music and films seem to resonate with the tensions of the time." Lipstiz, *Time Passages*, x.

22. Nelson George, *The Death of Rhythm and Blues* (New York: Penguin, 1988), 27.

23. "The R & B singers' fate could be servitude or self-sufficiency, depending on whether they knew how to take—and keep—control." Ibid., 83.

24. See www.doowopusa.org.

25. Anthony J. Gribin and Matthew M. Schiff, *The Complete Book of Doo-Wop* (Iola, WI: Krause Publications, 2000), 13–15.

26. "We can never go back to those times, but we can catch glimpses of who we were and what we were about" and "the medium that allows a recapturing of the past most easily is the music of our teenage generation." Ibid., 7.

27. "The entertainment industry [can colonize] cultural memory to create nostalgia (and secondary market demand) for the discarded husks of its own planned cultural obsolescence and turnover." Gage Averill, *Four Parts, No Waiting: A Social History of American Barbershop Harmony* (New York: Oxford University Press, 2003), 14.

28. "To tell the story of doo-wop is almost to describe it as a fall from grace: the vital music of African Americans [has been] converted into fodder for oldies radio and package shows." Melnick, "Story Untold," 138.

29. "To make noise is to interrupt a transmission, unplug, kill." Jacques Attali, *Noise: The Political Economy of Music* (Minneapolis: University of Minnesota Press, 1996), 47.

30. Fred Davis, *Yearning for Yesterday* (New York: Free Press, 1979), 37.

31. "The proclivity to appreciate attitudes toward former selves is closely related to nostalgia's . . . tendency to eliminate from memory or, at minimum, severely to mute the unpleasant, the unhappy, the abrasive, and most of all, those lurking shadows of former selves about which we feel shame, guilt or humiliation." Ibid., 37.

32. The following description of jazz musician Rahsaan Roland Kirk could easily apply to a doo-wop singer: "His art contained multi-layered and heavily coded covert messages about the past, but for a large part of his audience, Kirk's music inevitably appeared as just another novelty and diversion within the seemingly autonomous realms of commercialized leisure." Lipsitz, *Time Passages*, 4.

33. "Popular music is nothing if not dialogic, the product of an ongoing historical conversation in which no one has the first or the last word." Ibid., 99.

34. John Strausbaugh, *Rock 'Til You Drop: The Decline from Rebellion to Nostalgia* (London: Verso, 2001), 2–3.

35. Ibid., 120.

36. Gail Sheehy, *Passages: Predictable Crises of Adult Life* (New York: Dutton, 1977).

37. Nostalgia is "an emotionally charged form of *cultural memory* in which the past is idealized and invested with a present longing. Nostalgia [Mieke Bal argues] is a 'structure of relation to the past' rather than a set of explicit meanings." Averill, *Four Parts*, 14. See also Mieke Bal, *Acts of Memory: Cultural Recall in the Present*,

ed. Mieke Bal, Jonathan Crewe, and Leo Spitzer (Hanover: University Press of New England, 1999).

38. This is akin to "re-membering" which is part of the "postmodern turn" in theater, where "re-membering is not merely the restoration of some past intact, but setting it in living relationship to the present." Victor Turner, *From Ritual to Theatre: The Human Seriousness of Play* (New York: PAJ Publications, 1982), 86.

39. "Music is not primarily a thing or a collection of things, but an activity in which we engage." Christopher Small, *Music of the Common Tongue: Survival and Celebration in African American Music* (Hanover, NH: Wesleyan University Press, 1987), 50.

40. Kyra D. Gaunt, "Got Rhythm? Difficult Encounters in Theory and Practice and Other Participatory Discrepancies in Music," *City and Society* 14, no. 1 (2002): 131. See also Charles Keil, "Participatory Discrepancies and the Power of Music," *Cultural Anthropology* 2, no. 3 (1987): 275–83.

41. Mitchell Duneier, *Sidewalk* (New York: Farrar, Straus and Giroux, 1999), 352.

42. This is the "the Becker principle" (named for the sociologist Howard S. Becker). "Most social processes have a structure that comes close to insuring that a certain set of situations will arise over time. These situations practically require them to do or say certain things because there are other things going on that require them to do that, things that are more influential than the social condition of a fieldworker being present." Duneier, *Sidewalk*, 338.

43. Gaunt, "Got Rhythm?," 125–26.

44. Anne Tyler, *The Accidental Tourist* (New York: Alfred A. Knopf, 1985).

45. This is an allusion to "thick description," an important technique in the interpretive approach to anthropology. Clifford Geertz, *The Interpretation of Cultures* (New York: Basic Books, 1973).

46. This desire could be described as "the contemporary compulsion to move beyond." Homi K. Bhabha, *The Location of Culture* (New York: Routledge, 1994), 18.

47. Ibid., 2–13.

48. "Language and culture are irreducibly dialogical in nature." Bruce Mannheim and Dennis Tedlock, introduction to *The Dialogic Emergence of Culture,* ed. Tedlock and Mannheim (Urbana: University of Illinois Press, 1995), 3.

49. Ibid., 13.

50. "The voice, as the most, intimate, flexible and complex mode of articulation of the body, is fundamental to the creation of human societies." John Shepherd and Peter Wicke, *Music and Cultural Theory* (Cambridge, UK: Polity Press, 1997), 179.

51. Steven Feld and Aaron A. Fox, "Music and Language," *Annual Review of Anthropology* 23 (1994): 26.

52. "We must listen to the voices of those who appreciate and defend doo-wop, as well as to the voices of those who first recorded the form." Pruter, *Doowop*, 252.

1. The Roots of Vocal Harmony

1. Greg Woods, email to author, 2 February 2003.

2. Eileen Southern, *The Music of Black Americans* (New York: W. W. Norton, 1983), 58.

3. Ronald Radano and Philip Bohlman, "Music and Race, Their Past, Their Presence," in *Music and the Racial Imagination*, ed. Ronald Radano and Philip Bohlman (Chicago: University of Chicago Press, 2000), 49.

4. Lynn Abbott, " 'Play That Barber Shop Chord': A Case for the African-American Origin of Barbershop Harmony," *American Music* 10, no. 3 (1992): 289–325.

5. Barbershop quartet music is "a music of racial *encounter*, of a profound cultural intimacy, a short circuit in the hard-wiring of racial separation and segregation." Gage Averill, *Four Parts, No Waiting: A Social History of American Barbershop Harmony* (New York: Oxford University Press, 2003), 13.

6. Earl Carroll, interview by author, New York City, 26 February 1998.

7. "Owned and operated by black men, open from early morn until late at night, barbershops provided congenial meeting places where the musically inclined could discourse on music or practice in a back room without interruption." Southern, *Music of Black Americans*, 258.

8. Barbershops were the "unofficial headquarters for those who gathered to sing in harmony." Kip Lornell, *Happy in the Service of the Lord: African-American Sacred Vocal Harmony Quartets in Memphis* (Knoxville: University of Tennessee Press, 1995), 10.

9. Southern, *Music of Black Americans*, 34.

10. The term "barbershop quartet" was in use in the African American community possibly as far back as the 1870s; the actual musical practice likely has even older roots. Averill, *Four Parts*, 39–40.

11. "Germans and Austrians played a significant role in the maturation of American part-singing. Germans often worked as schoolteachers and tutors [and] ... formed concert and singing societies. Tours of German and Austrian minstrels [also] precipitated the formation of American quartets." Ibid., 22.

12. Eric Lott, *Love and Theft: Blackface Minstrelsy and the American Working Class* (New York: Oxford University Press, 1993), 148.

13. Southern, *Music of Black Americans*, 91.

14. Since the cakewalk was considered to be black satire of haughty white manners, there is a "remarkable kind of irony" in "white minstrels in blackface satirizing a dance satirizing themselves." Amiri Baraka, *Blues People* (New York: Morrow, 1963), 86.

15. Whites used not only blackface but "blackvoice" to portray African American culture on the minstrel stage. Averill, *Four Parts*, 33.

16. The great popularity of blackface minstrelsy can be attributed partly to an "industrial morality" imposed by capitalist forces on the white working class. "Whites get satisfaction in supposing the 'racial' Other enjoys in ways unavailable to them—through exotic food, strange and noisy music, outlandish bodily exhibitions, or remitting sexual appetite. And yet at the same time, because the Other personifies their inner divisions, hatred of their excess of enjoyment necessitates hatred of the Other." Lott, *Love and Theft*, 148.

17. "Nostalgic blackface songs" turned "the South into a kind of timeless lost home." Ibid., 190–91.

18. Close harmony is "a style of harmony singing in which the four voices remain relatively proximate to each other and generally do not exceed much more than an octave to an octave and a half from lowest to highest notes of a chord." Averill, *Four Parts*, 206.

19. Ibid., 31.

20. These elements correspond to early eighteenth-century accounts of the singing witnessed by European explorers of the African continent, who noted that the music was "distinctive for its high intensity and use of such special effects as falsetto, shouts, groans, and guttural tones." Southern, *Music of Black Americans*, 14.

21. Quartet singing may have been the only real avenue for black male singers in the late nineteenth century. "Male singers generally found it more difficult to succeed in the concert world than did the prima donnas. For that reason, they were more likely to join ensembles, minstrel troupes, or touring concert companies." Ibid., 245.

22. Averill, *Four Parts*, 87.

23. Robert W. Stephens, "The Mills Brothers," in *The Encyclopedia of African-American Culture and History*, ed. Jack Salzman, David Lionel Smith, and Cornel West (New York: Simon and Schuster, 1996), 1802.

24. Jay Warner, *The Da Capo Book of American Singing Groups* (New York: Da Capo Press, 1992), 44.

25. Marv Goldberg, *More Than Words Can Say: The Ink Spots and Their Music* (Lanham, MD: Scarecrow Press, 1998), viii–ix.

26. Southern, *Music of Black Americans*, 17.

27. Goldberg, *More Than Words*, 85.

28. In African American vocal music there is a "predilection for variety in timbre at all points along the continuum. A song might move from speechlike sounds . . . through ranges of the musical compass to screaming and yelling, all within the confines of a single performance." Southern, *Music of Black Americans*, 201.

29. Eventually Gabler started his own label, Commodore Records, which made new recordings by older jazz musicians such as Jelly Roll Morton and which inspired the creation of other like-minded independent labels including Blue Note and Signature. Geoffrey C. Ward, *Jazz: A History of America's Music* (New York: Alfred A. Knopf, 2000), 263–64.

30. Bill Godwin, remarks at concert, St. John's University, New York City, 18 November 2000.

31. The Deep River Boys started as the Hampton Institute Quartet, the Delta Rhythm Boys as the Dillard University Quartet. Southern, *Music of Black Americans*, 498–99.

32. Warner, *American Singing Groups*, 28.

33. Carroll interview.

34. Lornell, *Happy in the Service*, 1.

35. See Introduction, note 13.

36. Horace Clarence Boyer, *How Sweet the Sound: The Golden Age of Gospel* (Washington, DC: Elliott & Clark, 1995), 18, 47.

37. Warner, *American Singing Groups*, 3.

38. Gary Lewis, interview by author, New York City, 14 April 1998. Lewis's use of the word "roaming" resonates beyond a description of musical style. Gospel was the music of the Great Migration. It was the music of people on move, physically, spiritually, and socially. Definitions of the verb "to roam" include "to travel purposefully throughout a wide area unhindered" and "to contemplate a wide range of thoughts or memories" (*Webster's Third New International Dictionary*).

39. Warner, *American Singing Groups*, 57.

40. Portia Maultsby, interview in "Singing on the Corner," from *Let the Good Times Roll*, NPR, 2003.

41. Prentiss Barnes of the Moonglows (a big influence on the Cadillacs) remembers, "Back when the Moonglows first recorded . . . we relied on vocal backdrops, and we picked up quite a few from spiritual groups like the Dixie Hummingbirds and the Harmonizing Four. Even our idea of wearing matched suits came out of gospel, but in R & B, they were louder colors—reds, greens, blues." Jerry Zolten, *Great God A'mighty The Dixie Hummingbirds: Celebrating the Rise of Soul Gospel Music* (New York: Oxford University Press, 2003), 157.

42. Warner, *American Singing Groups*, 26.

43. Little Anthony Gourdine, lead singer of the Imperials, recalled how he created the song "I'm Alright": "I was influenced by the gospel singers there [at the Apollo]. The Imperials needed something to make the audience come up out of their seats. I just did a gospel thing, and fell to my knees and started reaching. I went to my old gospel roots and emotion went into the audience, and it totally blew the Apollo down. The Isley Brothers learned from us and did 'Shout'—the record that established their reputation as gospel-in-soul wailers." Quoted in Zolten, *Great God*, 262.

44. Carroll interview.

45. David Sanjek and Russell Sanjek, *American Popular Music Business in the 20th Century* (New York: Oxford University Press, 1991), 87.

46. Nelson George, *The Death of Rhythm and Blues* (New York: Penguin, 1988), 25.

47. Charlie Gillett, *The Sound of the City: The Rise of Rock and Roll* (New York: Pantheon Books, 1983), 121.

48. Gillett, *Sound of the City*, 159.

49. "There was no white equivalent of the Ravens' 'Bye Bye Baby Blues' on Savoy." George, *Death of Rhythm and Blues*, 26.

50. "There are elements in that song that lasted another twenty years." Bobby Jay, interview in *Life Could Be a Dream—The Doo Wop Sound*, DVD, White Star, 2003.

51. This circuit grew out of, and eventually was the up-market alternative to, a looser affiliation of small clubs and theaters that had supplanted the medicine shows, vaudevilles, and circuses of the early twentieth century. One of these affiliations was T.O.B.A., or Theatre Owners Booking Agency, which Baraka remembers performers referring to as "Tough On Black Asses." Baraka, *Blues People*, 89.

52. "The evolution of black male vocal group style during the 1950's indicated that important social and demographic changes had already coalesced to produce widespread black approval for a 'sweeter' strain of r & b, long before the industry began to pursue a similar strategy in its quest for a broader white audience." Brian Ward, *Just My Soul Responding: Rhythm and Blues, Black Consciousness, and Race Relations* (Berkeley: University of California Press, 1998), 56.

53. According to former Apollo Theatre owner Bobby Schiffman, the Orioles "were the innovators in rhythm and blues because they were the first ones who didn't try to represent melody as written. They were the ones who fucked over melody and did it their own way." Quoted in Ted Fox, *Showtime at the Apollo* (New York: Holt, Rinehart and Winston, 1983), 169.

54. "Sonny Til had a way he would lean to the side when he sang and he would point to the heavens and the women went nuts." Jay, *Life Could Be a Dream.*

55. Maultsby, "Singing on the Corner."

56. There was a social paradigm shift that accompanied this change in business practice. "The Negro as *consumer* was a new and highly lucrative slant, an unexpected addition to the strange portrait of the Negro the white American carried in his head." Baraka, *Blues People,* 101.

57. One piece of scholarship on female vocal harmony groups is Jane Hassinger, "Close Harmony: Early Jazz Styles in the Music of the New Orleans Boswell Sisters," in *Women and Music in Cross-Cultural Perspective,* ed. Ellen Koskoff (New York: Greenwood Press, 1987), 195–201. See also Averill, *Four Parts,* 126–31.

2. The Birth of Doo-Wop

1. Earl Carroll, interview by author, New York City, 26 February 1998.

2. This number comes from Jay Warner, *The Da Capo Book of American Singing Groups* (New York: Da Capo Press, 1992), 63. Other sources claim as many as 15,000 different groups, including Brian Ward, *Just My Soul Responding: Rhythm and Blues, Black Consciousness, and Race Relations* (Berkeley: University of California Press, 1998), 57.

3. It is not surprising that most of the writing about doo-wop has focused on specific urban areas. New York City, including Harlem and neighborhoods in Brooklyn and the Bronx, is featured in Philip Groia, *They All Sang on the Corner* (West Hempstead, NY: Phillie Dee Enterprises, 1983). In addition, there is Robert Pruter, *Doowop: The Chicago Scene* (Urbana: University of Illinois Press, 1996); Stuart L Goosman, "The Social and Cultural Organization of Black Group Vocal Harmony in Washington, D.C., and Baltimore, Maryland, 1945–60" (PhD diss., University of Washington, 1992); and Steve Propes, *L.A. R&B Vocal Groups, 1945–1965* (Winter Haven, FL: Big Nickel Publications, 2001), as well as short articles on the Philadelphia scene and the southern vocal groups of New Orleans, Nashville, and Houston in Anthony J. Gribin and Matthew M. Schiff, *The Complete Book of Doo-Wop* (Iola, WI: Krause Publications, 2000).

4. Guys used "to hang out on the corner, 'cause it was cooler." Don K. Reed, interview in *Life Could Be a Dream—The Doo Wop Sound,* DVD, White Star, 2003.

5. In Chicago, according to Jerry Butler, radio stations in the early 1950s played "a little bit of everything." Jerry Butler with Earl Smith, *Only the Strong Survive: Memoirs of a Soul Survivor* (Bloomington: Indiana University Press, 2000), 19.

6. The music that was offered in school was not necessarily to the liking of everyone. Jerry Butler recalled that sometimes they were asked to sing "old racist folk songs" like "Old Black Joe." Ibid., 26.

7. Carroll interview.

8. Goosman, "Social and Cultural Organization," 137.

9. There was "fluidity between sacred and secular." Ibid., 136.

10. Ibid. (abstract), 20–22, 30, 32.

11. Ibid., 58–59.

12. Carroll interview.

13. Gribin and Schiff, *Complete Book of Doo-Wop*, 122.

14. This area was "the kingdom of rhythm and blues." Groia, *They All Sang*, 103.

15. Ibid., 91–94.

16. Working on the harmony parts was referred to as "gangbanging for notes." Pruter, *Doowop*, 120–21.

17. Groia, *They All Sang*, 28, 42.

18. "All of that tile and porcelain was tailor-made for singing." Johnny Keyes, *Du-Wop* (Chicago: Vesti Press, 1987), 3.

19. Butler, *Only the Strong*, 26.

20. Emma Patron and Reather Turner, interview in *Life Could Be a Dream*.

21. Warner, *Da Capo Book*, 81.

22. Reed, *Life Could Be a Dream*.

23. "It was often the ingenious chants that attracted attention to their records." Gillett, *Sound of the City*, 31.

24. "The one who knew the words to the song was the lead singer. The remaining three or four singers imitated the sound that the horns made in the background, in harmony." Keyes, *Du-Wop*, preface (n.p.).

25. "Harmonies turned the corner from rhythm and blues to doo-wop with the invocation of 'blow harmonies.'" Anthony J. Gribin and Matthew M. Schiff, *Doo-Wop: The Forgotten Third of Rock 'n Roll* (Iola, WI: Krause Publications, 1992), 17.

26. "Like the blues, vocal harmony has a strong folk character" because "there was a body of songs and song motifs that was shared among the groups." Pruter, *Doowop*, 8.

27. "The music business in the era that I came along in the 1950s was populated by children." Bobby Jay, interview in *Life Could Be a Dream*.

28. Ninety-one percent of doo-wop records were on independent labels. Gribin and Schiff, *Doo-Wop*, 80–83.

29. Warner, *Da Capo Book*, 64–65.

30. Goosman, "Social and Cultural Organization," 151–55.

31. Carroll interview.

32. This company issued the Cadillacs' albums under the Jubilee label and their singles under the Josie label.

33. Earl Carroll, phone interview by Radioactive Gold Radio Network, 23 November 2002.

34. Groia, *They All Sang*, 72–73.

35. Bill Millar, *The Drifters: The Rise and Fall of the Black Vocal Group* (New York: Macmillan, 1971), 91. See also Warner, *Da Capo Book*, 133.

36. "The acceleration to form groups was equaled only by the haste of record companies to sign them . . . [and] many groups gathered in a studio did not even know each other's names." Millar, *Drifters*, 56.

37. The "interchangeability" of parts in the auto manufacturing process is similar to what goes on in doo-wop songwriting. The same argument might be made for the group members themselves. Bernard Gendron, "Theodor Adorno Meets the Cadillacs," in *Studies in Entertainment*, ed. Tania Modleski (Bloomington: Indiana University Press, 1986), 20.

38. "Doo-wop may have developed on the streets but it came to fruition in the recording studio." Pruter, *Doowop*, xiii.

39. Carroll interview. The doo-wop literature is rife with tales of alleged copyright theft. The story of the Moonglows and the song "Sincerely" may be the most famous. Pruter, *Doowop,* 60.

40. Previously, Exclusive Records had released what are now more-obscure versions of "Gloria," in 1945 by the Buddy Baker Sextet featuring Herb Jeffries on vocals and in 1946 by Ray Anthony.

41. Bobby Phillips, interview by author, New York City, 14 April 1998.

42. According to the singer Johnny Keyes, "A street song is an original that everyone sings, and a hundred people take credit for writing it." Pruter, *Doowop*, 8.

43. Gribin and Schiff, *Doo-Wop*, 117.

44. Black-owned record companies also exploited black singers, as was the case with Vee Jay records and the Spaniels. Todd R. Baptista, *Group Harmony: Behind the Rhythm and the Blues* (New Bedford, MA: TRB Enterprises, 1996), 19.

45. Cleveland Freeman, interview by author, Westbury, NY, 29 March 2003.

46. One way to refer to I–vi–IV–V is as a "circular progression" or "perpetual progression." Such progressions occur in western classical music (for example, the ostinato, passacaglia, chaconne).

47. Gribin and Schiff, *Doo-Wop*, 130–46, and United in Group Harmony Association's Top 500 Songs, www.ugha.org, 24 November 2002.

48. Rodgers and Hart's "Blue Moon" is a good example.

49. Most jazz musicians, however, refer to this progression as I–vi–*ii*–V, since ii–V harmonic movement is basic to jazz grammar.

50. Basing "is one of the most elemental of continuities in African American group song." Goosman, "Social and Cultural Organization," 211–13.

51. In the doo-wop songwriting process Tin Pan Alley tunes were often "flattened out" harmonically, meaning a more complex chord progression was reduced to the I–vi–IV–V template. An example of this process is a recording by the Jaguars of "The Way You Look Tonight." See Various Artists, *The Doo Wop Box, Volume 3: 101 More Vocal Group Gems from the Golden Age of Rock-N-Roll*, Rhino CD R2-71463, 2000.

52. For example, "Mr. Lee" by The Bobbettes uses the I–vi–IV–V progression in the chorus and a blues progression in the verses; the introduction in the Imperials' version of "When You Wish upon a Star."

53. Enthusiastic responses to the channel section of a song were witnessed at the Apollo Theatre. Groia, *They All Sang*, 108.

54. Cholly Atkins and Jacqui Malone, *Class Act: The Jazz Life of Choreographer Cholly Atkins* (New York: Columbia University Press), xviii.

55. Carroll phone interview.

56. Carroll interview.

57. Al "Diz" Russell, interview by author, New York City, 27 October 2000.

58. Unfortunately, the Regals' original recording of "Got the Water Boilin' Baby" is extremely rare, so I have not been able to substantiate Carroll's and Russell's recollections.

59. What goes around comes around. According to Carroll, "The Spaniels took [the vocal arrangement for] 'Stormy Weather' from us. We were on a show together in Connecticut an' I wondered why they kept telling us, 'Sing that one more time, jus' one more time eh?'" Quoted in Bill Millar, *The Coasters* (London: W. H. Allen, 1975), 143.

60. The African tradition of composition favors "improvis[ing] on a song already in existence." It is a communal process with a long history. Eileen Southern, *The Music of Black Americans* (New York: W. W. Norton, 1983), 172.

61. "Got the Water Boilin' Baby" does list Russell as cowriter, and with a recent re-release by Atlantic Records he is receiving royalties for the first time. Joe Pinchot, "Russell Is the Keeper of Orioles' Legacy," *(Sharon, PA) Herald*, 14 January 1999.

62. Carroll interview.

63. "Closing out the program had to be the greatest stage performance ever presented in the history of Rhythm and Blues with the possible exceptions of the Temptations and James Brown." Groia, *They All Sang*, 11.

64. George Lipsitz, *Time Passages: Collective Memory and American Popular Culture* (Minneapolis: University of Minnesota Press, 1990), 120.

65. Carroll interview.

66. "The makers of recorded music didn't let concerns of class or racism deny them a profit." Nelson George, *The Death of Rhythm and Blues* (New York: Penguin, 1988), 7.

67. Carroll interview.

68. Ibid.

69. Ibid.

70. Phillips interview.

71. Acoustic space is "the profile of a sound over a landscape. The acoustic space of any sound is that area over which it may be heard before it drops below the ambient sound level." Murray R. Schafer, *The Soundscape: Our Sonic Environment and Tuning of the World* (Rochester, VT: Destiny Books, 1977), 271. There is a distinction between different kinds of "landscapes" and the nature of the acoustic spaces associated with them. "The only place where sound can be naturally bounded is the interior space." Murray R. Schafer, *Voices of Tyranny, Temples of Silence* (Indian River, Ontario: Arcana Editions, 1992), 26.

72. "Reverberation and echo give the illusion of permanence to sounds and also the impression of acoustic authority." Schafer, *Soundscape*, 219.

73. Schafer, *Soundscape*, 219.

74. Our voice comes "back to us with the properties of the immediate environment embedded within it" Truax, *Acoustic Communication*, 32–33.

75. Gillett, *Sound of the City*, viii.

76. Keyes, *Du-Wop*, 1.

77. Acoustemology is the study of "local conditions of acoustic sensation, knowledge, and imagination embodied in the culturally particular sense of place." Steven Feld, "Waterfalls of Song: An Acoustemology of Place Resounding in Basavi, Papua New Guinea," in *Senses of Place*, ed. Steven Feld and Keith H. Basso (Santa Fe, NM: School of American Research Press, 1996), 91.

78. There is a state of "acoustic knowing, of sounding as a condition of and for knowing, of sonic presence and awareness as potent shaping forces in how people make sense of experiences." Ibid., 97.

79. Ward, *Just My Soul Responding*, 70.

80. "Vocal groups symbolized and . . . [eventually] sang of an idealized vision of a united, harmonious black community which was seldom seen in the real world." Ibid., 71.

81. Steven Feld, *Sound and Sentiment: Birds, Weeping, Poetics, and Song in Kaluli Expression* (Philadelphia: University of Pennsylvania Press, 1982), 136.

82. There can be "a tension between literal and connotative, obvious and ambiguous, and explicit and obfuscated. This, in great part, is the source for aesthetic tension in song." Ibid., 144.

83. The phrase "vocal landscapes of memory" is Steven Feld's. My thanks to him for coining it in response to my paper for his "Anthropology of Sound" course, spring 1999, New York University.

3. Shortcut to Nostalgia

1. The nucleus of the Coasters came from the Robins, a group that had formed in Los Angeles in late 1940s. They were a vocal group with several hits on the R&B chart that were written by the white songwriters Jerry Leiber and Mike Stoller. In 1955 the group became the Coasters, as in West Coast, and Leiber and Stoller began orienting material toward a younger, and whiter, audience. Bill Millar, *The Coasters* (London: W. H. Allen, 1975), 71–72.

2. Carroll always introduces the song "Gloria" in oldies shows as "the national anthem of the doo-wops."

3. "Gloria" was a popular song title in the doo-wop world. There are at least thirty-four different records with that title, many of which bear no resemblance to the Cadillacs' record. Anthony J. Gribin and Matthew M. Schiff, *The Complete Book of Doo-Wop* (Iola, WI: Krause Publications, 2000), 212–13.

4. Millar has suggested that Earl Carroll's racially accessible vocal style made "Gloria" popular with the white groups. "Carroll's voice had little social context. There were no fierce black inflections . . . it was light, happy, and patently youth-ful . . . his lack of distinction provided the model for a great many street-corner teams, both black and white" (*The Coasters,* 142). However, it is important to note that Carroll's was only one of several black styles admired and copied by white singers.

5. There were a fair number of Jewish singers if not wholly Jewish groups, only not on the scale of the Italian contribution. The Escorts, for example, were a Jew-ish vocal trio from Brooklyn who recorded an up-tempo version of "Gloria" in 1962. Jay Warner, *The Da Capo Book of American Singing Groups* (New York: Da Capo Press, 1992), 375–76.

6. Groia remembers his discovery of rhythm and blues on the radio as a teen-ager in Queens in 1954. This included the distinctive delivery of black personality DJs like Tommy Smalls, who would say, "Sit back, relax and enjoy the wax; from three-oh-five to five-three-oh; it's The Dr. Jive Show!" Quoted in Philip Groia, *They All Sang on the Corner* (West Hempstead, NY: Phillie Dee Enterprises, 1983), 8–9. Meanwhile, Earl Carroll, in a different New York neighborhood, was listening to the same programs. Earl Carroll, interview by author, New York City, 26 February 1998.

7. Vito Picone, speaking at "Italian Americans and Early Rock and Roll," a symposium sponsored by the John D. Calandra Italian American Institute and the

Catholic Center at Queens College, Flushing, NY, 10 May 2003, transcribed by author.

8. Picone remembers, "I used to despise the white artists who were attempting to simulate the black sound, via the so-called 'cover' records . . . [w]hat made me think that other people would feel differently about *me* singing black music, I'll never know." Quoted in Ed Engel, *White and Still All Right* (Scarsdale, NY: Crackerjack Press, 1977), unpaginated.

9. There is another doo-wop copyright saga here. "Daddy's Home" is very similar to "A Thousand Miles Away." Even though he wrote it, Sheppard did not own the copyright on the earlier song and the publishing company sued him for plagiarism when the second song came out. Bill Millar, *The Drifters: The Rise and Fall of the Black Vocal Group* (New York: Macmillan, 1971), 128.

10. The song was no. 1 on both the Pop and the R & B charts; the Elegants were only the second white group, after Danny and the Juniors, to accomplish this feat. Warner, *Da Capo Book,* 175. Picone referred to Sheppard as his mentor not only for his song-writing advice but also for his help in signing a deal with Hull Records. Picone, "Italian Americans."

11. Nick Santamaria, speaking at the "Italian Americans and Early Rock and Roll" symposium.

12. Joseph Sciorra, "Who Put the Wop in Doo-Wop? Some Thoughts on Italian Americans and Early Rock and Roll," *Voices in Italian Americana* 13, no. 1 (2002): 14.

13. Ibid., 15.

14. Jennifer Guglielmo and Salvatore Salerno, *Are Italians White? How Race Is Made in America* (New York: Routledge, 2003).

15. John A. Jackson, *American Bandstand: Dick Clark and the Making of a Rock 'n' Roll Empire* (New York: Oxford University Press, 1997), 26.

16. Ibid.

17. Picone, ibid.

18. Santamaria, ibid.

19. Keir Keightley, "You Keep Coming Back Like a Song: Adult Audiences, Taste Panics, and the Idea of the Standard," *Journal of Popular Music Studies* 13, no. 1 (2001): 12–16.

20. Warner, *Da Capo Book,* 72.

21. Gribin and Schiff, *Complete Book of Doo-Wop,* 199.

22. Warner, *Da Capo Book,* 90.

23. Gribin and Schiff, the most assiduous of the doo-wop historians, divide the music's history into three periods: paleo-doo-wop (1952–54), classical doo-wop (1955–59), and neo-doo-wop (1960–63). Even though this song was first released

in 1958, its double-release history and musical characteristics place it in the last category. Anthony J. Gribin and Matthew M. Schiff, *Doo-Wop: The Forgotten Third of Rock 'n Roll* (Iola, WI: Krause Publications, 1992), 23–46.

24. "We wanted to hear only songs by vocal groups, preferably black, with full harmony and growling bass." Donn Fileti, "Slim's and the First Doo Wop Revival," in *The Doo Wop Box: 101 Vocal Group Gems from the Golden Age of Rock 'N' Roll* booklet to 4-CD box set (Los Angeles: Rhino Records, 1993), 29.

25. Nostalgia is a "deeply social emotion," and there is something about our secret selves that is "yearning to be made public." Fred Davis, *Yearning for Yesterday* (New York: Free Press, 1979), vii, 43.

26. There has been a similar "practice of commodity fetishism" among working-class salsa record collectors in Cali, Colombia. Lise A. Waxer, *The City of Musical Memory: Salsa, Record Grooves, and Popular Culture in Cali, Colombia* (Middletown, CT: Wesleyan University Press, 2002), 118.

27. For instance, Motown stalwarts the Four Tops signed their first recording contract in 1956 with Chess Records. Harold Melvin and the Blue Notes, who had many hits in 1970s with the Philadelphia International, made their first record in 1955. Warner, *Da Capo Book*, 257, 388.

28. The Ronettes and the Crystals are two girls groups Spector worked with.

29. Alan Betrock, *Girl Groups: The Story of a Sound* (London: Putnam, 1983), 8.

30. Warner, *Da Capo Book*, 449.

31. The music business reflected "the integrationist aspirations of a new generation of blacks." Brian Ward, *Just My Soul Responding: Rhythm and Blues, Black Consciousness, and Race Relations* (Berkeley: University of California Press, 1998), 159.

32. "It was unfortunate for many of us who found nowhere to go, didn't have an audience anymore, didn't have record companies who were receptive to what we did best. It just changed." Bobby Jay, interview in *Life Could Be a Dream—The Doo Wop Sound*, DVD, White Star, 2003.

33. Carroll interview.

34. Ibid.

35. The movie starred Allan Freed and a host of rock and roll luminaries including Chuck Berry, Ritchie Valens, Jackie Wilson, Harvey Fuqua of the Moonglows, Jimmy Clanton, Sandy Stewart, and Jo-Ann Campbell. The Cadillacs performed two Coasters-style numbers including "Please Mr. Johnson," a cult favorite among vocal group enthusiasts.

36. "It was a great move because those guys wasn't only singing, they were acting and that was something that I wanted to do, wanted to get into." Carroll interview.

37. Carroll's first official record date with the Coasters was 25 September 1961. Their only charting song in this era was "Love Potion Number 9" in 1971. Millar, *The Coasters*. See also www.allmusic.com.

38. Bobby Phillips, interview by author, New York City, 14 April 1998.

39. "It hurts an artist who's been popular to not have anything going and you're still in that world. And you feel that you should still be there and there's nothing to back it up. And it's horrible. You begin to look for substitutes—substitute strength." Jimmie Castor, interview in *Life Could Be a Dream*.

40. He died of a heroin overdose in 1968 at the age of 26. Warner, *Da Capo Book*, 244.

41. Al "Diz" Russell, interview by author, New York City, 27 October 2000.

42. "The doo wop groups were hurt more than the pop and vocal bands [in the sixties] in that they were invariably of draft age and couldn't stay together long enough to succeed before the Viet Nam buildup started." Warner, *Da Capo Book*, 322.

43. Bobby Jay, interview by author, New York City, 21 October 2000.

44. Most notably, he recorded as a member of Brooklyn's Jive Five in 1962.

45. Navarro would eventually leave the music business and start a successful movie casting company, Navarro/Bertoni & Associates, in Manhattan.

46. J. R. Bailey, who had been a Cadillac intermittently for the previous fifteen years, wrote the song. He had a career as solo singer in the late 1960s and also wrote "Everybody Plays the Fool," a big hit for the Main Ingredient in 1972.

47. Phillips interview.

48. Carroll interview.

49. He "fanned the smoldering ember into a raging fire. Doo-wopps [*sic*] were bigger than they had been in years." Gribin and Schiff, *Complete Book of Doo-Wop*, 200.

50. Jay interview.

51. The 1970s were a "nostalgic orgy." Davis, *Yearning for Yesterday*, 4.

52. Nostalgia satisfies the individual and societal need for "continuity of identity." Ibid., 33.

53. "Rarely in modern history has the common man had his fundamental, taken-for-granted convictions about man, woman, habits, manners, law, society, and God . . . so challenged, disrupted, and shaken" as in the 1960s. Ibid., 106.

54. Similar films released at the time include *Sweet Toronto* (1970), which starred John Lennon and the Plastic Ono Band but featured his heroes Chuck Berry, Bo Diddley, Jerry Lee Lewis, and Little Richard, and *The London Rock and Roll Show*, the film of a concert featuring Bo Diddley, Jerry Lee Lewis, Little Richard, and Bill Haley and the Comets held at Wembley Stadium in 1972.

55. Sha Na Na's "look refers neither to the [actual] performance practices associated with the music they perform nor to the typical appearance of its audiences but, rather, to a stereotypical 'Italian-Americanicity' that has no basis in lived reality." Philip Auslander, "Good Old Rock and Roll: Performing the 1950s in the 1970s," *Journal of Popular Music Studies* 15, no. 2 (2003): 166.

56. Manhattan Transfer eventually mastered a broader repertoire that would include the pop vocal music of the 1940s as well as acclaimed vocal arrangements of contemporary jazz material such as Weather Report's "Birdland."

57. "The doo-wop romance of the street corner echoes that of the earlier barbershop revival. Indeed, the number of early barbershoppers who spoke of hearing African American 'blades' harmonizing on the streets, or the promoters who discovered black harmony groups on corners or in bars, would support speculation that the rhetoric of authenticity that surrounds the street corner may have had black ambulatory harmony quartets as its original reference." Gage Averill, *Four Parts, No Waiting: A Social History of American Barbershop Harmony* (New York: Oxford University Press, 2003), 155–56.

58. "Race was a kind of shorthand for an array of social, cultural, and economical deprivals." Jonathan Rieder, *Canarsie: The Jews and Italians of Brooklyn against Liberalism* (Cambridge: Harvard University Press, 1985), 92–93.

59. For example, "A Little Street Where Old Friends Meet" written by Gus Hahn and Harry Woods in 1932.

60. Vance plays the character of Professor Plano in *American Hot Wax*, the film biography of Alan Freed (1978), for which the vocal group the Planotones was created.

61. Richard Nader remembers that "he [Ricky Nelson] disrupted the nostalgic atmosphere of the evening." Quoted in Roger Catlin, "Doo-wop Regains the Ears of American Listeners," *Hartford Courant,* 9 August 2000.

62. According to Reeves, "It's very difficult for a person who was popular back in the sixties to have a hit record today. If it happens, you better consider yourself very fortunate. I just recorded two sides. I think they're both good and they're not like the old stuff. But they wouldn't accept it . . . 'I like your new things, but I'd rather play your old things.' And then if you try to record in the oldie vein you're out of date to them. They say, 'Here you come again with those doo-wop tunes; I can't believe it.'" Quoted in Bruce Pollack, *Working Musicians* (New York: Harper Entertainment, 2002), 343.

63. Catlin, "Doo-wop Regains."

64. According to Nader, "Nobody had seen any of these acts on TV since Dick Clark played them in 1960, '61 and '62. And it was perfectly suited for the PBS demographic, [people] in their '40s, '50s and '60s; and the slow songs of the late

'50s and early '60s are more in tune with their physical movements and capacities and memories than the fast songs." Quoted in Catlin, "Doo-wop Regains."

65. Jay interview.

4. The Doo-Wop Community

1. Eddie Jones, interview by author, New York City, 12 April 1998.

2. Bobby Phillips, interview by author, New York City, 14 April 1998.

3. Nick Santamaria, speaking at "Italian Americans and Early Rock and Roll," a symposium sponsored by the John D. Calandra Italian American Institute and the Catholic Center at Queens College, Flushing, NY, 10 May 2003; transcribed by author.

4. Anonymous review of Blues Estafette, Utrecht, Netherlands, 23 November 1997, posted on www.bluesworld.com.

5. Ibid.

6. Scott Schinder, "Concert Preview," *Time Out New York*, 18 January 2001.

7. The Diamonds are a group "that every true fan of doo-wop music loves to hate, because they covered so many records by black groups and usually outsold them." Anthony J. Gribin and Matthew M. Schiff, *The Complete Book of Doo-Wop* (Iola, WI: Krause Publications, 2000), 67.

8. Dave Somerville, interview in *Life Could Be a Dream—The Doo Wop Sound*, DVD, White Star, 2003.

9. I have borrowed the term "mediator" from Jerome Harris, who coined it in his study of the international jazz community, which he subdivides into "art makers," "art users (audiences)," and "various intermediary elements," or "mediators." Harris, "Jazz on the Global Stage," in *The African Diaspora: A Musical Perspective*, ed. Ingrid T. Monson (New York: Garland, 2000), 104.

10. See the Afterword for more about Don K. Reed's "Doo-Wop Shop."

11. According to Jim Dawson, "Doo-wop singles were the first rock 'n' roll records to become valuable as collectibles." One such rare recording was "Stormy Weather" by the Five Sharps, which may have started this trend in the early 1960s. "It was the inspiration that turned record collecting into a passionate profession and sent young, mostly white fans scurrying into junk shops and Salvation Army stores looking for used records." Excerpt from Doo-Wop Society of Southern California website, accessed 18 March 2005 (no longer available).

12. The fact that most promoters are white and male exemplifies how the racial make-up of the music business hierarchy has changed little since the 1950s. "Here in NYC, the oldies circuit is still run by white males. It's still built around black headline acts but black promoters are unable to raise the capital or to get the white management of the artists to cooperate." Greg Woods, email to author, 24 July 2002.

13. *Doo-Wop at the Garden XX,* New York City, 17 October 2000.

14. Jay Warner, *The Da Capo Book of American Singing Groups* (New York: Da Capo Press, 1992), 39.

15. Santamaria, "Italian Americans" symposium.

16. Gary Lewis, interview by author, New York City, 14 April 1998; Phillips interview.

17. Vito Picone, speaking at "Italian Americans" symposium.

18. John Pareles and Jesse McKinley "Great Pretenders: Pop Imitators Sing the Same Old Song," *New York Times,* 28 May 1998.

19. Jon "Bowzer" Bauman, email to author, 6 October 2006.

20. Bennett quoted in Russell Nichols, "My Tunes," *Boston Globe,* 29 October 2006.

21. Robbins quoted in ibid.

22. Baptista quoted in ibid.

23. Reed quoted in ibid.

24. Katherine Rizzo, "'50s Rockers Fight Against Imposters," *Seattle Times,* 23 March 1999.

25. This demographic group is often referred to the "Reagan Democrats." Marvin Gottlieb, "The Durability of Doo-Wop," *New York Times,* 17 January 1993.

26. Nelson George, *The Death of Rhythm and Blues* (New York: Penguin, 1988), 92–93.

27. Cleveland Freeman, a black musician with much more experience than I on the circuit, claims the racial profile is about 75 percent white musicians.

28. Anthony J. Gribin and Matthew M. Schiff, *Doo-Wop: The Forgotten Third of Rock 'n Roll* (Iola, WI: Krause Publications, 1992), 80–83.

29. Other MDs include Al Browne (the Crests), Jesse Stone (many Atlantic groups), Richard Barrett (the Teenagers), Buck Ram (the Platters), William "Prez" Tyus (the Students), and Eddie Jones (the Chantels).

30. Carl Vreeland, interview by author, Jamesburg, NJ, 13 March 2003.

31. In the Afterword I discuss singers' aging and its impact on the doo-wop community.

32. Vreeland interview.

33. Ibid.

34. Ibid.

35. Jim Wacker, interview by author, Upper Marlboro, MD, 5 April 2003.

36. Ibid.

37. Ibid.

38. Anthony Vigliotti, interview by author, Wilmington, DE, 1 February 2003.

39. Paul Page, interview by author, New York City, 23 June 2003.

40. Ibid.

41. Ibid.

42. Several of the black band members I have met on the circuit grew up in the 1970s in the Jamaica section of Queens. Their neighbors and jamming partners included well-known jazz musicians like drummer Lenny White, bassist Marcus Miller, and saxophonist Najee.

43. Cleveland Freeman, interview by author, Westbury, NY, 29 March 2003.

44. Ibid.

45. Greg Woods, email to author, 2 February 2003.

46. Greg Woods, interview by author, Wilmington, DE, 1 February 2003.

47. Freeman interview.

48. Vreeland interview.

49. Woods interview.

50. Page interview.

51. A class is "a coherent group of people with common traits and concerns." Richard Florida, *The Rise of the Creative Class: And How It's Transforming Work, Leisure, Community and Everyday Life* (New York: Basic Books, 2002), xi. I relate my personal experiences as a member of the band in Chapter 5.

52. "Though [jazz musicians'] activities are formally within the law, their culture and way of life are sufficiently bizarre and unconventional for them to be labeled as outsiders by more conventional members of community." The way of life of any group "arises essentially in response to a problem faced in common by a group of people, insofar as they are able to interact and communicate with one another effectively." Howard Becker, "The Culture of a Deviant Group: The 'Jazz' Musician," in *The Subcultures Reader,* ed. Ken Gelder and Sarah Thornton (London: Routledge, 1997), 55–56.

53. A member of the Tokens band whom I did not know said this to me backstage before an 18 January 2004 show at the Mohegan Sun Casino in Uncasville, CT.

54. Page interview.

55. "The process of self-segregation is evident in certain symbolic expressions, particularly in the use of occupational slang." Becker, *Deviant Group,* 65.

56. Page interview.

57. This might be also termed a "counter-strategy" for "contesting [in this case a past] racialized regime of representation." Stuart Hall, "The Spectacle of the 'Other,'" in *Representation: Cultural Representations and Signifying Practices,* ed. Stuart Hall (London: Sage Publications, 1997), 269.

58. "Do these images evade the difficult questions dissolving the harsh realities of racism into a liberal mishmash of 'difference'? Do these images *appropriate* 'difference' into a spectacle in order to sell a product? Or are they genuinely a political

statement about the necessity for everyone to accept and live with 'difference" in an increasingly diverse, culturally pluralistic world?" Ibid., 273–74.

5. The Oldies Circuit

1. Emmett Till was a black teenager from Chicago who was brutally murdered for whistling at a white woman while visiting relatives in Mississippi in 1955. The white male suspects were all acquitted, though the case was reopened in 2004. Till's murder became one of the galvanizing events of the civil rights movement.

2. They are referring to a 1998 incident in which three white men in the small town of Jasper, Texas, chained a black man to the back of their pickup truck and dragged him to his death.

3. The Crests, originally from the Lower East Side of Manhattan, were one of first racially integrated groups and are known for the song "Sixteen Candles" (1958). Jay Warner, *The Da Capo Book of American Singing Groups* (New York: Da Capo Press, 1992), 128–30.

4. Gary Lewis, interview by author, New York City, 14 April 1998.

5. The Delta Rhythm Boys were one of the premier black vocal groups of 1940s and were a strong influence on doo-wop groups (see Chapter 1). The Lamplighters were a 1950s–era black group from Los Angeles with several hits on the rhythm and blues chart. Warner, *Da Capo Book*, 235–36.

6. This song would eventually be the B side of the million-selling hit "You Belong to Me" by the Duprees, a recording for which Jones initially received no composer credit and for which he has never received any royalties.

7. Little Anthony and the Imperials from Brooklyn were led by "Little" Anthony Gourdine and are best known for "Tears on My Pillow" (1958). Warner, *Da Capo Book*, 238–41.

8. Eddie Jones, interview by author, New York City, 12 April 1998. See also Steve Propes, *L A R&B Groups* (Winter Haven, FL: Big Nickel Publications, 2001), 101.

9. Brown had previously worked with the Five Satins and with 1970s soul group New York City.

10. "Rehearsals constitute an essential component of quartet music culture . . . a creative environment in which the leader, the background song arranger, and the other group members can work cooperatively on innovative song arrangements . . . providing opportunities for socializing and camaraderie." Ray Allen, *Singing in the Spirit: African-American Sacred Quartets in New York City* (Philadelphia: University of Pennsylvania Press), 58.

11. Anthony J. Gribin and Matthew M. Schiff, *The Complete Book of Doo-Wop* (Iola, WI: Krause Publications, 2000), 38. Kip Lornell, *Happy in the Service of the*

Lord: African-American Sacred Vocal Harmony Quartets in Memphis (Knoxville: University of Tennessee Press, 1995), 129.

12. There is a "common concern musicians and listeners have in bringing into existence an ideal society . . . the musicking can exhilarate us with a vision of that ideal which is not just intimated to us but actually brought into existence for as long as the performance lasts." Christopher Small, *Music of the Common Tongue: Survival and Celebration in African American Music* (Hanover, NH: Wesleyan University Press, 1987), 86–70.

13. This is in the tradition of the "ritual jive talk" of Louis Armstrong, "who started musicians referring to themselves as cats . . . [and] who popularized such ritualized greetings as What you say, Gates; Well, what you know, Jim." Albert Murray, *Stomping the Blues* (New York: Da Capo Press, 1976), 238.

14. Marshall and Jean Stearns, *Jazz Dance: The Story of American Vernacular Dance* (New York: Da Capo Press, 1994), 27.

15. Cleveland Freeman, interview by author, Westbury, NY, 29 March 2003.

16. Carl Vreeland, interview by author, Jamesburg, NJ, 13 March 2003.

17. Greg Woods, email to author, 19 August 2002.

18. In the "historical trajectory" of the "musico-linguistic" approach to ethnography, thirty years ago "speech and song were implicitly assumed to be normative poles of a single objective continuum of sonic communication but recent research has moved beyond this 'bipolar model.'" Steven Feld and Aaron A. Fox, "Music and Language," *Annual Review of Anthropology* 23 (1994): 36.

19. Musical semantics, however, although oriented more toward emotionality than rationality, still acquires additional meaning from its nonmusical context. Musical meaning "is constituted in relation to the structures of the human world and the states of being that flow from them and sustain them." John Shepherd and Peter Wicke, *Music and Cultural Theory* (Cambridge, UK: Polity Press, 1997), 129. The sound of speech also has emotional impact, but not on the level of intensity of singing. It is not an either/or situation, but a matter of degree.

20. "The rules may 'frame' the performance, but the 'flow' of action and interaction within that frame may conduce to hitherto unprecedented insights and even generate new symbols and meanings, which may be incorporated into subsequent performances." Victor Turner, *From Ritual to Theatre: The Human Seriousness of Play* (New York: PAJ Publications, 1982), 79.

21. Goffman actually calls it "keying," which he defines as "the set of conventions by which a given activity, one already meaningful in terms of some primary framework, is transformed into something patterned on this activity but seen by the participants to be something quite else . . . a rough musical analogy is intended."

Erving Goffman, *Frame Analysis: An Essay on the Organization of Experience*, (Boston: Northwestern University Press, 1986), 44.

22. *Webster's Third New International Dictionary.*

23. "In the clash of continuities and discontinuities with which life confronts us, nostalgia clearly attends more to the pleas for continuity." Fred Davis, *Yearning for Yesterday* (New York: Free Press, 1979), 33.

24. The Ronettes were one of the preeminent black girl groups. They hailed from Washington Heights in Manhattan, and their hits included "Be My Baby" (1963). Warner, *Da Capo Book*, 440–42.

25. The decision was eventually overturned on appeal. John Caher, "Ronettes' Profits limited by 1963 Contract," *New York Law Journal*, 21 October 2002.

26. The Students were a black group who formed in the late 1950s in Cincinnati.

27. Micky Borack formed the group in 1961 in Queens with Jerry Landis (Paul Simon's alias) as lead singer. Warner, *Da Capo Book*, 465.

28. I have withheld the names of all the individuals involved in this encounter because of the sensitive nature of the subject matter.

29. The Dubs were formed in Harlem in the mid-1950s and are known for the song "Could This Be Magic?" (1957). Warner, *Da Capo Book*, 168–69.

30. This is a "matter of ritual" because "most of the slouching about, the jive talk, the joking, and even the nonchalance is as deliberately stylized as is most of the stage business on the bandstand during a performance for a regular audience." Murray, *Stomping*, 230.

31. The story of Herb Reed and the Platters, one of most popular vocal groups of all time, with hits like "Only You" (1955) and "Twilight Time" (1958), was also discussed in Chapter 4. The Five Keys were another very influential African American vocal group from the early 1950s known for the song "The Glory of Love" (1951) and others. This Teenagers group features the original tenor Herman Santiago.

32. This information was posted on www.city-data.com.

33. These on-stage and back-stage conversations are akin to what Scott has termed *public transcripts*, which he defines as "a shorthand way of describing the open interaction between subordinates and those who dominate," and *hidden transcripts*, "which is discourse that takes place 'offstage,' beyond direct observation by powerholders." James Scott, *Domination and the Arts of Resistance: Hidden Transcripts* (New Haven, CT: Yale University Press, 1990), 2–4.

34. "The frontier between the public and the hidden transcripts is a zone of constant struggle . . . not a solid wall," Ibid., 14.

35. This quote is from the poem *Burnt Norton*, no. 1 of *Four Quartets* (1935).

Afterword: The Persistence of Harmony

1. Carl Vreeland, interview with author, Jamesburg, NJ, 13 March 2003.

2. John Blacking, *How Musical Is Man?* (Seattle: University of Washington Press, 1973).

3. Richard Huff, "Oldies Suddenly a Thing of the Past in WCBS Shift," *New York Daily News*, 4 June 2005.

4. Cynthia Daniels, "The Doo-Wop Is Gone," *New York Newsday*, 5 June 2005.

5. Greg Woods, email to author, 4 June 2005.

6. Jay Traynor, email to author, 6 June 2005.

7. Paul Page, interview with author, New York, NY, 23 June 2003.

8. Freeman, interview with author, Westbury, NY, 29 March 2003.

9. Earl Carroll, Tass Filipos, Peter Millrose, and I co-wrote the lyrics.

10. Carroll, a third partner, David Sykes, and I are equal co-owners of the master recording. Phillips and Lewis will each receive a relatively generous royalty rate after expenses are recovered.

11. The most successful new doo-wop recording of the post-oldies era by an oldies group is probably "Morse Code of Love" by the Capris, issued on the Ambient Sound label in 1982. Despite its being newly composed and recorded, many oldies stations added it to their playlists.

12. Johnny Zacchio, phone message to author, 1 October 2004.

13. Anonymous Collectable Records employee, phone conversation with author, 15 November 2004.

14. Steve Percy, email to author, 27 June 2005.

15. Liesl Schillinger, "The Long Jump," *New York Times*, 12 September 2004.

INDEX

acoustemology, 161n.77
acoustic spaces, 59, 62, 161n.71
African Americans: barbershop
quartets, 24–27, 153n.7; as
consumers, 39, 157n.56; in
doo-wop audience, 97–99;
increasing white access to
culture of, 8; Italian Americans
associate with, 66–67;
migration north, 33, 34, 80;
minstrelsy, 25; new urban
identity for, 36; political radicalism associated with, 10, 150n.20;
sacred and secular music come
together, 8; vocal harmony in
daily life of, 5, 40. *See also* race;
segregation
Albanese, Rob, 132, 133
Allen, Ray, 170n.10
American Bandstand (television
program), 66–67, 135
American Graffiti (film), 77–78, 79
"American Pie" (McClean), 78–79
Andrews Sisters, 39
Angels, 136
Anka, Paul, 58
Apollo Theatre (Harlem): Atkins works
at, 54; black audience at, 98; on
chitlin' circuit, 37; fervent
performance styles at, 34, 87;
Freeman frequents, 104; Italian
Americans attend, 65; revue
format of shows at, 86; rhythm
and blues at, 35; sacred and
secular music come together at, 8;
white groups at, 67
Armstrong, Louis, 171n.13

Artists Rights Enforcement Corporation, 124
Atkins, Cholly, 53–54, 55, 73, 114
Atlantic Records, 46, 125
"attainable happy ending" message, 6, 7
audience, 96–100; African American,
97–99; age of, 99; demographic
characteristics of, 80, 96, 97;
enthusiastic responses to subpar
performances, 135; European,
99–100; identification with
singers, 97, 98–99; in music
making process, 146; political
sentiment of, 96; vocal behavior
to, 121, 122–23; why they like
doo-wop, 97
authenticity: group membership and
name ownership and, 92; Nader
on, 91; versus nostalgia, 91, 97;
oldies work adds to, 104; race and,
99; record collectors on, 70; Sha
Na Na claims, 79; of Charlie
Thomas's Drifters, 130
authorship, 49–51
Avalon, Frankie, 73, 74
Averill, Gage, 151n.27, 153n.5, 154n.18,
166n.57
Azusa Street Revival, 32

"Baby It's You" (Shirelles), 119
Bailey, J. R., 165n.46
Balsamo, Vito, 50, 64, 89
Baltimore, 40
bands, 100–107; composition of, 100;
freelance lifestyle of, 106–7;
hierarchy in, 100; in musician
class, 105–7; "next gig" anxiety in,

members of, 110–11

other group of, 92

recordings of: "Better than Ever,"
145; box set, 82; *The Cadillacs
Meet the Orioles*, 48; "Deep in the
Heart of the Ghetto Parts 1 and 2,"
75–76, 165n.46; "The Girl That I
Love," 115; "Gloria," 48–51, 52–53,
61–62, 63–64, 68, 84, 89, 113,
115, 116, 117, 137, 162n.4; *Have
You Heard the News?*, 144; "Jay
Walker," 74; "Peek-a-boo," 74, 115;
"Please Mr. Johnson," 74, 164n.35;
"Speedoo," 54–56, 87, 113, 115, 118,
129, 135, 137, 138, 144, 145; "Zoom,"
x, 87, 113, 115, 116, 145

shows of: *The Big Five* show format
of, 114–18; closing shows, 137;
European performances, 100; in
Go Johnny Go film, 73, 74, 164n.35,
Fig. 2; at Netherlands blues
festival, 86–87; offstage discourse, 127–28; on oldies circuit,
x, xi, 84; opening shows, 137; on
PBS *Doo Wop 50* fund-raiser, 83;
rehearsals, 111–13; at Rhythm and
Blues Foundation event, Fig. 9; at
taping of 2005 PBS special at
Sands Casino, Fig. 6; as tough act
to follow, 137; voices at, 21

Cadillacs Meet the Orioles, The (album),
48

cakewalk, 25, 154n.14

Capris, 3, 46, 65, 67, 68, 70, 75, 173n.11

Carey, J. C., 95

Carey, Jacob, 95

Carnations, 41–42, 46

Carroll, Earl "Speedo": on Anka trying
to learn trade secrets, 58; on
Atkins, 54; on author as his "baby
brother," 116, 122; author meets,
x–xi; author's interviews with,
xi–xiii; on barbershops in African

American communities, 24; on
black hotels, 58; Cadillacs' break
up in 1960s, 63, 74; in Cadillacs'
publicity photo from mid-1950s,
Fig. 1; at Cadillacs' shows, 115, 116,
117–18; in Carnations, 41–42, 46;
changes in voice of, 144; with
Coasters, 74, 76, 78, 82, 164n.36,
165n.37; in Coasters' suit against
Atlantic Records, 125; and *The
Crazy Cadillacs* album, 47; dances
"the Itch," 118; education of, 113;
and *The Fabulous Cadillacs*
album, 47; in "Gloria," 49, 52–53,
62, 89, 113, 116, 117, 162n.4; on
gospel music, 32, 34; identifies
with Harlem, 40; insider racial
discourse of, 115; on interracial
audiences, 57; in *Let the Good
Times Roll* film, 78; in *Life Could
Be a Dream* documentary, 133;
on *Mr. Lucky*, 145; on Navarro
claiming songwriting credit, 48,
50, 51; on New York musical map,
41; offstage discourse by, 127,
128; on opportunities for black
entertainers, 73–74; performs in
schools, 41; in reunion of Cadillacs
in 1970s, 82; on rhythm and blues,
35; Rhythm and Blues Foundation
grant for, 82; as school custodian,
82, 111, 119; in Speedo and the
Cadillacs, 110; on "Speedoo," 54–55;
as star on oldies circuit, 82;
survival instinct of, 139; at taping of
2005 PBS special at Sands Casino,
Fig. 3, Fig. 7, Fig. 8; on touring
in 1950s and 1960s, 109–10; in
unwritten vamp section for
"Speedoo," 138; way of speaking
of, 117; weekly earnings with the
Cadillacs, 73

car shows, 90

Deep River Boys, 31, 155n.31
Dells, 71, 81
Delphonics, 105
Delta Rhythm Boys, 31, 37, 111, 155n.31, 170n.5
Del-Vikings, 134
Demens, 111
Desires, 42
Desjardins, Bob, 103
Diablos, 149n.3
dialog, 20–21
Diamonds, 88–89, 167n.7
"Diana" (Anka), 58
Diddley, Bo, 78
DiMucci, Dion, 64
Dinwiddie Colored Quartet, 26
Dion and the Belmonts, 64
disc jockeys, 9, 89, 90
DISCoveries (magazine), 70
Dixie Hummingbirds, 32, 34, 155n.41
Dixon, Luther, 72, 131–32
Domino, Fats, 73, 78, 88, 119
Dominoes, 35, 71
doo-wop
    community, 85–108 (*See also*
        audience; bands; mediators;
        singers); author's role in, xiv; as
        celebration of human voice, 21–22;
        collective nostalgia in, 17; dancing
        and sex as aspects of, 16; elements
        of, x; as in state of flux, 15; as
        subculture, ix; survival instinct
        in, 139; transcending differences
        in, 18
    defining, 1–6; name, 1–2, 76; as
        vocal group rhythm and blues, 1,
        4, 11, 15
    history of: amateur vocalizing in
        development of, 48; birth of,
        40–62; continuing appeal, 141;
        decline in face of British invasion,
        4, 72; digital availability of,
        141–42; drafting of group mem-

bers, 165n.42; emergence of, 2–3;
in Europe, 99–100; evolves into
silky soul, 105; female groups,
43–44; future of, 143–44; golden
age of, 12; Italian American,
64–68; new recordings, 145;
number one hits, 13–14; original
group members, 92, 94–95, 97,
141, 142, 147; periodization of,
163n.23; popularization of "doo-
wop," 44; race in demise of,
72–73; revival in early 1960s, 69;
revival in late 1960s and 1970s,
76–80; roots of, 2; short duration
of, 68; on the "street corner,"
40–45, 62, 79–80, 166n.57; in
vocal harmony tradition, 2, 23
legal issues: authorship, 49–51;
copyright, 11–12, 49–51; group-
name ownership, 11–12, 46–47,
91–93; litigating for reparation
and recompense, 124–26;
royalties, 73, 82, 83, 96, 124–25
musical characteristics of, 3, 34;
cyclical harmonic structure, 51;
flexibility in choosing harmony
notes, 112; gospel influence, 32;
hierarchy in arrangements, 61; ice
cream changes, 51–53; meter, 71;
nonsense syllables, 61–62;
I-vi-IV-V chord progression, 51–53,
69, 159n.46; simplicity of lyrics,
98; song structure, 71; vocal
choreography, 53–55
nostalgic associations of, 63–84 (*See
also* oldies circuit); careers revived
by, 12; economic consequences of,
13–15; of word *doo-wop*, 2
social characteristics of: "attainable
happy ending" message, 7;
collective nostalgia, 17–18; as
communal, 18; cross-generational
popularity, 99; crossover realities,

doo-wop (cont.)

56–58; as dance music, 53; fifteen minutes of fame for groups, 139; fluid nature of group personnel, 47, 91–92; group ethos, 60–61; group names develop lives of their own, 47–48; human quality of, 141; male bonding, 67, 80; as music of first generation of rock and rollers, 14; as oldies, 11–15; racial interdependence in, 116; reputations as blessing and curse, 146; sartorial practice, 34, 155n.41; semantic anxiety of *doo-wop*, 15; as shorthand for all things 1950s, 12; sonically signifies time and place of its origins, 58–62; as sonic embodiment of African American experience, 5–6; teenage pop culture associated with, 4–5; tension between lives of songs and singers, 141–42; unplanned obsolescence, 11; as urban phenomenon, 3, 59–60; vocal behavior, 121–24

writings about, xiii, 157n.3; magazines, 77

"Doo Wop (That Thing)" (Hill), 13

Doo Wop 50 (PBS), 82–83, 89

Doo Wop 51 (PBS), 83, 88

Doo-Wop Hall of Fame, 95, 104

Doo Wop Preservation Society, 12

Doo-Wop Shop, The (WCBS-FM radio program), 77, 142–43

Dorsey, Thomas, 33

Downbeat (magazine), 29, 30

Drake, Laverne, 41

Drifters: with Atlantic Records, 46; Diamonds tour with, 88; different groups of, 92, 93, 102–3, 147; hit records of, 130; and ice cream changes, 53; lead singers of, 130; Lewis as member of, 111; McPhat-ter as lead singer of, 35, 130; Shirley Alston Reeves sings songs of, 119; "There Goes My Baby," 53; Charlie Thomas's, 93, 130; "Under the Boardwalk," 53, 130

drugs, 74–75

Du Bois, W. E. B., 7, 32, 150n.13

Dubs, 127, 128, 129, 172n.31

Duck and Cover (film), 6–7

Duneier, Mitchell, 18

Duprees, 126, 170n.6

Earl Theater (Philadelphia), 38

"Earth Angel" (Penguins), 31

Ebonairs, 42

echo, 123

"echo chamber" effect (reverb), 42, 59, 62

Echoes of the Past (magazine), 77

Eckstine, Billy, 35, 36

Edsels, 46, 68–69

El Dorados, 46

Elegants, 64–65, 67, 92, 103, 163n.10

Eliot, T. S., 140

Ellington, Duke, 28

End (record label), 45

Escorts, 162n.5

ethnographic intimacy, 1, 18–22

Evans, Ronnie, 119

"Everybody Loves a Lover" (Shirelles), 119

Excellents, 134

Exclusive Records, 48–49

Fabian, 73, 74

Fabulous Cadillacs, The (album), 47

Fabulous Hubcaps, 129

Fagan, Garth, 146–47

Feld, Steven, xv, 162n.83

festivals, 4

Fileti, Donn, 69, 70, 164n.24

Fisk Jubilee Singers, 32

Fi-tones, 47, 128
Five Crowns, 42, 46, 47
Five Jones Boys, 33
Five Keys, 128–29, 172n.31
Five Platters, Inc., 94
Five Red Caps, 31
Five Sharps, 167n.11
Flamingos, 53, 95, 134
Flash Cadillac, 79
Fletcher, Wilber, 128
Fletcher Gospel Singers, 128
Fogerty, John, 125
folk music, 5
"Foolish Little Girl" (Shirelles), 119
Four Bells, 42
Four Blue Birds, 33
Four Southern Singers, 33
Four Tops, 164n.27
Four Vagabonds, 31
Fox Theater (Detroit), 37
Fredericks, Alan, 68, 76
Freed, Alan, 9, 50, 54, 55, 73, 86,
    164n.35, 166n.60
Freeman, Cleveland, 51, 104, 105, 106,
    107, 120
frenzy, music-related, 7–8, 15, 32

Gabler, Milt, 30, 155n.29
Gaines, Lee, 37
Gaining, Cub, 41, 47
Gallagher, Jimmy, 89
gangs. See street gangs
"Garden Party" (Nelson), 81
Gardner, Carl, 96, 125
Gardner, Veta, 96
Garnes, Sherman, 149n.3
"Gee" (Crows), 41, 56
German close harmony singing, 24,
    26, 153n.11
Gershwin, George, 51
Gilmore, Randy, 138
girl groups, 71–72; choreography of,
    132; Lauryn Hill's video and, 13;

origins of, 43–44; range of
emotional experience in music
of, 2. *See also* Shirelles; *and other
groups by name*
"Girl That I Love, The" (Cadillacs),
    115
Gladiolas, 88
"Gloria" (Cadillacs), 48–51, 52–53,
    61–62, 63–64, 68, 84, 89, 113, 115,
    116, 117, 137, 162n.4
"Gloria" (Channels), 79
"Gloria" (Manhattan Transfer), 50, 79
"Gloria" (Mills Brothers), 49, 117
"Gloria" (Three Blazers), 49
"Glory of Love, The" (Five Keys),
    172n.31
Godwin, Bill, 30–31
Goffin, Gerry, 72
Goffman, Erving, 171n.21
Go Johnny Go (film), 73, 74, 164n.35,
    Fig. 2
Golden Gate Quartet, 33
Goosman, Stuart L., 149n.10
Gordy, Berry, 72
gospel music, 71
gospel quartets, 8, 32–35, 114
Gossert, Gus, 76, 165n.49
Gourdine, Little Anthony, 35, 111,
    156n.43, 170n.7
Grease (musical), 53, 77
"Great Pretender, The" (Platters), 96
Green, Cal, 109
Greenberg, Florence, 131–32
Greene, Jerry, 68
Gregory, Barry, 130
Gribin, Anthony J., 3, 163n.23
Groia, Philip, 162n.6
Group Harmony Review (radio pro-
    gram), 90
group-name ownership, 11–12, 46–47,
    91–93
Gunter, Cornell, 74, 93
Guy, Billy, 125

Kenny, Bill, 29–30
Keyes, Johnny, 159n.42
Keynotes, 42
King, B. B., 36, 87
King, Ben E., 46, 104, 130, 150n.16
King, Carole, 72
King, Martin Luther, Jr., 7
Kirk, Rahsaan Roland, 151n.32
Kramer, Bill J., 103
Kucinich, Dennis, 94

Laboe, Art, 69, 70
Ladders, 42
Laddins, 42, 75
Lamplighters, 111
Lanham Act (1946), 94
Laverne and Shirley (television program), 78
lawyers, 89, 90, 124–26
Lee, Beverly, 72, 95
Legends, 42
Leiber, Jerry, 53, 162n.1
Let the Good Times Roll (film), 78
Levy, Morris, 131
Lewis, Earl, 79, 89
Lewis, Gary, 110–11; author's interviews with, xii; at Cadillacs' shows, 116, 118; education of, 113; in "Gloria," 113; on gospel music and roaming, 33, 155n.38; on *Mr. Lucky*, 145; offstage discourse by, 127; on other group of Cadillacs, 92; at taping of 2005 PBS special at Sands Casino, Fig. 5, Fig. 7; on touring in 1950s and 1960s, 109–10
Lewis, Rudy, 130
Life Could Be a Dream (documentary), 132–33
Limelights, 65, 99
Lincolns, 46
"Lion Sleeps Tonight, The" (Tokens), 136

litigating for reparation and recompense, 124–26
Little Anthony and the Imperials, 35, 111, 156n.43, 170n.7
Little Caesar and the Romans, 69
"Little Darlin'" (Diamonds), 88
"Little Darlin'" (Gladiolas), 88
"Little Girl of Mine" (Cleftones), 136
Little Richard, 57, 73, 78, 119
"Little Star" (Elegants), 65, 92
London Rock and Roll Show, The (film), 165n.154
"Looking for an Echo" (Vance), 81
Lornell, Kip, 153n.8
Los Angeles, 40
Lott, Eric, 25
Lubinsky, T. J., 83
Lucas, George, 77, 79
Lymon, Frankie, 74–75, 129, 131, 149n.3

Maestro, Johnny, 136
magazine and fanzine editors and writers, 89
major scale, 52
male bonding, 67, 80
"Mama Said" (Shirelles), 119, 120
managers, 89, 90, 126
Manhattan Transfer, 50, 79, 99, 166n.56
Mariners, 31
Marshak, Larry, 93–94, 102, 141
Marshall, Maithe, 37
Marvelettes, 103
Matadors, 42
McClean, Don, 78–79
McGuire Sisters, 50
McPhatter, Clyde, 35, 130
MCs, 135–36
mediators: defined, 85; in doo-wop community, 89–96; managers, 89, 90, 126; promoters, 89, 90–91, 98, 167n.12
Mello-Moods, 42

Melnick, Jeffrey, 151n.28
Melvin, Harold, 164n.27
Mercury Records, 57, 75
Micky B. (DJ), 126
Miller, Marcus, 169n.42
Millrose, Peter, x
Mills Brothers, 27–28; as ancient
    history to oldies band members,
    105; crossover appeal of, 31;
    "Gloria," 49, 117; humming by, 44;
    "Paper Doll," 28, 29; Ravens
    compared with, 36, 37
minor scale, 52
minstrelsy, 25–26, 80, 154n.16
Mississippi Mudmashers, 33
"Money Honey" (Drifters), 130
Moonglows, 44, 50, 81, 155n.41,
    159n.39
Moore, Johnny, 49, 130
"Morse Code of Love" (Capris), 173n.11
Moten, Fred, 150n.20
Motown, 2, 11, 13, 54, 72, 129
"Mr. Lee" (Bobbettes), 43, 119, 120,
    160n.52
Mr. Lucky (Cadillacs' album), 144–46
"Mr. Lucky" (Cadillacs' single), 145
musical directors and musician
    contractors, 100, 105
musical semantics, 122, 171n.19
"musico-linguistic approach, 171n.18
muting of the negative, 15
"My Boyfriend's Back" (Angels), 136
Mystics, 134
"My True Story" (Jive Five), 136

Nader, Deborah, 90
Nader, Richard, 77, 78, 90–91, 99, 142,
    166n.61, 166n.64
Najee, 169n.42
"Nature Boy" (Cole), 57
Navarro, Esther, 46; affair with Jessie
    Powell, 132; Cadillacs as salaried
    employees under, 73; Cadillacs

break with, 58, 75; on Cadillacs'
    name, 46; in film industry,
    165n.45; songwriter's credit
    claimed by, 48, 49–50, 51, 54, 55,
    117, 137
Nelson, Rick, 81, 166n.61
neo-doo-wop, 69
*New Grove Dictionary of Music and
    Musicians, The,* 3
New York City: *The Doo-Wop Shop*
    canceled, 142–43; gospel music in,
    34; musical map in 1950s, 41–42;
    oldies audience in, 96, 97; Times
    Square Record Store, 68–69; as
    vocal group center, 40. *See also*
    Apollo Theatre (Harlem)
Nite, Norm N., 77
nonsense syllables, 61–62
Norwood, Charles, 94
nostalgia, 63–84; in African Ameri-
    cans, 98; audience response
    framed by, 135; authenticity versus,
    91, 97; author's original definition
    of, xi; in barbershop quartets, 24;
    collective, 16–18, 78; as cultural
    memory, 151n.37; dangers of
    excessive sentimentality, 15;
    defined, 13; divisive political issues
    submerged beneath, 96; doo-
    wop's nostalgic associations, 2, 12,
    13–15; fifties-centric, 14, 77–80,
    142; growing old trope reaffirms,
    116; in Ink Spots, 29, 30; in Mills
    Brothers, 28; in minstrelsy, 25;
    nostalgic tourism, 85, 100; oldies
    shows as, 14, 81–82, 123; perform-
    ers' professional lives extended by,
    86; promoters use as rhetorical
    device, 90; record collecting in,
    68–70; rock-era, 142; as social
    emotion, 164n.25; the South as
    object of, 26; for youth, 16–17
novelty songs, 63, 74, 115

Picone, Vito, 64–65, 66, 67, 92–93, 103, 163n.8
Pitt, Eugene, 136
Planotones, 81, 166n.60
Platters: as ancient history to oldies band members, 105; band members for, 102; different groups of, 92, 94, 128, 147; female members of, 85; Five Platters, Inc., 94; "The Great Pretender," 96; and ice cream changes, 53; "Only You," 172n.31; original members of, 95; "Twilight Time," 129
"Please Mr. Johnson" (Cadillacs), 74, 164n.35
Politi, Paul Leo, 69
Polydor (record label), 75–76
popular music: class shift in audience, 4; digital editing in, 141; each generation and music of its youth, ix, 14, 16–17; racial double helix in, 6–11; rhythmic changes in 1950s, 70–73; shift from adult to teen orientation in, 49; Tin Pan Alley, 36, 38, 48, 51, 52, 71, 160n.51. *See also* jazz; rhythm and blues; rock music; soul music; vocal harmony
Porter, Bob, 145
Powell, Jessie, 100, 132, 137
preservation societies, 12, 27, 90
Presley, Elvis, 8, 73, 126
primitivism, 150n.18
"Promise to Remember" (Teenagers), 52
promoters, 89, 90–91, 98, 137, 167n.12
Pruter, Robert, 153n.52, 158n.26, 159n.38
Puzey, Leonard, 37

race: and barbershop quartets, 24–27; boundaries crossed on radio, 64, 65, 162n.6; Carroll's insider racial

discourse, 115; continuing tensions on oldies circuit, 136–37; delineation of music along racial lines, 56; in doo-wop's demise, 72–73; and ethnographic intimacy, 18–19; historical and social issues at oldies circuit shows, 139; images of racial interaction on oldies circuit, 107–8, 116, 169n.58; interracial relationships, 131–32; racial double helix in American culture, 6–11; racial interaction on oldies circuit, 126–29. *See also* African Americans
"race music," 35
radio: big band music programs in 1950s, 68; black stations of 1950s, 40, 157n.5; college stations, 90, 143; disc jockeys, 9, 89, 90; doo-wop audience listens to, 96; in doo-wop music business, 45; *The Doo-Wop Shop*, 77, 142–43; gospel music on, 32; Internet, 143, 145; mainstream, 142; Mills Brothers on, 27–28; oldies, 13, 90, 142–43; payola, 35, 45–46; racial boundaries crossed on, 64, 65, 162n.6; rhythm and blues on, 35; specialty programs, 143; WCBS-FM, 77, 142–43
Ram, Buck, 46, 94, 168n.29
"Rama Lama Ding Dong" (Edsels), 68–69
Ramblers, 46
R & B Magazine, 77
Ravens, 35, 36–37
record collecting, 68–70, 89, 167n.11
Record Collector's Monthly (magazine), 77
Record Exchanger (magazine), 77
recording industry: barbershop quartets in, 26; cover versions, 9, 57–58, 65, 88, 89, 145, 163n.8; doo-wop audience buys records,

96; gospel music in, 32, 34; independent companies, 35, 45–46, 47; making rock and roll profitable, 72. *See also labels by name*

Red Robin (record label), 45

Reed, Don K., 77, 83, 133, 142–43

Reed, Herb, 95, 96, 128, 172n.31

Reeves, Shirley Alston, 118–19; author works with, 109, 118–21, 123, 124, 126–27, 130, 146; band members of, 100–101, 103–4; on biographical films, 131–32; creative limitations of oldies circuit for, 81–82, 166n.602; on "50 percent of something," 124–25; and ownership of Shirelles name, 95, 118; with Shirelles, 72; as sounding better than in 1960s, 144

Regals, 54–55, 75, 160n.58

Regal Theater (Chicago), 37

Reicheg, Richard, 81

reissues, 90

release, the, 52–53

Relic Records, 69

re-membering, 152n.38

Rene, Leon, 48–49, 50, 117

reverb ("echo chamber" effect), 42, 59, 62

Rhino records, 90

rhythm and blues, 35–39; backbeat accents in, 49; backlash against, 9, 11, 15; cover versions, 65, 163n.8; doo-wop as, 1, 4, 11, 15; Italian Americans listen to, 64, 162n.6; music-related frenzy in, 7–8, 15; new dance steps inspired by, 53; oldies band members' relation to, 104–5; in rock's origins, 4, 9, 11; sexuality in, 9–10, 38–39; sweeter strain of, 38, 156n.52; three feel of, 71; white teenagers adopt, 8–9, 11, 56

Rhythm and Blues Foundation, 82, 90, 92, Fig. 9

Ricks, Jimmy, 37

Riley, Billy Lee, 55, 100

Risky Business, 126

Robbins, Harvey, 95–96

Robins, 162n.1

Robinson, Bill "Bojangles," 41, 55, 118

rockabilly, 3, 56, 100

Rock Magazine, 93

rock music: African American origins of, x; British invasion, x, 4, 72; doo-wop as music of first generation of rock and rollers, 14; doo-wop in emergence of rock and roll, 2–3; historiography, 5; middle-aged musicians, 16; rhythm and blues in origins of, 4, 9, 11; rhythm and form of, 70–71; rhythmic accentuation in, 3; rock and roll becomes, 4; rock-era nostalgia, 142; as youth music, 16

Rolling Stone (magazine), 5

Ronettes, 124, 125, 172n.24

Rose, Irving "Slim," 68, 69, 76

Royal Theater (Baltimore), 38

royalties, 73, 82, 83, 96, 124–25

Rubin, Chuck, 124–25, 126

Ruffin, David, 75

Ruiz, Katrina, 107

Ruiz, Richard, 107

Russell, Al "Diz," 55, 75, 160n.1

Rydell, Bobby, 12, 73

Salutations, 50, 64, 89, 117

Santamaria, Nick, 65–66, 67, 75, 86, 92

Santiago, Herman, 172n.31

"Save the Last Dance for Me" (Drifters), 130

Savoys, 42

Scepter records, 131–32

Schafer, Paul, x

vocal behavior, 121–24
vocal choreography, 53–55
Vocaleers, 47
Vocal Group Hall of Fame, 94
vocal harmony: in African American daily life, 5, 40; barbershop quartets, 23–27, 80, 81; doo-wop in tradition of, 2, 23; female groups, 39; folk characteristic of, 158n.26; golden age of, 40; Italian American, 64–68; jazz-era quartets, 27–32; minstrelsy, 25–26, 80, 154n.16; roots of, 23–39; stylistic transition in postwar era, 49; as way of being in the world, 140. *See also* close harmony singing; doo-wop; girl groups
Vocaltones, 47
voice: doo-wop community as celebration of, 21–22, 152n.50; vocal behavior, 121–24; vocal choreography, 53–55. *See also* singing
Vreeland, Carl, 100–102, 104, 105, 120, 130–31, 141, 144, 168n.27

Wacker, Jim, 102–3, 104, 105
Wanderers, 42
Warner, Jay, 157n.2
Washington, Baby, 136
Washington, D.C., 40

Waters, Muddy, 4, 36, 87
Watkins, Glenn, 150n.18
WCBS-FM radio, 77, 142–43
weddings, 101–2
Whirlers, 42
Whirlin' Disc (record store), 146
White, Lenny, 169n.42
white flight, 80
Why Do Fools Fall in Love (film), 131
Williams, Joe, 55
Williams, Maurice, 88
Williams, Tony, 95
Willingham, Johnny "Gus," 47
Willows, 42
"Will You Love Me Tomorrow" (Shirelles), 72, 95, 103, 118, 119, 132
Wilson, Timothy, 129
Woods, Greg, 23, 104–5, 106, 120, 143, 167n.12
World Trade Center attack, 112, 127
"Worst That Could Happen, The" (Brooklyn Bridge), 136

Yesterday's Memories (magazine), 77
"You Belong to Me" (Duprees), 126, 170n.6
"You Send Me" (Cooke), 34, 65

"Zoom" (Cadillacs), x, 87, 113, 115, 116, 145

John Michael Runowicz, who holds a PhD in
ethnomusicology from New York University, is a
professional musician and independent scholar.
He grew up in Franklinville, New Jersey, and
has lived and worked in the New York City area
since 1983, as a singer, songwriter, and guitarist.
Starting in 1987 he has performed with the doo-
wop group Speedo and the Cadillacs as guitarist,
second tenor, and musical director.